Mind Over Mission: A Strategic Guide to Self-Mastery

by

Dorian Steele

Front Matter

This work is dedicated to those who understand that true strength lies not in the absence of fear, but in the courage to act with clarity and presence, even when the path is uncertain. It is for the sentinels of their own lives, those who stand watch over their inner landscape, ever vigilant, ever growing, and ever ready to engage with the world with wisdom, fortitude, and compassion. May you find in these pages a reflection of your own journey, and a renewed sense of your inherent capacity for greatness.

The goal is not to wage war, but to engage with life with the precision of a strategist and the calm awareness of a mindful warrior. It is about building an integrated self—one that is prepared, resilient, purposeful, and capable of navigating the complexities of existence with both unwavering resolve and profound inner peace. This is your mission, should you choose to accept it.

This book will guide you through a comprehensive operational framework for self-mastery, integrating the "how-to" of strategic planning with the "how-to" of mindful living. We will explore the foundational elements of readiness, from optimizing sleep and nutrition to mastering the power of your breath and establishing disciplined routines. You will learn to sharpen your mind through cognitive fortification, employing tactics like visualization and reframing to build mental agility and resilience. Emotional fortitude will be cultivated by understanding and navigating your inner spectrum with clarity and Stoic resilience. The core of strategic execution will be detailed, from mission definition and intelligence gathering to operational planning and resource allocation. Crucially, we will delve into adaptive warfare, learning to maintain situational awareness, prepare for the unexpected, and learn from setbacks. Finally, we will explore the integration of contemplation into action, fostering a state of mindful presence that enhances decision-making and cultivates compassion.

Contents

Chapter 1: The Foundation of Readiness: Building Unshakeable Habits 5

The Sentinel's Slumber: Mastering Sleep for Peak Performance 6

Fueling the Machine: Strategic Nutrition for Cognitive and Physical Prowess 13

Chapter 2: Sharpening the Mind: Cognitive Fortification and Mental Agility 48

Cognitive Reframing: Rewiring Thought Patterns for Resilience 80

Chapter 3: Emotional Fortitude: Mastering the Inner Landscape 100

Stoic Resilience: Cultivating Inner Calm Amidst Adversity 120

Chapter 4: Strategic Execution: Planning and Implementing for Success 144

Chapter 5: Adaptive Warfare: Navigating Change and Overcoming Obstacles 190

Chapter 6: The Mindful Warrior: Integrating Contemplation into Action 235

Chapter 7: Sustaining the Campaign: Long-Term Mastery and Continuous Growth 270

Chapter 8: The Integrated Self: Living a Life of Purpose and Mastery 306

References 345

Chapter 1: The Foundation of Readiness: Building Unshakeable Habits

The Sentinel's Slumber: Mastering Sleep for Peak Performance

In the demanding theater of personal growth, where the mind is the primary weapon and the body the crucial vessel, sleep stands as the bedrock of readiness. Just as a seasoned military unit cannot execute a complex operation without adequate rest and recovery, an individual striving for self-mastery must prioritize and optimize their sleep. Without sufficient, quality sleep, our cognitive functions falter, our emotional resilience erodes, and our physical stamina dwindles. This is not merely a matter of comfort; it is a fundamental strategic imperative for anyone seeking to perform at their peak. The operations of our lives, whether mental, emotional, or physical, are entirely dependent on the restorative power of the sentinel's slumber.

The science behind sleep is a fascinating, intricate dance of neurobiology and physiology. Our sleep doesn't unfold as a monolithic block of unconsciousness but rather progresses through distinct cycles, each with unique benefits. These cycles, typically lasting around 90-110 minutes, repeat several times throughout the night and are broadly categorized into Non-Rapid Eye Movement (NREM) sleep and Rapid Eye Movement (REM) sleep. NREM sleep is further divided into stages. Stage N1, the lightest stage, is the transition from wakefulness to sleep, characterized by a slowing of brain waves and muscle relaxation. Stage N2, a deeper stage, accounts for the largest portion of our sleep and involves further slowing of brain activity and the emergence of sleep spindles and K-complexes, which are thought to play a role in memory consolidation. Stage N3, often referred to as deep sleep or slow-wave sleep (SWS), is the most physically restorative phase. During SWS, the body repairs tissues, builds bone and muscle, strengthens the immune system, and conserves energy. This is the stage where growth hormone is released and where we feel most refreshed upon waking if we've had enough of it.

Following NREM sleep, we enter REM sleep. This stage is characterized by rapid eye movements, increased brain activity that closely resembles wakefulness, and muscle paralysis. Despite the brain's heightened activity, REM sleep is crucial for cognitive functions, particularly memory consolidation, learning, emotional processing, and dreaming. It's during REM sleep that we process the day's experiences, solidify new knowledge, and even work through emotional challenges. A healthy sleep cycle typically involves progressing through these stages multiple times. For instance, the initial sleep cycles may have longer periods of deep NREM sleep, while later cycles tend to feature longer REM periods. Disruptions to this natural architecture can significantly impair our ability to function optimally.

Unfortunately, modern life presents a formidable array of sleep disruptors, often stemming from our own habits and environments. The omnipresent glow of electronic screens, emitting blue light, is a notorious offender. This blue light suppresses the production of melatonin, a hormone essential for signaling to the body that it's time to sleep. Late-night consumption of caffeine and alcohol, while seemingly conducive to relaxation for some, can fragment sleep, leading to more awakenings and reduced time spent in restorative deep and REM sleep. Irregular sleep schedules, perhaps necessitated by shift work or inconsistent social demands, throw our body's natural circadian rhythm—the internal 24-hour clock that regulates sleep-wake cycles—out of sync. Stress and anxiety are also major culprits; a mind racing with worries about the past or future makes it exceedingly difficult to surrender to sleep. Even environmental factors like an uncomfortable mattress, an inadequately darkened room, or disruptive noise can significantly detract from sleep quality. Understanding these common disruptors is the first step in dismantling their hold on our rest.

Mastering sleep hygiene, therefore, becomes a critical strategic objective for self-mastery. It involves a multifaceted approach, focusing on establishing a consistent sleep schedule, creating a sleep-conducive environment, and developing effective pre-sleep rituals. The cornerstone of good sleep hygiene is consistency. Going to bed and waking up around the same time every day, even on weekends, helps regulate your circadian rhythm, making it easier to fall asleep and wake up naturally. This consistency signals to your body when it's time for rest, reinforcing the natural sleep-wake cycle. Even if you have a late night, try to maintain your regular wake-up time to prevent significant disruption.

The sleep environment plays a pivotal role in the quality of rest achieved. The ideal sleep sanctuary is cool, dark, and quiet. A slightly cooler room temperature, generally between 60-67 degrees Fahrenheit (15-19 degrees Celsius), is often optimal for sleep as our body temperature naturally drops as we prepare to sleep. Darkness is equally crucial; even small amounts of light can interfere with melatonin production. Blackout curtains, an eye mask, or ensuring all electronic devices are turned off and their indicator lights are covered can make a significant difference. Minimizing noise is also important. If complete silence is impossible, consider using earplugs or a white noise machine to mask disruptive sounds. Ensuring your mattress and pillows are comfortable and supportive is also essential for physical comfort and uninterrupted sleep.

Beyond environmental controls and a consistent schedule, pre-sleep rituals are powerful tools for signaling to the body and mind that it's time to wind down. These rituals are about creating a transition period, moving from the demands of the day to a state of relaxation. This could involve a warm bath, reading a physical book (avoiding screens), gentle stretching, listening to calming music, or practicing mindfulness or meditation. Engaging in these calming activities for 30-60 minutes before bed can significantly improve sleep onset and quality. The key is to make these rituals enjoyable and consistent, creating a predictable pathway to slumber. It's also important to avoid stimulating activities close to bedtime, such as intense exercise, engaging in emotionally charged conversations, or consuming heavy meals.

The benefits of prioritizing sleep extend far beyond simply feeling less tired. For individuals in high-pressure professions, athletes, and leaders, the impact of sufficient sleep on cognitive function and performance is profound. Consider the military context: alertness, decision-making, reaction time, and the ability to process complex information are all critically dependent on well-rested personnel. A sleep-deprived soldier is a liability, prone to errors in judgment and slower to respond. Similarly, in civilian life, a lack of sleep impairs our ability to concentrate, solve problems, and learn new information. It diminishes our creativity, increases our susceptibility to stress, and negatively impacts our mood and emotional regulation.

Athletes, who often push their bodies to the extreme, are acutely aware of sleep's importance. Elite athletes consistently report prioritizing 8-10 hours of sleep per night. They understand that sleep is when muscle repair occurs, energy stores are replenished, and cognitive recovery takes place. For example, studies have shown that restricting sleep in athletes can lead to decreased endurance, slower reaction times, and impaired accuracy. Conversely, athletes who extend their sleep duration often report improved performance metrics, faster recovery from training, and fewer injuries. This isn't exclusive to physical performance; mental acuity is equally vital in competitive arenas, and sleep is the primary driver of that acuity.

High-performing individuals in fields like business and science also emphasize sleep as a non-negotiable component of their success. They recognize that sleep deprivation leads to poor decision-making, reduced productivity, and increased errors. Many successful entrepreneurs and CEOs have spoken openly about making sleep a priority, understanding that being well-rested allows them to think more clearly, be more creative, and operate more effectively throughout their demanding days. They treat sleep not as a luxury but as a strategic investment in their performance and well-being. For instance, Arianna Huffington, founder of The Huffington Post, has become a vocal advocate for sleep after experiencing burnout. She realized that by sacrificing sleep, she was actually hindering her productivity and overall effectiveness. Her personal journey underscores the transformative power of prioritizing rest.

The physiological mechanisms underlying these benefits are robust. During deep sleep (NREM Stage 3), the brain clears out metabolic waste products that accumulate during waking hours, including beta-amyloid, a protein linked to Alzheimer's disease. This "housekeeping" function of sleep is crucial for maintaining brain health and cognitive function. REM sleep, as mentioned, is vital for consolidating memories, strengthening neural connections, and enhancing learning. Furthermore, sleep plays a critical role in regulating hormones that control appetite, stress, and growth. Insufficient sleep can disrupt these hormonal balances, leading to increased cravings for unhealthy foods, elevated cortisol levels (the stress hormone), and impaired immune function.

To further illustrate the practical application of these principles, consider the science of sleep extension in athletes. Studies published in journals like *Sleep* have demonstrated that when athletes increase their sleep duration to 9-10 hours per night, they experience significant improvements in performance. For instance, basketball players showed increased sprint times, improved shooting accuracy, and faster reaction times when they slept longer. Similarly, swimmers demonstrated quicker start times and more efficient turns. These are tangible, measurable improvements directly attributable to prioritizing sleep. It's a clear demonstration that for peak performance, whether on the field or in the boardroom, sleep is not a passive state but an active, crucial component of training and preparation.

The challenges of achieving optimal sleep can be significant, but by applying strategic principles and consistent effort, it is possible to master this fundamental aspect of readiness. The journey begins with understanding the architecture of sleep and the myriad ways it can be disrupted. From there, implementing evidence-based strategies for sleep hygiene—establishing a consistent schedule, optimizing the sleep environment, and creating calming pre-sleep rituals—becomes paramount. The rewards are substantial: enhanced cognitive function, improved emotional regulation, increased physical stamina, and a greater capacity for resilience and peak performance in all areas of life. By treating sleep as the strategic imperative it is, we lay a solid foundation for the unshakeable habits that will carry us through our personal campaigns for mastery. The sentinel's slumber is not an indulgence; it is the essential preparation for the missions that lie ahead.

Fueling the Machine: Strategic Nutrition for Cognitive and Physical Prowess

Just as an advanced military operation relies on meticulous logistical planning and the provision of high-grade sustenance for its personnel, so too does our pursuit of peak performance in personal development demand strategic nutritional foresight. Our bodies and minds are complex machines, and the fuel we provide them directly dictates their efficiency, resilience, and sustained operational capacity. Moving beyond mere caloric intake, strategic nutrition is about understanding the intricate interplay between the foods we consume and our cognitive acuity, our physical endurance, and our overall emotional equilibrium. It's about viewing every meal and snack as a deliberate choice to either enhance or detract from our ability to engage effectively with the challenges and opportunities of our lives. In essence, we are what we eat, and when we aim for superior performance, our dietary choices must reflect that ambition.

The cornerstone of strategic nutrition lies in achieving a robust balance of macronutrients: carbohydrates, proteins, and fats. These are not simply categories of food but essential building blocks and energy sources that serve distinct, yet interconnected, roles. Carbohydrates are our primary source of energy, particularly for the brain, which relies almost exclusively on glucose for its fuel. Opting for complex carbohydrates – such as whole grains, legumes, and vegetables – is paramount. These foods release glucose into the bloodstream slowly and steadily, preventing the sharp spikes and subsequent crashes in energy and mood that are characteristic of refined sugars and processed starches. Think of it as supplying a steady burn for a long-duration mission, rather than a short, explosive burst followed by depletion. Complex carbohydrates provide sustained energy, allowing for prolonged periods of concentration and physical activity, and they are also rich in fiber, which aids digestion and promotes satiety, helping to manage hunger and prevent overeating.

Protein, on the other hand, is the fundamental building material for our bodies. It is essential for muscle repair and growth, hormone production, enzyme function, and even neurotransmitter synthesis – the chemical messengers that govern our mood and cognitive processes. Adequate protein intake is crucial for recovery after physical exertion and for maintaining muscle mass, which is vital for metabolic health and strength. For cognitive function, specific amino acids derived from protein are precursors to neurotransmitters like dopamine and serotonin, which play significant roles in focus, motivation, and mood regulation. Sources of high-quality protein include lean meats, poultry, fish, eggs, dairy products, legumes, nuts, and seeds. Distributing protein intake throughout the day, rather than consuming it all in one meal, can help maintain stable energy levels and support muscle protein synthesis more effectively.

Fats, often unfairly maligned, are indispensable for optimal health and performance. They are critical for hormone production, nutrient absorption, and the structural integrity of cell membranes, including those in the brain. The brain itself is composed of a significant amount of fat, and the quality of these fats directly impacts cognitive function. Omega-3 fatty acids, found in fish such as salmon and mackerel, as well as in flaxseeds and walnuts, are vital for brain health. They are incorporated into brain cell membranes, supporting fluidity and communication between neurons, and have anti-inflammatory properties that can protect against cognitive decline. Healthy fats also contribute to satiety, helping to regulate appetite and prevent unhealthy snacking. Sources of healthy fats include avocados, nuts, seeds, olive oil, and fatty fish. It's crucial to prioritize unsaturated fats (monounsaturated and polyunsaturated) and limit saturated and trans fats, which can negatively impact cardiovascular health and cognitive function.

Beyond macronutrient balance, the specific quality of our food choices significantly influences our cognitive and physical prowess. The concept of micronutrients – vitamins and minerals – is equally vital. These often-overlooked components are not direct energy sources but act as catalysts and cofactors in countless metabolic processes, including energy production, neurotransmitter synthesis, and antioxidant defense. For instance, B vitamins are crucial for energy metabolism and the production of neurotransmitters. Iron is essential for oxygen transport to the brain and muscles, while magnesium plays a role in over 300 enzymatic reactions in the body, including those involved in energy production and nerve function. Antioxidants, such as vitamins C and E, and various phytonutrients found in fruits and vegetables, combat oxidative stress, a byproduct of cellular metabolism that can damage cells and contribute to aging and disease, including cognitive decline. A diet rich in a variety of colorful fruits, vegetables, and whole foods ensures a broad spectrum of micronutrients, supporting optimal bodily function and protecting against cellular damage.

The impact of nutrition on cognitive function is a rapidly expanding field of research, often referred to as neuro-nutrition. Foods that support brain health are often those that reduce inflammation, provide antioxidants, and supply the necessary building blocks for neurotransmitters. Fatty fish, rich in omega-3s, are consistently linked to improved memory and reduced risk of cognitive decline. Berries, packed with anthocyanins and other antioxidants, have been shown to enhance communication between brain cells and improve cognitive performance. Dark leafy greens, like spinach and kale, provide vitamins K, lutein, folate, and beta-carotene, which are associated with slower cognitive decline. Nuts and seeds, besides healthy fats, offer vitamin E, which may protect against cellular damage from free radicals. Even the hydration status of the body is critical; dehydration, even mild, can impair attention, memory, and other cognitive functions.

Conversely, certain dietary patterns can actively hinder our cognitive and physical capabilities. Diets high in processed foods, refined sugars, and unhealthy fats are associated with increased inflammation, oxidative stress, and impaired metabolic function. These can lead to energy slumps, difficulty concentrating, irritability, and an increased risk of chronic diseases that compromise long-term well-being. The "sugar crash" is a perfect example of how refined carbohydrates can negatively impact cognitive performance, leading to brain fog and decreased alertness. Furthermore, consistent consumption of these types of foods can contribute to insulin resistance, a condition that not only increases the risk of type 2 diabetes but also negatively affects brain health and cognitive function.

Developing a strategic approach to nutrition requires practical meal planning and mindful eating habits. This is not about restrictive dieting but about making conscious, informed choices that align with our performance goals. The concept of "eating the rainbow" – consuming a wide variety of fruits and vegetables of different colors – is a simple yet effective strategy for ensuring a broad intake of essential vitamins, minerals, and antioxidants. Incorporating lean protein sources at each meal helps to stabilize blood sugar and promote satiety. Choosing whole grains over refined grains provides sustained energy and fiber. Healthy fats should be integrated thoughtfully, using olive oil for cooking and dressings, snacking on nuts and seeds, and including fatty fish in the diet regularly.

Practical strategies for meal planning can make adhering to these principles much more manageable. Preparing meals in advance, often referred to as "meal prepping," can be a powerful tool, especially for individuals with busy schedules. Dedicating a few hours on a weekend to wash and chop vegetables, cook grains, and prepare protein sources can save significant time and prevent impulsive, less healthy choices during the week. This also ensures that nutritious options are readily available when hunger strikes.

Another key aspect is mindful eating – paying attention to the sensory experience of eating, recognizing hunger and fullness cues, and savoring each bite. This practice not only enhances enjoyment but also improves digestion and can help prevent overconsumption. It involves eating without distractions, such as screens, and focusing on the food itself. This shift in approach transforms eating from a mere biological necessity into a deliberate act of self-care and performance enhancement.

Considering the demands of high-performance environments, the timing of nutrient intake also becomes relevant. Consuming a balanced meal or snack containing carbohydrates and protein before demanding cognitive or physical tasks can provide the necessary fuel for optimal performance. Similarly, post-activity nutrition, focusing on replenishing glycogen stores with carbohydrates and facilitating muscle repair with protein, is crucial for recovery and adaptation. For cognitive tasks requiring sustained focus, steady energy release from complex carbohydrates is more beneficial than the rapid influx from simple sugars.

In military contexts, ration packs are meticulously designed to provide sustained energy, essential micronutrients, and a balance of macronutrients that can withstand harsh conditions and varying operational demands. These rations are the product of extensive research into human physiology and performance under stress. Applying similar principles to our daily nutrition means recognizing that our own "operations" – whether they involve intense mental work, physical training, or navigating complex interpersonal dynamics – require fuel that supports endurance, clarity, and resilience.

For example, an individual preparing for a mentally demanding day might start with oatmeal topped with berries and nuts, providing complex carbohydrates for sustained energy, antioxidants from berries, and healthy fats and protein from nuts. For a mid-morning snack, a hard-boiled egg or a small handful of almonds would offer a protein and healthy fat boost to maintain focus. Lunch could consist of grilled chicken or lentil salad with a variety of colorful vegetables and a source of whole grains like quinoa. An afternoon snack might be Greek yogurt with fruit, offering protein and natural sugars for a gentle energy lift. Dinner should again focus on lean protein, plenty of vegetables, and a moderate portion of complex carbohydrates. Staying adequately hydrated throughout the day with water is also a critical, yet often overlooked, component of strategic nutrition.

The scientific basis for these recommendations is robust. Research published in peer-reviewed journals consistently demonstrates the link between dietary patterns and cognitive function. Studies examining the Mediterranean diet, for instance, which emphasizes fruits, vegetables, whole grains, legumes, nuts, seeds, and olive oil, have shown associations with improved cognitive function and a reduced risk of dementia. This dietary pattern is rich in antioxidants, anti-inflammatory compounds, and healthy fats, all of which are beneficial for brain health. Similarly, research on athletes highlights the importance of carbohydrate availability for endurance and the critical role of protein in muscle recovery and adaptation.

Ultimately, strategic nutrition is about empowering ourselves with knowledge and making deliberate choices that serve our long-term goals. It's a continuous process of learning, adapting, and refining our approach based on how our bodies and minds respond. By viewing food not just as sustenance but as a powerful tool for enhancing cognitive and physical prowess, we can build a foundation of readiness that supports sustained peak performance in all facets of our lives. This mindful approach to fueling the machine ensures that we are operating at our optimal capacity, ready to engage with the demands of our personal campaigns with clarity, energy, and resilience. It transforms the mundane act of eating into a proactive strategy for self-mastery, ensuring that our internal machinery is primed for success.

The ability to regulate one's physiological and psychological state is a hallmark of elite performance, whether on the battlefield or in the boardroom. Just as a seasoned commander maintains composure amidst chaos, a disciplined individual can harness internal resources to navigate stress and enhance clarity. Central to this mastery is an often-underutilized yet universally accessible tool: the breath. Our breath is a constant companion, an automatic process that sustains life. Yet, when we consciously engage with it, it transforms from a passive biological function into an active instrument of control, a direct command to our nervous system. This is the essence of the breath as a command – the deliberate and strategic use of our respiratory patterns to influence our mental landscape, emotional equilibrium, and physical readiness.

The intimate link between breath and our internal state is not merely anecdotal; it is deeply rooted in our physiology. The autonomic nervous system, responsible for regulating involuntary bodily functions, is intricately connected to our breathing patterns. The sympathetic nervous system, our "fight or flight" response, is associated with shallow, rapid breathing, increasing heart rate and preparing the body for action. Conversely, the parasympathetic nervous system, often referred to as the "rest and digest" system, is activated by slow, deep breaths, which signal safety and calm to the brain, lowering heart rate and promoting relaxation. By consciously altering our breathing, we can, in effect, send targeted signals to our nervous system, shifting from a state of arousal and stress to one of calm and focus. This provides a powerful, immediate mechanism for self-regulation, allowing us to regain control when faced with overwhelming circumstances.

Consider the soldier on the front lines, facing a barrage of incoming fire. Their instinct might be to hyperventilate, their breathing shallow and rapid. This physiological response, while natural, exacerbates fear and impairs cognitive function. The trained soldier, however, understands the power of controlled breathing. By deliberately slowing their exhalation, engaging their diaphragm, and focusing on a steady rhythm, they can actively counter the body's stress response. This isn't about suppressing fear; it's about managing the physiological cascade that accompanies it, creating the mental space needed to assess the situation, make sound decisions, and execute their mission effectively. This principle translates directly to civilian life. Whether facing a high-stakes presentation, a difficult conversation, or simply the daily grind of deadlines and pressures, conscious breathing can act as an anchor, stabilizing our internal environment and allowing us to respond with measured intention rather than reactive emotion.

The most fundamental yet profoundly effective breathwork technique is diaphragmatic breathing, often called belly breathing. This contrasts with the shallow chest breathing that often accompanies stress or exertion. Diaphragmatic breathing involves the active engagement of the diaphragm, a large, dome-shaped muscle located at the base of the lungs. When we inhale deeply, the diaphragm contracts and flattens, drawing air down into the lungs and causing the abdomen to expand outward. During exhalation, the diaphragm relaxes and returns to its dome shape, pushing air out of the lungs. This type of breathing is naturally occurring during sleep and in infants, signifying a state of relaxation.

To practice diaphragmatic breathing, find a comfortable position, either sitting or lying down. Place one hand on your chest and the other on your abdomen, just below your rib cage. As you inhale slowly through your nose, focus on allowing your abdomen to rise, pushing your hand outward. Your chest hand should remain relatively still. As you exhale slowly through your mouth or nose, feel your abdomen fall. The key is to make the exhalation slightly longer than the inhalation, which helps to further activate the parasympathetic nervous system. For instance, inhale for a count of four, and exhale for a count of six. Consistency is crucial. Aim to incorporate this practice into your routine, perhaps for a few minutes upon waking, before bed, or during moments of perceived stress. The immediate effect is a calming sensation, a reduction in heart rate, and a sense of grounding. Over time, regular practice can retrain your breathing patterns, making you naturally more resilient to stress.

Beyond simple diaphragmatic breathing, a vast array of breathwork techniques, known collectively as pranayama in yogic traditions, offers more sophisticated methods for influencing our physiology and mental state. Pranayama literally translates to "life force control" or "breath extension." These techniques are not simply exercises but sophisticated practices designed to purify the body, balance energy channels, and cultivate mental clarity and emotional stability.

One widely accessible and beneficial pranayama technique is **Alternate Nostril Breathing (Nadi Shodhana)**. This practice is believed to balance the hemispheres of the brain and calm the nervous system. It involves using the fingers of one hand to alternately close and open the nostrils while breathing. To perform Nadi Shodhana, sit comfortably with your spine erect. Close your right nostril with your right thumb and inhale slowly and deeply through your left nostril. At the peak of your inhalation, close your left nostril with your ring finger, release your thumb from the right nostril, and exhale slowly through the right nostril. Then, inhale through the right nostril. At the peak of this inhalation, close your right nostril with your thumb, release your ring finger from the left nostril, and exhale through the left nostril. This completes one round. Continue for several rounds, maintaining a smooth, controlled rhythm. Nadi Shodhana is particularly effective for reducing anxiety, improving focus, and preparing the mind for meditation or demanding tasks. Its ability to harmonize the subtle energies of the body is reflected in its calming and centering effects.

Another powerful technique is **Box Breathing (Sama Vritti Pranayama)**, which is highly favored in military and law enforcement circles for its efficacy in stabilizing the mind under pressure. This method involves creating an equal rhythm for inhalation, holding the breath, exhalation, and holding the breath again. A common pattern is to inhale for a count of four, hold for four, exhale for four, and hold for four. This rhythmic pattern creates a predictable cadence that can override anxious thought patterns and promote a sense of control. The breath holds, when performed comfortably and without strain, further engage the parasympathetic nervous system and can lead to a deeper sense of calm. Practicing Box Breathing for even a few minutes can significantly reduce feelings of overwhelm and sharpen mental acuity. Its simplicity makes it an invaluable tool that can be employed almost anywhere, anytime.

The physiological benefits of conscious breathing are well-documented. Studies have shown that deep, slow breathing can reduce heart rate variability, a marker of stress, and increase heart rate variability, a marker of resilience. It has been demonstrated to lower blood pressure, decrease cortisol levels (the primary stress hormone), and improve oxygenation of the blood, leading to enhanced cognitive function and reduced fatigue. The act of focusing on the breath itself also serves as a form of mindfulness, anchoring the individual in the present moment and disrupting the cycle of rumination and worry that often accompanies stress.

Psychologically, the impact is equally profound. By consciously engaging in controlled breathing, we are essentially sending a message of safety to the brain. This can interrupt the stress response cascade, preventing the overactivation of the amygdala, the brain's fear center. This leads to a reduction in anxiety, a greater sense of emotional regulation, and an improved ability to manage difficult emotions. Furthermore, the increased oxygen flow to the brain can enhance cognitive functions such as attention, concentration, memory, and problem-solving. It allows for greater clarity of thought and a more objective perspective when facing challenges.

Consider the application of breathwork in high-stress professions. Navy SEALs, for instance, often employ techniques similar to Box Breathing to maintain composure and focus during intense operations. Police officers and firefighters utilize controlled breathing to manage the emotional toll of traumatic events and to remain effective in critical situations. The rationale is simple: when the mind is calm and the body is physiologically stable, decision-making improves, reaction times can be more precise, and the capacity to endure prolonged periods of stress is enhanced. This deliberate cultivation of internal equilibrium is a force multiplier, amplifying an individual's inherent capabilities.

The integration of conscious breathing into daily life is not about reserving it for moments of crisis. It's about building a foundation of resilience that can be accessed proactively. Small, consistent practices can yield significant results.

Here are some practical exercises to begin integrating conscious breathing:

1. **The Mindful Breath Check-in**: Several times a day, pause for 30 seconds to a minute. Simply bring your awareness to your breath. Notice the sensation of the air entering and leaving your body. Are you breathing shallowly or deeply? Is your breath fast or slow? Without judgment, simply observe. This awareness itself can begin to shift your breathing pattern towards greater calm.

2. **Pre-Meeting/Task Breathwork**: Before entering a stressful meeting, engaging in a difficult conversation, or starting a demanding cognitive task, take 1-3 minutes to practice diaphragmatic breathing or Box Breathing. Focus on slowing your exhale. This simple act can significantly alter your internal state, preparing you for optimal engagement.

3. **Transition Breaths**: Use transitions in your day as natural triggers for breathwork. As you move from one activity to another – for example, finishing one task and starting another, or leaving home for work – take 3-5 deep diaphragmatic breaths. This helps to release the residual stress from the previous activity and to arrive fully present for the next.

4. **Evening Wind-Down Breathing**: Before sleep,

dedicate 5-10 minutes to slow, deep breathing. Focus on exhaling longer than you inhale. This signals to your body that it is time to relax and prepare for rest, improving sleep quality and facilitating recovery.

5. **During Physical Activity**: Even during moderate exercise, conscious breathing can enhance performance and endurance. Focus on synchronizing your breath with your movement, aiming for deep, rhythmic inhalations and exhalations. For example, during walking, inhale for two steps, exhale for two steps. This mindful engagement with breath can transform physical exertion into a more meditative experience.

6. **Stress Inoculation with Breathing**: Identify common stressors in your life. Before encountering these situations, or immediately after, practice specific breathwork techniques designed to counteract the physiological effects of stress. This is akin to inoculating your system against the negative impacts of stress, building tolerance and resilience over time.

The breath is an ever-present resource, a direct conduit to our nervous system's control center. By understanding and actively employing breathwork techniques, we equip ourselves with a potent tool for self-regulation, stress management, and cognitive enhancement. It is a fundamental pillar of readiness, enabling us to approach challenges with a calm, focused, and resilient mindset, much like the disciplined warrior who masters their internal environment to dominate the external one. This mastery of the breath is not a passive byproduct of training, but a deliberate, practiced skill that underpins our ability to perform at our peak, regardless of the circumstances. It is the first command we can issue to ourselves, setting the stage for all subsequent actions.

The deliberate cultivation of a structured daily routine serves as a potent strategic advantage, not merely for managing time, but for building unwavering momentum and achieving consistent progress toward our objectives. Just as a well-drilled military unit operates with predictable precision, an individual who establishes and adheres to a disciplined daily march can harness their internal resources to overcome inertia, enhance focus, and systematically chip away at even the most formidable goals. This is not about rigid, joyless adherence to a schedule, but about architecting a personal framework that prioritizes high-impact activities, fosters well-being, and creates a reliable rhythm for personal growth and performance. The psychological underpinnings of habit formation are critical here; by understanding how habits are formed, reinforced, and sustained, we can design a routine that works *for* us, rather than one that we merely struggle against.

At its core, establishing a routine is an act of self-command, an assertion of control over the variables that influence our effectiveness and overall state of being. In a world often characterized by external demands, distractions, and unforeseen circumstances, a consistent personal routine acts as an internal anchor. It provides a predictable flow to our days, reducing the cognitive load associated with constant decision-making about what to do next. This mental economy is invaluable, freeing up cognitive resources that can then be directed towards more challenging tasks and creative endeavors. Think of it as building a well-maintained supply line for your personal campaign – ensuring that essential resources, be they focused work periods, physical activity, or mental replenishment, are consistently available when needed.

The strategic advantage of routine becomes particularly evident when considering the psychological principles of habit formation. Our brains are wired for efficiency; they seek to automate repetitive actions to conserve energy. Habits are the neural pathways that facilitate this automation. By consciously designing our daily activities to align with our goals, we are essentially creating positive feedback loops that reinforce desired behaviors. Two powerful techniques in habit formation are **habit stacking** and the implementation of **reward systems**.

Habit stacking, a concept popularized by James Clear in "Atomic Habits," involves linking a new habit you want to form to an existing habit you already perform consistently. The formula is straightforward: "After [CURRENT HABIT], I will [NEW HABIT]." For example, if you want to establish a practice of journaling, you could stack it with your morning coffee ritual: "After I pour my morning coffee, I will write for five minutes." Or, if you aim to incorporate a short period of mindful breathing, you might say, "After I brush my teeth in the morning, I will practice three minutes of diaphragmatic breathing." The existing habit acts as a trigger or cue for the new behavior, making it far more likely to be remembered and executed. The key is to choose a current habit that is already deeply ingrained and to place the new habit immediately afterward. This leverages the momentum of the established behavior and reduces the friction associated with initiating something new.

Consider the soldier rising before dawn. Their morning routine – from donning gear to preparing their station – is often a sequence of ingrained habits performed with minimal conscious thought. This allows them to be mission-ready with remarkable speed and efficiency. We can apply this principle to our civilian lives by carefully sequencing our day. If your goal is to increase physical fitness, you might stack a short home workout with the act of getting dressed for work: "After I put on my work clothes, I will do 20 squats and 10 push-ups." Or, if you want to dedicate time to learning a new skill, you might stack it with your evening routine: "After I finish dinner, I will spend 15 minutes reading my industry journal." This strategic layering of habits transforms routine from a burden into a supportive structure.

Complementing habit stacking is the strategic use of reward systems. Our brains are motivated by anticipation and the experience of reward, a principle deeply understood in behavioral psychology and military training alike. When a behavior is followed by a positive outcome, the likelihood of that behavior being repeated increases. Rewards can be external (e.g., a treat, a small purchase) or internal (e.g., a sense of accomplishment, increased energy). For habit formation, the most effective rewards are often immediate and intrinsically linked to the habit itself, or at least to the progress it represents.

For instance, if your goal is to complete a challenging project, you might reward yourself with a short break to listen to uplifting music after each hour of focused work. This immediate positive reinforcement can make the task feel less daunting and more enjoyable. For a fitness goal, the reward might be tracking your progress and acknowledging the milestone achieved – perhaps a new pair of workout shoes after a month of consistent exercise. The key is to make the reward meaningful and to ensure it doesn't undermine the habit itself. A reward of unhealthy food after a workout, for example, would create conflicting signals.

The power of rewards lies in their ability to shift our perception of effort. What might otherwise feel like a chore can be reframed as an opportunity to earn a positive experience. This is particularly important when establishing habits that require sustained effort over time. The initial stages of habit formation often involve a significant degree of willpower and deliberate action. A well-designed reward system can help bridge the gap between the initial effort and the eventual intrinsic satisfaction that comes from mastery. It's about giving your brain a reason to embrace the new behavior.

Designing a personal schedule that incorporates these principles requires a strategic approach. It begins with identifying your core objectives and the key activities that will move you closer to them. This involves a period of honest self-assessment and planning. What are your non-negotiable priorities? What tasks require focused, uninterrupted attention? What activities are essential for your physical and mental well-being?

A military planning process often begins with defining the mission objective and then breaking it down into phases and specific tasks. Similarly, we can define our overarching goals – career advancement, improved health, skill development – and then identify the daily or weekly actions that contribute to these goals. This might involve blocking out specific times for deep work, scheduling regular exercise sessions, dedicating time for learning, and ensuring adequate periods for rest and recovery.

Consider the concept of **time blocking**. This involves allocating specific blocks of time in your calendar for particular activities. Instead of having a vague to-do list, you assign concrete time slots for tasks. For example, your calendar might include:

7:00 AM - 7:30 AM: Morning routine (including journaling and mindful breathing)

7:30 AM - 8:00 AM: Breakfast and preparing for the day

8:00 AM - 9:30 AM: Focused work block 1 (e.g., strategic planning)

9:30 AM - 9:45 AM: Short break and stretch

9:45 AM - 11:00 AM: Focused work block 2 (e.g., addressing key emails)

11:00 AM - 12:00 PM: Physical activity

12:00 PM - 1:00 PM: Lunch and mental decompression

This approach provides a visual representation of your day and ensures that critical activities are not overlooked. It also helps to guard against the encroachment of less important tasks and distractions. The effectiveness of time blocking is amplified when it is integrated with habit stacking and reward systems. For instance, you might stack a short reading session into a 30-minute block designated for "skill development," with the reward of a few minutes of social media engagement afterward.

The psychological principle of **commitment and consistency** also plays a crucial role in establishing a sustainable routine. Once we commit to a course of action, especially publicly or to ourselves, we feel an internal pressure to remain consistent with that commitment. This is why articulating your intentions, perhaps by sharing your new routine with a trusted friend or family member, can be so powerful. It creates accountability. Furthermore, when we consistently engage in a behavior, it gradually becomes a part of our identity. We start to see ourselves as "someone who exercises daily" or "someone who prioritizes learning." This shift in self-perception reinforces the habit and makes it more resilient to disruption.

The design of a routine should also be flexible enough to accommodate the realities of life. While discipline is key, rigid adherence can lead to burnout and discouragement when unforeseen events occur. The goal is to create a structure that provides a strong framework but allows for adaptation. If a particular time block is disrupted, the intention is to return to the established routine as soon as possible, rather than abandoning it altogether. This is akin to a military unit that might adjust its operational plan due to enemy action but remains focused on the ultimate objective. The resilience lies in the ability to course-correct without losing sight of the mission.

Furthermore, a balanced routine incorporates not only productive work but also elements that support recovery and rejuvenation. Burnout is the enemy of sustained performance. Therefore, intentionally scheduling periods for rest, relaxation, and activities that bring joy and fulfillment is not a luxury; it is a strategic imperative. This might include spending quality time with loved ones, engaging in hobbies, spending time in nature, or simply allowing for unstructured downtime. These periods of respite are essential for replenishing mental and physical energy, preventing fatigue, and maintaining long-term motivation. Without them, even the most well-intentioned routine can become unsustainable.

The process of establishing and refining a daily routine is an iterative one. It requires ongoing evaluation and adjustment. What is working well? What are the friction points? Are the chosen habits supporting your overall goals, or are they becoming ends in themselves? Regularly reviewing your schedule and making necessary modifications ensures that your routine remains effective and aligned with your evolving priorities. This continuous improvement mindset, common in high-performing organizations and military operations, is crucial for long-term success.

In practice, this might involve a weekly review session where you assess the past week's adherence to your routine and identify any adjustments needed for the upcoming week. Perhaps a particular work block was consistently interrupted, suggesting a need to reschedule or delegate tasks. Or perhaps you found that a planned exercise session felt forced, indicating a need to adjust the intensity or duration, or even the type of activity. This self-awareness and willingness to adapt are hallmarks of a disciplined and effective individual.

The psychological benefit of establishing such a routine extends beyond mere productivity. It cultivates a profound sense of order and control in one's life. In an often chaotic world, having a predictable structure for your day can significantly reduce anxiety and feelings of overwhelm. It provides a stable platform from which to face challenges, knowing that essential aspects of your life are well-managed. This internal sense of order can then radiate outwards, influencing your interactions with others and your ability to navigate external complexities. It is the creation of a personal sanctuary of order, a reliable base camp from which to launch your daily efforts.

Ultimately, cultivating the daily march is about harnessing the power of consistent, deliberate action. It is about understanding that small, sustained efforts, amplified by the principles of habit formation and strategic planning, can lead to extraordinary results over time. By designing a personal schedule that is both disciplined and adaptable, we empower ourselves to move forward with clarity, purpose, and resilience, building an unshakeable foundation for readiness in all aspects of life. This disciplined approach to our days is not about restriction, but about liberation – freeing ourselves from the tyranny of reactive living and enabling proactive engagement with our goals and aspirations. It is a practical application of strategic thinking to the most fundamental arena of all: our own lives.

The first sliver of dawn, that ethereal moment when night concedes to day, holds an immense, often underestimated, power. It is not merely the transition from darkness to light, but a critical inflection point in our daily campaign. How we greet this nascent light, how we navigate those initial moments upon waking, sets the strategic tone for the entire day. This is the domain of the morning ritual, the deliberate architecture of our awakening. Far from being a mere sequence of actions, a well-crafted morning routine is our personal declaration of intent, a proactive engagement with the day ahead that can transform it from a series of reactions into a series of purposeful strides. It is the first, most crucial opportunity to establish dominance over our own consciousness and direct our energies toward our objectives.

Consider the soldier, roused by the bugle call, not with grogginess and reluctant movement, but with ingrained discipline. Their actions are precise, efficient, and geared towards immediate readiness. They don't question the process; they embody it. We, too, can cultivate this level of intentionality in our mornings. The goal is not to mimic a military reveille, but to harness the same spirit of preparedness and focused energy. It is about consciously choosing how we emerge from sleep, rather than allowing the default state of inertia to dictate our trajectory. This requires a mindful transition, a deliberate disengagement from the dream state and an engaged embrace of the waking world. The temptation to hit the snooze button, to cling to the vestiges of slumber, is a subtle but potent act of surrendering control before the day has even truly begun. Each press of that button is a small concession to inertia, a signal to our subconscious that the day's demands are secondary to the comfort of continued rest.

The cornerstone of any effective morning ritual is mindful waking. This means moving beyond the jarring intrusion of an alarm clock if possible, or at least approaching it with intention. If an alarm is necessary, consider its sound. Is it a jarring, aggressive blare, or a gentle, escalating tone? Many modern devices offer 'smart' alarms that aim to wake you during a lighter sleep cycle. Whatever the method, the intent is to transition into wakefulness as smoothly as possible. Once awake, resist the urge to immediately grab your phone. The digital world, with its influx of notifications, emails, and social media updates, is a powerful disruptor of the nascent calm. It pulls your focus outwards, scattering your attention before you've even had a chance to orient yourself. Instead, allow yourself a few moments of stillness. Simply breathe. Become aware of your physical presence in the world.

Hydration is another fundamental, yet often overlooked, element of the morning ritual. Our bodies are naturally dehydrated after a night's sleep. Reintroducing fluids is a vital step in reawakening our physiology. Think of it as priming the engine. A large glass of water, perhaps infused with lemon for an added boost of vitamin C and a touch of alkalizing effect, is an excellent way to kickstart your system. This simple act signals to your body that you are beginning the day with care and attention. It aids in flushing out toxins and preparing your digestive system for nourishment. Some proponents of morning rituals even advocate for warm water, believing it to be more easily absorbed and more soothing to the system. Regardless of temperature, the consistent act of hydrating upon waking is a powerful statement of self-care and physical readiness.

Following hydration, introducing gentle physical movement is paramount. This is not about an intense workout, though that can certainly be incorporated later in the day. It's about rousing the body, increasing circulation, and activating the neuromuscular pathways. Light stretching, a few yoga poses, or even a short walk can make a significant difference. The aim is to connect with your physical self, to feel the body reawaken and become responsive. Consider movements that promote spinal mobility, awaken the major muscle groups, and encourage deep breathing. Think of it as a gradual build-up of energy, rather than an immediate demand for peak performance. This gentle activation helps to shake off the stiffness of sleep and prepare the body for the demands ahead. Even five to ten minutes of mindful movement can have a profound impact on your physical and mental state, bridging the gap between dormancy and dynamic engagement.

For instance, a simple sequence could include: lying on your back and gently drawing your knees to your chest, followed by a gentle spinal twist. Then, transitioning to a cat-cow stretch on your hands and knees to mobilize the spine, and finally, a few sun salutations to awaken the entire body. The key is to listen to your body and choose movements that feel nourishing and energizing. This physical awakening also has a direct impact on mental clarity. As blood flow increases to the brain, cognitive functions are enhanced, preparing you for more demanding mental tasks.

Beyond the physical, the morning ritual offers a critical window for mental and emotional preparation. This is where contemplation and intention setting come into play. This period, however brief, allows you to align your inner state with your outward actions. Meditation, even for just a few minutes, can be incredibly powerful. It's a practice of observing thoughts without judgment, of anchoring yourself in the present moment. This cultivates a sense of calm and resilience, equipping you to better handle the inevitable stresses and distractions that the day will bring. By practicing mindfulness, you train your brain to be less reactive and more responsive. You build the capacity to choose your response, rather than being swept away by impulse or external stimuli.

Alternatively, or in addition to meditation, journaling can be a potent tool. Writing down your thoughts, feelings, or a simple gratitude list can provide clarity and perspective. It's a way to externalize your inner landscape, to understand what's occupying your mind and to consciously direct your focus. Setting intentions for the day is perhaps the most direct way to imbue your morning with purpose. This involves articulating what you want to achieve, how you want to feel, or what qualities you wish to embody. It could be as simple as "Today, I will approach challenges with patience," or "My intention is to be fully present in my interactions." This deliberate act of setting a course, even a micro-course, provides a compass for your day. It transforms amorphous desires into actionable intents.

Think about the strategic value of this mental preparation. A military commander doesn't launch an operation without a clear mission briefing and an understanding of their objectives. Similarly, by setting intentions, you provide yourself with a personal mission statement for the day. This clarity of purpose acts as a powerful filter, helping you to prioritize tasks and make decisions that are aligned with your desired outcomes. It's about being the architect of your day, not just a passive participant.

The cumulative effect of these elements – mindful waking, hydration, gentle movement, and mental preparation – is a profound shift in your baseline state. Instead of waking up feeling reactive, scattered, or already behind, you emerge from your morning ritual feeling grounded, focused, and in command. This initial advantage can cascade throughout the day, influencing your productivity, your decision-making, and your overall well-being. When you start your day with intention, you are less likely to be derailed by minor setbacks. You have built an internal reservoir of calm and focus that can buffer against external pressures.

Many highly successful individuals attribute a significant portion of their achievements to the consistency and intentionality of their morning routines. While the specifics vary, the underlying principles remain consistent. For example, some leaders begin their day with an hour of exercise, followed by reading and journaling, before even checking their emails. Others prioritize quiet contemplation and meditation, using the early morning hours for deep thinking and strategic planning. The common thread is the deliberate carving out of time for self-development and mental preparation, insulating this crucial period from the demands of the external world. These are not simply habits of convenience; they are strategic investments in personal effectiveness.

Consider the ripple effect. A morning that begins with a sense of calm and control is more likely to lead to focused work sessions. Focused work sessions often result in greater productivity and higher quality output. This sense of accomplishment can then fuel positive momentum throughout the day, leading to better interactions with colleagues, improved problem-solving, and a greater overall sense of fulfillment. Conversely, a morning that begins with chaos – a frantic rush, a bombardment of notifications, a feeling of being immediately overwhelmed – can set a tone of reactivity that is difficult to shake. The scattered energy of the morning can persist, leading to fragmented attention, missed opportunities, and a general feeling of being on the back foot.

The design of your personal morning ritual should be a deeply individualized process. There is no one-size-fits-all solution. The most effective routine is one that resonates with your personal values, your lifestyle, and your goals. Experimentation is key. What time do you naturally wake up most refreshed? What activities genuinely make you feel energized and centered? Start small. You don't need to overhaul your entire morning overnight. Implement one or two new practices at a time and observe their impact. Perhaps begin by committing to drinking a glass of water immediately upon waking. Once that becomes automatic, add five minutes of mindful breathing. Gradually build your ritual, ensuring that each element feels sustainable and beneficial.

It's also important to acknowledge that life is not always predictable. There will be days when your meticulously planned morning is disrupted by unforeseen circumstances – a child's illness, an urgent work matter, or simply a night of poor sleep. In such instances, the principle of strategic flexibility comes into play. The goal is not perfection, but consistency and resilience. If your full ritual isn't possible, do what you can. Perhaps all you have time for is a few deep breaths and a glass of water. The act of still attempting *something* intentional, even in a compressed form, is far more valuable than abandoning the entire practice. This approach prevents a minor disruption from becoming a total derailment. It reinforces the idea that your routine is a supportive structure, not a rigid cage.

The true power of the morning ritual lies in its ability to cultivate a proactive mindset. By consciously choosing how you begin your day, you are asserting your agency. You are signaling to yourself and to the world that you are the author of your own experience. This intentionality extends beyond mere task completion; it shapes your perception of yourself and your capabilities. When you consistently start your day feeling prepared and purposeful, you build self-efficacy, the belief in your ability to succeed. This internal locus of control is a powerful driver of sustained performance and personal growth.

Think of your morning ritual as the initial deployment of your strategic assets. It's about ensuring your primary resource – your own mind and body – is optimally prepared before engaging the challenges of the day. It's an investment in your cognitive capital, your emotional equilibrium, and your physical vitality. By dedicating these precious early moments to intentional self-care and preparation, you create a foundation of readiness that will serve you throughout the hours that follow. The first light of dawn, when met with purpose and discipline, can indeed be the harbinger of a victorious day. It is the moment when you claim ownership of your time, your energy, and your potential, setting the stage for a day lived with intention, focus, and resilience. This is not about striving for an unattainable ideal, but about the practical, actionable steps that empower you to meet each day with your best self, ready to engage, adapt, and achieve.

Chapter 2: Sharpening the Mind: Cognitive Fortification and Mental Agility

The mind, in its capacity for thought, analysis, and decision-making, is akin to a sophisticated command center, a strategic theater where every thought, every perception, and every action plays out. Within this theater, attention is the most precious and finite resource. Much like a military unit needing to maintain focus on its objective amidst the chaos and sensory overload of a battlefield, our minds must constantly navigate a complex landscape of internal and external stimuli. Understanding this dynamic is foundational to fortifying our cognitive capabilities and achieving mental agility. The very notion of a "battlefield of the mind" isn't hyperbole; it's a functional description of the continuous struggle to maintain focus against a barrage of competing demands.

Central to this understanding is the concept of cognitive load. This term, borrowed from cognitive psychology, refers to the total amount of mental effort being used in the working memory. Our working memory is the mental workspace where we hold and process information actively. It's like a temporary workbench; while it's incredibly powerful, its capacity is inherently limited. When we overload this workbench with too many tasks, too much information, or too many distractions, our ability to process anything effectively plummets. This is precisely what happens when our cognitive load becomes excessive. Imagine trying to assemble a complex piece of equipment with a constant stream of radio chatter, unexpected enemy movements, and incomplete schematics – it's a recipe for error and inefficiency. Similarly, when our minds are burdened by excessive cognitive load, our ability to think clearly, solve problems, and retain information degrades.

Cognitive load theory categorizes this mental burden into three types: intrinsic, extraneous, and germane. Intrinsic cognitive load is the inherent difficulty of the subject matter itself. Learning advanced calculus, for example, has a higher intrinsic load than learning basic arithmetic due to the complexity of the concepts and the number of elements that must be held in mind simultaneously. Germane cognitive load refers to the mental effort devoted to processing information and constructing mental schemas – essentially, the effort used for learning and understanding. This is the type of load we want to optimize, as it leads to deeper comprehension and skill acquisition.

Extraneous cognitive load, however, is the detrimental type. It's the mental effort imposed by the way information is presented or by irrelevant distractions that interfere with our ability to engage with the core material. This is where the battlefield analogy becomes particularly potent. Extraneous cognitive load is like the enemy artillery fire that forces your troops to divert attention and resources away from their primary mission. In our daily lives, extraneous load is often generated by our environment, our habits, and the very design of the information systems we interact with.

Consider the ubiquitous nature of distractions in the modern world. Every ping of a notification from a smartphone, every pop-up advertisement on a website, every unexpected email notification, every tangential thought that drifts into our consciousness – these are all potential sources of extraneous cognitive load. Each interruption, no matter how brief, requires our brain to disengage from the current task, process the new stimulus, and then attempt to re-engage with the original task. This process isn't seamless. It involves a mental "context switch," which expends precious mental energy and inevitably leads to a reduction in performance. Neuroscientific research has shown that the brain doesn't truly multitask; instead, it rapidly switches attention between tasks. This switching incurs a "switch cost," a measurable loss of time and efficiency.

The neurological basis of attention helps us understand why these distractions are so detrimental. Attention is a complex cognitive function mediated by a network of brain regions, including the prefrontal cortex, the parietal lobe, and the anterior cingulate cortex. These areas work in concert to select relevant information, inhibit irrelevant stimuli, and maintain focus over time. When we are exposed to a constant stream of stimuli, especially those that are novel, unpredictable, or emotionally salient (like social media updates or urgent work emails), these attentional networks are constantly being pulled in different directions. This sustained activation and redirection can lead to mental fatigue, a state where our ability to exert control over our attention diminishes.

Think of your attentional capacity as a spotlight. In an ideal scenario, this spotlight is focused on the task at hand, illuminating only what is relevant and necessary. However, when extraneous cognitive load increases, it's as if numerous smaller, unexpected lights are flashing all around, constantly trying to capture the spotlight's attention. Each flash forces the spotlight to shift, to acknowledge the new stimulus, and then to struggle to return to its original position. Over time, the constant shifting can make the spotlight unsteady, its beam wavering and its intensity diminished.

The prevalence of digital devices and the interconnected nature of modern life have amplified these challenges significantly. We are often expected to be constantly available, to respond immediately to communications, and to process vast amounts of information from multiple sources simultaneously. This creates a perpetual state of high cognitive load for many individuals. The very tools designed to enhance productivity can, if not managed consciously, become significant drains on our mental resources. This is particularly true for tasks that require deep concentration, such as writing, coding, complex problem-solving, or strategic planning.

Identifying common cognitive drains is the first step in mitigating their impact. These drains can manifest in various ways:

Constant Connectivity: The expectation of immediate responses to emails, messages, and social media platforms forces frequent context switching and fragments attention.

Information Overload: The sheer volume of data we encounter daily, from news feeds to research papers, can overwhelm our working memory.

Multitasking Illusion: Believing we can effectively juggle multiple demanding tasks simultaneously, leading to reduced efficiency and increased errors.

Unmanaged Notifications: Digital alerts that interrupt our workflow without a clear purpose or immediate necessity.

Internal Distractions: Wandering thoughts, worries, or rumination that pull our focus away from the present task.

Environmental Noise: Physical distractions such as loud colleagues, background chatter, or a cluttered workspace.

Ambiguous Goals: Lacking clarity on what needs to be achieved, leading to inefficient use of mental energy as we try to decipher our purpose.

The neurological underpinnings of attention also highlight the importance of novelty and unpredictability. Our brains are wired to pay attention to things that are new, surprising, or potentially threatening. This evolutionary advantage, designed to help us detect danger or opportunity, can be hijacked by the constant stream of novel stimuli from our digital environment. Social media feeds, for instance, are designed to be inherently engaging by presenting a constantly changing array of content, often with elements of surprise and social validation (likes, comments), which triggers dopamine release in the brain and reinforces the habit of checking. This creates a feedback loop that can be difficult to break, further exacerbating cognitive load and depleting attentional resources.

Understanding these mechanisms is not about advocating for a complete disconnect from the digital world, but about cultivating a more strategic and mindful approach to our engagement with it. It's about recognizing that our attention is a vital component of our cognitive arsenal, and just as we would protect and maintain our physical equipment, we must actively manage and protect our mental focus. This requires developing an awareness of when our cognitive load is becoming excessive and when our attention is being depleted by unnecessary drains.

This awareness forms the bedrock for developing strategies to enhance concentration and cognitive efficiency. Without understanding the dynamics of cognitive load and the mechanisms of attention, any attempts to improve focus will be akin to trying to win a battle without understanding the terrain or the enemy's tactics. The goal is to move from a reactive state, where our attention is dictated by external stimuli and internal impulses, to a proactive state, where we consciously direct our focus towards our most important objectives. This involves not only minimizing extraneous load but also optimizing our environment and our mental practices to support deep work and sustained concentration.

The principle is simple: by reducing the mental "noise" and the demand on our working memory, we free up cognitive resources. This allows our brains to engage more effectively with the tasks that truly matter, fostering deeper learning, more creative problem-solving, and more effective decision-making. It's about creating the optimal conditions for our minds to perform at their peak, much like a well-maintained and strategically deployed unit operating with clear objectives and minimal interference. The battlefield of the mind is always active, but by understanding its dynamics, we can learn to navigate it with greater skill, resilience, and ultimately, greater success. The subsequent sections will delve into specific exercises and techniques to achieve this, building upon this foundational understanding of cognitive load and the critical nature of attention. This initial insight into the mind's limitations and vulnerabilities is the first step in building a more robust and agile cognitive system, prepared to meet the demands of any challenge. It requires a shift in perspective, viewing our mental energy not as an inexhaustible resource, but as a valuable commodity that must be managed with deliberate intent and strategic foresight.

Drawing directly from the rigorous pre-mission planning protocols honed over centuries of military operations, we can extract a profoundly effective cognitive strategy: tactical visualization, or mental rehearsal. This isn't mere daydreaming; it is a deliberate, systematic process of simulating a future event or task in exquisite detail within the mind's theater. Just as a special forces unit will walk through every possible scenario of an upcoming operation, from insertion points to exfiltration routes, from enemy engagement protocols to contingency plans for equipment failure, so too can we prepare our minds for success by rehearsing it before the fact.

The essence of tactical visualization lies in creating a high-fidelity mental simulation. This involves engaging as many senses as possible within this internal rehearsal. What do you see? What do you hear? What do you feel – both physically and emotionally? For a soldier preparing for a complex infiltration, this might mean visualizing the texture of the rope they will rappel down, the faint smell of damp earth at the extraction point, the precise sequence of hand signals they will use, and the internal calm they aim to maintain despite potential enemy proximity. The goal is to make the mental simulation as close to the real-world experience as possible, thereby desensitizing the mind to novelty and stress, and imprinting the successful sequence of actions.

The scientific underpinnings of this practice are robust and deeply rooted in our understanding of neuroplasticity and motor learning. When we vividly imagine performing an action, our brain actually activates many of the same neural pathways that would be engaged if we were physically performing it. Studies have shown that individuals who engage in mental rehearsal for skills like archery, basketball shooting, or even playing a musical instrument demonstrate significant performance improvements compared to those who do not visualize. This phenomenon is often attributed to the brain's ability to "practice" and refine motor sequences, strengthen neural connections, and optimize the pathways involved in task execution without the physical strain or risk of actual performance. In essence, the brain learns by imagining, creating a neurological blueprint for success.

Consider the impact on confidence and self-efficacy. By mentally walking through a challenging task and envisioning a positive and successful outcome, we build a powerful internal narrative of capability. Each successful mental rehearsal reinforces the belief that the task is achievable, that we possess the necessary skills, and that we can handle potential obstacles. This internal reinforcement is crucial for overcoming the psychological barriers that often accompany difficult endeavors, such as performance anxiety or fear of failure. When faced with the actual event, the mind is not encountering the situation for the first time; it has already navigated it numerous times in a controlled, internal environment, reducing the element of surprise and increasing the sense of preparedness.

The application of tactical visualization extends far beyond the traditional domains of military or athletic performance. In the realm of personal development and professional life, it can be a game-changer for complex problem-solving. Before a critical negotiation, a challenging presentation, or a high-stakes meeting, one can engage in tactical visualization. Walk through the entire scenario: the initial greetings, the key points to be made, the potential questions or objections from the other party, and how you will respond calmly and effectively. Visualize yourself articulating your arguments clearly, confidently, and persuasively. Imagine the positive reception of your ideas and the successful achievement of your objectives. Focus not just on the outcome, but on the process – how you will maintain composure, listen actively, and adapt your strategy as needed.

For instance, if you are preparing for a job interview, the visualization might involve seeing yourself walking into the interview room, shaking hands confidently, making eye contact with the interviewer, and clearly articulating your qualifications and enthusiasm for the role. You might visualize yourself answering behavioral questions with specific, compelling examples drawn from your experience, demonstrating your problem-solving skills, your teamwork abilities, and your leadership potential. You can even visualize yourself handling difficult questions with grace and honesty. The more detailed and emotionally resonant the visualization, the more potent its effect. Feel the sense of calm assurance as you speak, the positive affirmation from the interviewer, and the ultimate satisfaction of having performed exceptionally. This mental preparation can significantly reduce interview jitters and improve your ability to think on your feet.

Similarly, when facing performance anxiety, such as public speaking, tactical visualization can be a powerful antidote. Instead of dwelling on the fear of forgetting lines or being judged, a speaker can visualize the entire speech unfolding perfectly. Picture the audience engaged, nodding in agreement, and responding positively. Imagine the feeling of confidence as you deliver your message, the clarity of your voice, and the sense of accomplishment after the applause. This mental rehearsal helps to reframe the experience from one of potential threat to one of opportunity and control. It allows the brain to create a new, positive association with the act of public speaking, overriding the anxious default response.

The process of tactical visualization also involves a conscious effort to identify potential obstacles and mentally rehearse strategies to overcome them. In a military context, this might be visualizing how to react to an unexpected ambush or a sudden communication breakdown. In personal life, it could involve anticipating potential roadblocks to a project – a delay in receiving necessary information, resistance from a colleague, or an unforeseen technical issue – and mentally rehearsing your calm and effective responses to each. This proactive approach to problem-solving makes you more resilient and adaptable when challenges inevitably arise. You are not merely hoping for the best; you are preparing for a range of possibilities, thereby increasing your capacity to navigate them successfully.

To effectively implement tactical visualization, several key elements are crucial. Firstly,

clarity of objective is paramount. You must know precisely what you are aiming to achieve. Without a clear target, the visualization will be unfocused and less effective. Secondly, **detail and sensory engagement** are vital. The more vividly you can immerse yourself in the imagined scenario, the more the brain will treat it as a real experience. Engage all your senses: what do you see, hear, smell, taste, and touch? What are your internal thoughts and feelings? Thirdly, **positive focus** is essential. While it is beneficial to anticipate obstacles, the overarching narrative of the visualization should be one of success and effective execution. Focus on how you will overcome challenges, not on the challenges themselves overwhelming you. Fourthly, **repetition** is key. Like any skill, tactical visualization becomes more potent with practice. Regularly engaging in mental rehearsal strengthens the neural pathways and enhances your ability to achieve a deep state of focused imagination.

Let's delve deeper into the sensory and emotional components. Imagine you are preparing for a challenging hike. Instead of just thinking "I will hike up the mountain," a tactical visualization would involve:

Visuals: Seeing the trail ahead, the dappled sunlight through the trees, the texture of the rocks underfoot, the panoramic view from the summit.

Sounds: Hearing the crunch of leaves and gravel under your boots, the chirping of birds, the rush of wind, your own steady breathing.

Physical Sensations: Feeling the weight of your backpack, the exertion in your legs, the warmth of the sun on your skin, the cool breeze, the sweat on your brow.

Emotions: Experiencing a sense of determination as you begin, focus as you navigate tricky sections, moments of awe at the scenery, and the profound satisfaction and exhilaration upon reaching the summit.

By immersing yourself in these sensory details and emotional states, you create a richer, more impactful mental simulation. This process not only primes your mind and body for the physical exertion but also builds the mental resilience needed to push through fatigue or moments of doubt. You are, in essence, creating a memory of success before the event even occurs.

Furthermore, tactical visualization can be a powerful tool for developing specific mental skills, such as **decision-making under pressure**. Imagine a scenario where you need to make a critical decision quickly. Mentally rehearse the process: identifying the core problem, rapidly assessing available information, considering potential options and their likely consequences, and then making a decisive choice. Visualize yourself remaining calm and focused, even as the stakes are high. This practice helps to build the mental discipline required to perform effectively when time is limited and the consequences of error are significant.

The integration of mindfulness, which we've touched upon in earlier sections concerning attention, further enhances the efficacy of tactical visualization. A mindful approach ensures that during the visualization, you are fully present in the imagined scenario, noticing details without judgment and observing your internal reactions with curiosity rather than aversion. This heightened awareness allows for a more authentic and impactful rehearsal, enabling you to identify potential points of mental friction or emotional distress and proactively address them within the simulation.

For individuals struggling with procrastination, tactical visualization can be used to mentally rehearse the process of starting and completing a task. Visualize yourself sitting down to work, resisting the urge to distract yourself, and making steady progress. Focus on the feeling of accomplishment as you complete small milestones. This can help to break down daunting tasks into manageable steps and build the momentum needed to overcome inertia.

The principle is one of preparation meeting opportunity. By dedicating time to mentally rehearse desired outcomes and the processes that lead to them, we are actively shaping our mental landscape and influencing our future performance. This isn't about guaranteeing a specific result, as external factors are always at play. Instead, it's about maximizing our internal readiness, building confidence, refining our approach, and increasing our capacity to adapt and succeed in the face of whatever challenges arise. Tactical visualization is not a passive wish; it is an active, strategic deployment of our mental faculties, preparing the mind to execute flawlessly when the moment of truth arrives. It is the unseen training that often makes the visible success possible. It's about commanding your inner world to prepare for the outer one, ensuring that when the mission calls, your mind is already a veteran of success.

The preceding exploration has underscored the power of tactical visualization – the art of mentally rehearsing future events to optimize performance and build confidence. Now, we pivot to a foundational cognitive discipline that complements and enhances this proactive mental preparation: the cultivation of mindful awareness, or as it's often termed, the observer's stance. This approach, deeply rooted in ancient contemplative traditions, particularly Buddhism, offers a profound method for understanding and navigating the complexities of our own minds and the external world with clarity and equanimity. It is, in essence, about learning to witness our internal and external experiences without immediate judgment or reaction, akin to a skilled scout meticulously observing and reporting battlefield conditions without allowing personal bias or emotional response to color the assessment.

Mindfulness, at its core, is the practice of bringing one's attention to the present moment, deliberately and non-judgmentally. This isn't about emptying the mind or achieving a state of blissful detachment. Rather, it is about cultivating a clear, objective awareness of whatever is arising, be it a thought, an emotion, a physical sensation, or an external stimulus. Imagine a seasoned reconnaissance operative tasked with gathering intelligence. Their primary objective is to observe accurately – the terrain, enemy movements, the disposition of forces – and to report these facts without embellishment or distortion. They are trained to recognize what is truly present, rather than what they *wish* were present or *fear* might be present. Similarly, the observer's stance in mindfulness encourages us to become impartial witnesses to our own inner landscape.

This practice involves a deliberate shift in our relationship with our thoughts and feelings. Typically, we are deeply identified with our mental content. A fleeting anxious thought can feel like an absolute truth, and an emotional surge can dictate our entire perception of reality. Mindfulness invites us to step back, to observe these phenomena as passing events, like clouds drifting across the sky. We learn to notice the *process* of thinking, the *arising and passing* of emotions, rather than being swept away by their content. This cultivates a crucial distinction between *being* the thought or emotion and *observing* the thought or emotion. This subtle yet powerful shift is the bedrock of mental agility and emotional resilience.

Developing this observer's stance requires consistent practice. One fundamental technique is **body scanning**. This involves systematically bringing attention to different parts of the body, noticing any sensations present – warmth, coolness, tingling, pressure, or even the absence of sensation. The key is to observe these sensations without trying to change them, judge them, or analyze them. For instance, while scanning your feet, you might notice a feeling of tightness. Instead of immediately thinking, "My feet are too tight, I need to stretch," or "This tightness means something is wrong," the mindful approach is to simply acknowledge, "There is a sensation of tightness in my feet." This non-judgmental observation creates space around the experience, preventing it from escalating into a narrative of discomfort or anxiety. This detailed, moment-by-moment awareness of physical experience trains the mind to be present and observant, a skill directly transferable to keenly observing external situations.

Another cornerstone of mindfulness is **breath awareness**. The breath is a constant, anchoring presence that is always available. By directing attention to the physical sensations of breathing – the rise and fall of the chest, the feeling of air entering and leaving the nostrils – we anchor ourselves in the present moment. When the mind inevitably wanders, as it will, the practice is not to chastise oneself for wandering, but to gently, with curiosity, notice that the mind has wandered, and then to bring the attention back to the breath. This repeated act of noticing and returning is the core exercise of mindfulness, strengthening the neural pathways associated with focused attention and self-awareness. It's like repeatedly returning your gaze to a fixed point in the distance, training your visual focus.

This practice of returning our attention to the breath or bodily sensations is fundamentally about **de-escalating emotional reactivity**. When we are caught in a strong emotion, such as anger or fear, our physiological responses are activated, and our cognitive processes become narrowly focused on the perceived threat. Mindfulness interrupts this cycle by creating a pause. By stepping back and observing the physiological sensations associated with the emotion – the racing heart, the tense muscles, the shallow breath – we begin to recognize that these are *sensations*, not necessarily objective reality. This recognition allows us to respond from a more considered place, rather than react impulsively.

Consider a scenario where you receive an email that triggers an immediate sense of frustration. Your initial, unmindful reaction might be to fire back an angry reply. However, by employing the observer's stance, you can pause. You notice the heat rising in your chest, the clenching of your jaw. You acknowledge these sensations without immediately acting on them. You observe the thought, "This is unfair!" without automatically accepting it as the absolute truth. This pause, facilitated by mindful awareness, allows you to access a broader range of options. You can then choose to reread the email more calmly, consider the sender's perspective, or formulate a measured response that aligns with your long-term goals, rather than one driven by immediate emotional impulse. This capacity to observe and regulate one's internal state is crucial for effective decision-making, especially under pressure.

A critical distinction to cultivate within this practice is between **observation and analysis**. Observation is about noticing what *is*. It is a direct, uninterpreted awareness of experience. Analysis, on the other hand, involves interpretation, judgment, and the construction of narratives. For example, observing your breath is noticing the in-and-out movement. Analyzing your breath might involve thinking, "My breath is too shallow, which means I'm stressed," or "This is the most perfect breath I've ever taken." While analytical thinking has its place, in the context of cultivating mindful awareness, we are learning to prioritize direct observation. This allows us to gather information about our internal and external environment without the immediate overlay of our personal biases, beliefs, and past experiences, which often distort our perception.

This skill of dis-identifying from our thoughts and emotions is profoundly liberating. We are not our thoughts, nor are we our feelings. We are the awareness that witnesses them. This realization can significantly reduce suffering, as much of our distress arises from our resistance to or over-identification with our mental and emotional states. By becoming a detached observer, we can begin to see that difficult emotions are transient and that negative thoughts are not necessarily accurate reflections of reality.

The ability to observe without judgment is perhaps the most challenging, yet most rewarding, aspect of mindfulness. It asks us to approach our experiences, even the uncomfortable ones, with a sense of gentle curiosity. When you notice a judgmental thought arise – perhaps a critical assessment of yourself or someone else – the mindful approach is to simply observe that judgmental thought itself, acknowledging its presence without getting caught in its content. You might note, "There is a thought of judgment about X," or "The mind is engaged in criticism right now." This doesn't mean you condone the judgment; it means you are observing the *process* of judgment occurring within you. This practice gradually weakens the habitual tendency to automatically endorse every thought as truth.

This cultivated detachment is not about becoming cold or uncaring. Instead, it fosters a deeper, more authentic form of empathy and connection. When we are less reactive to our own internal states, we are better able to understand and connect with the experiences of others. We can recognize that they, too, are subject to the ebb and flow of thoughts and emotions. This empathetic understanding, grounded in the recognition of shared human experience, is far more profound than a reaction based on superficial judgment or immediate emotional resonance.

Furthermore, the observer's stance directly enhances our problem-solving capabilities and decision-making processes. When faced with a complex situation, our habitual response might be to panic, to become overwhelmed, or to jump to conclusions based on limited information or emotional bias. By cultivating mindful awareness, we create the mental space to observe the situation more clearly and comprehensively. We can step back from the immediate emotional charge and assess the facts objectively. We can identify our own assumptions and biases that might be clouding our judgment. This allows us to consider a wider range of solutions and to make more rational, effective decisions.

Imagine preparing for a critical negotiation. Without mindfulness, you might enter the room already feeling defensive or anxious, projecting these feelings onto the other party and limiting your ability to listen effectively. With the observer's stance, you can bring a calm, observant awareness to the interaction. You notice your own internal reactions – a tightening in your stomach, a tendency to interrupt – and you can choose to respond differently. You observe the other party's words and body language without immediately interpreting them through the lens of your own anxieties. This objective observation allows you to understand the situation more fully, identify opportunities, and respond strategically rather than reactively.

The development of present-moment awareness, facilitated by practices like breath awareness and body scanning, is crucial for improving decision-making by reducing the influence of past regrets and future anxieties. When we are fully present, our decisions are based on the current reality, not on hypothetical scenarios or past mistakes. This allows for more agile and adaptive responses to evolving circumstances. It's akin to a pilot flying an aircraft, who must constantly assess the present conditions – airspeed, altitude, weather – to make immediate, effective course corrections, rather than dwelling on a past miscalculation or worrying about a hypothetical future emergency.

This consistent practice of observing without judgment also builds a profound sense of self-compassion. We often hold ourselves to impossibly high standards, and when we inevitably fall short, we engage in harsh self-criticism. Mindfulness teaches us to approach our own perceived flaws and mistakes with the same gentle curiosity and acceptance we might offer a dear friend. When a thought arises, "I made a mistake on that project," the mindful response is not self-recrimination, but observation: "Ah, a thought that I made a mistake. What can I learn from this?" This shift in internal dialogue transforms the experience of error from a source of shame into an opportunity for growth and learning.

Moreover, the observer's stance can be integrated with the tactical visualization discussed earlier. While tactical visualization focuses on rehearsing future success, mindful awareness provides the clear, objective perspective needed to observe the visualization itself. During mental rehearsal, one can practice noticing the quality of the visualization: are the images clear? Are the emotions felt authentic? Are there moments of resistance or distraction? By observing these aspects of the mental rehearsal with mindful awareness, we can refine the visualization process itself, making it more potent and effective. For instance, if during visualization you notice a persistent feeling of self-doubt creeping in, mindful observation allows you to acknowledge this doubt without letting it derail the rehearsal. You can then gently redirect your attention, or even visualize yourself meeting that doubt with calm acceptance and continued forward momentum.

In essence, cultivating the observer's stance is about developing a more sophisticated and refined form of attention. It's about shifting from an automatic, reactive mode of consciousness to a deliberate, observant mode. This allows us to engage with life more fully, to understand ourselves and our circumstances more clearly, and to respond with greater wisdom and effectiveness. It is the foundation upon which many other cognitive enhancements can be built, ensuring that as we sharpen our mental acuity and strategic thinking, we do so from a place of clarity, balance, and self-awareness. The observer's stance is not merely a technique; it is a way of being, a conscious choice to engage with reality, both internal and external, with open eyes and an impartial mind, prepared to witness and respond with clarity and purpose. This cultivated detachment from immediate, often misleading, mental chatter is what allows for true insight and robust, unshakeable composure in any situation. It is the quiet strength that underpins all effective action.

The preceding exploration has underscored the power of tactical visualization – the art of mentally rehearsing future events to optimize performance and build confidence. Now, we pivot to a foundational cognitive discipline that complements and enhances this proactive mental preparation: the cultivation of mindful awareness, or as it's often termed, the observer's stance.

This approach, deeply rooted in ancient contemplative traditions, particularly Buddhism, offers a profound method for understanding and navigating the complexities of our own minds and the external world with clarity and equanimity. It is, in essence, about learning to witness our internal and external experiences without immediate judgment or reaction, akin to a skilled scout meticulously observing and reporting battlefield conditions without allowing personal bias or emotional response to color the assessment.

Mindfulness, at its core, is the practice of bringing one's attention to the present moment, deliberately and non-judgmentally. This isn't about emptying the mind or achieving a state of blissful detachment. Rather, it is about cultivating a clear, objective awareness of whatever is arising, be it a thought, an emotion, a physical sensation, or an external stimulus. Imagine a seasoned reconnaissance operative tasked with gathering intelligence. Their primary objective is to observe accurately – the terrain, enemy movements, the disposition of forces – and to report these facts without embellishment or distortion. They are trained to recognize what is truly present, rather than what they *wish* were present or *fear* might be present. Similarly, the observer's stance in mindfulness encourages us to become impartial witnesses to our own inner landscape.

This practice involves a deliberate shift in our relationship with our thoughts and feelings. Typically, we are deeply identified with our mental content. A fleeting anxious thought can feel like an absolute truth, and an emotional surge can dictate our entire perception of reality. Mindfulness invites us to step back, to observe these phenomena as passing events, like clouds drifting across the sky. We learn to notice the *process* of thinking, the *arising and passing* of emotions, rather than being swept away by their content. This cultivates a crucial distinction between *being* the thought or emotion and *observing* the thought or emotion. This subtle yet powerful shift is the bedrock of mental agility and emotional resilience.

Developing this observer's stance requires consistent practice. One fundamental technique is **body scanning**. This involves systematically bringing attention to different parts of the body, noticing any sensations present – warmth, coolness, tingling, pressure, or even the absence of sensation. The key is to observe these sensations without trying to change them, judge them, or analyze them. For instance, while scanning your feet, you might notice a feeling of tightness. Instead of immediately thinking, "My feet are too tight, I need to stretch," or "This tightness means something is wrong," the mindful approach is to simply acknowledge, "There is a sensation of tightness in my feet." This non-judgmental observation creates space around the experience, preventing it from escalating into a narrative of discomfort or anxiety. This detailed, moment-by-moment awareness of physical experience trains the mind to be present and observant, a skill directly transferable to keenly observing external situations.

Another cornerstone of mindfulness is **breath awareness**. The breath is a constant, anchoring presence that is always available. By directing attention to the physical sensations of breathing – the rise and fall of the chest, the feeling of air entering and leaving the nostrils – we anchor ourselves in the present moment. When the mind inevitably wanders, as it will, the practice is not to chastise oneself for wandering, but to gently, with curiosity, notice that the mind has wandered, and then to bring the attention back to the breath. This repeated act of noticing and returning is the core exercise of mindfulness, strengthening the neural pathways associated with focused attention and self-awareness. It's like repeatedly returning your gaze to a fixed point in the distance, training your visual focus.

This practice of returning our attention to the breath or bodily sensations is fundamentally about **de-escalating emotional reactivity**. When we are caught in a strong emotion, such as anger or fear, our physiological responses are activated, and our cognitive processes become narrowly focused on the perceived threat. Mindfulness interrupts this cycle by creating a pause. By stepping back and observing the physiological sensations associated with the emotion – the racing heart, the tense muscles, the shallow breath – we begin to recognize that these are *sensations*, not necessarily objective reality. This recognition allows us to respond from a more considered place, rather than react impulsively.

Consider a scenario where you receive an email that triggers an immediate sense of frustration. Your initial, unmindful reaction might be to fire back an angry reply. However, by employing the observer's stance, you can pause. You notice the heat rising in your chest, the clenching of your jaw. You acknowledge these sensations without immediately acting on them. You observe the thought, "This is unfair!" without automatically accepting it as the absolute truth. This pause, facilitated by mindful awareness, allows you to access a broader range of options. You can then choose to reread the email more calmly, consider the sender's perspective, or formulate a measured response that aligns with your long-term goals, rather than one driven by immediate emotional impulse. This capacity to observe and regulate our internal state is crucial for effective decision-making, especially under pressure.

A critical distinction to cultivate within this practice is between **observation and analysis.** Observation is about noticing what *is*. It is a direct, uninterpreted awareness of experience. Analysis, on the other hand, involves interpretation, judgment, and the construction of narratives. For example, observing your breath is noticing the in-and-out movement. Analyzing your breath might involve thinking, "My breath is too shallow, which means I'm stressed," or "This is the most perfect breath I've ever taken." While analytical thinking has its place, in the context of cultivating mindful awareness, we are learning to prioritize direct observation. This allows us to gather information about our internal and external environment without the immediate overlay of our personal biases, beliefs, and past experiences, which often distort our perception.

This skill of dis-identifying from our thoughts and emotions is profoundly liberating. We are not our thoughts, nor are we our feelings. We are the awareness that witnesses them. This realization can significantly reduce suffering, as much of our distress arises from our resistance to or over-identification with our mental and emotional states. By becoming a detached observer, we can begin to see that difficult emotions are transient and that negative thoughts are not necessarily accurate reflections of reality.

The ability to observe without judgment is perhaps the most challenging, yet most rewarding, aspect of mindfulness. It asks us to approach our experiences, even the uncomfortable ones, with a sense of gentle curiosity. When you notice a judgmental thought arise – perhaps a critical assessment of yourself or someone else – the mindful approach is to simply observe that judgmental thought itself, acknowledging its presence without getting caught in its content. You might note, "There is a thought of judgment about X," or "The mind is engaged in criticism right now." This doesn't mean you condone the judgment; it means you are observing the *process* of judgment occurring within you. This practice gradually weakens the habitual tendency to automatically endorse every thought as truth.

This cultivated detachment is not about becoming cold or uncaring. Instead, it fosters a deeper, more authentic form of empathy and connection. When we are less reactive to our own internal states, we are better able to understand and connect with the experiences of others. We can recognize that they, too, are subject to the ebb and flow of thoughts and emotions. This empathetic understanding, grounded in the recognition of shared human experience, is far more profound than a reaction based on superficial judgment or immediate emotional resonance.

Furthermore, the observer's stance directly enhances our problem-solving capabilities and decision-making processes. When faced with a complex situation, our habitual response might be to panic, to become overwhelmed, or to jump to conclusions based on limited information or emotional bias. By cultivating mindful awareness, we create the mental space to observe the situation more clearly and comprehensively. We can step back from the immediate emotional charge and assess the facts objectively. We can identify our own assumptions and biases that might be clouding our judgment. This allows us to consider a wider range of solutions and to make more rational, effective decisions.

Imagine preparing for a critical negotiation. Without mindfulness, you might enter the room already feeling defensive or anxious, projecting these feelings onto the other party and limiting your ability to listen effectively. With the observer's stance, you can bring a calm, observant awareness to the interaction. You notice your own internal reactions – a tightening in your stomach, a tendency to interrupt – and you can choose to respond differently. You observe the other party's words and body language without immediately interpreting them through the lens of your own anxieties. This objective observation allows you to understand the situation more fully, identify opportunities, and respond strategically rather than reactively.

The development of present-moment awareness, facilitated by practices like breath awareness and body scanning, is crucial for improving decision-making by reducing the influence of past regrets and future anxieties. When we are fully present, our decisions are based on the current reality, not on hypothetical scenarios or past mistakes. This allows for more agile and adaptive responses to evolving circumstances. It's akin to a pilot flying an aircraft, who must constantly assess the present conditions – airspeed, altitude, weather – to make immediate, effective course corrections, rather than dwelling on a past miscalculation or worrying about a hypothetical future emergency.

This consistent practice of observing without judgment also builds a profound sense of self-compassion. We often hold ourselves to impossibly high standards, and when we inevitably fall short, we engage in harsh self-criticism. Mindfulness teaches us to approach our own perceived flaws and mistakes with the same gentle curiosity and acceptance we might offer a dear friend. When a thought arises, "I made a mistake on that project," the mindful response is not self-recrimination, but observation: "Ah, a thought that I made a mistake. What can I learn from this?" This shift in internal dialogue transforms the experience of error from a source of shame into an opportunity for growth and learning.

Moreover, the observer's stance can be integrated with the tactical visualization discussed earlier. While tactical visualization focuses on rehearsing future success, mindful awareness provides the clear, objective perspective needed to observe the visualization itself. During mental rehearsal, one can practice noticing the quality of the visualization: are the images clear? Are the emotions felt authentic? Are there moments of resistance or distraction? By observing these aspects of the mental rehearsal with mindful awareness, we can refine the visualization process itself, making it more potent and effective. For instance, if during visualization you notice a persistent feeling of self-doubt creeping in, mindful observation allows you to acknowledge this doubt without letting it derail the rehearsal. You can then gently redirect your attention, or even visualize yourself meeting that doubt with calm acceptance and continued forward momentum.

In essence, cultivating the observer's stance is about developing a more sophisticated and refined form of attention. It's about shifting from an automatic, reactive mode of consciousness to a deliberate, observant mode. This allows us to engage with life more fully, to understand ourselves and our circumstances more clearly, and to respond with greater wisdom and effectiveness. It is the foundation upon which many other cognitive enhancements can be built, ensuring that as we sharpen our mental acuity and strategic thinking, we do so from a place of clarity, balance, and self-awareness. The observer's stance is not merely a technique; it is a way of being, a conscious choice to engage with reality, both internal and external, with open eyes and an impartial mind, prepared to witness and respond with clarity and purpose. This cultivated detachment from immediate, often misleading, mental chatter is what allows for true insight and robust, unshakeable composure in any situation. It is the quiet strength that underpins all effective action.

Having established the importance of mindful awareness as an observer, we now turn our attention to a more active, yet equally crucial, cognitive skill:

Cognitive Reframing: Rewiring Thought Patterns for Resilience.

While mindfulness teaches us to observe our thoughts and emotions with equanimity, cognitive reframing empowers us to consciously reshape the narrative we tell ourselves about challenging events. This is akin to a military commander receiving new intelligence on the battlefield and adapting the operational plan accordingly. The initial assessment of the situation might be dire, but with a strategic shift in perspective, a new course of action becomes viable, even advantageous. Our internal landscape, much like a battlefield, can be influenced by the interpretations we apply. The way we frame a situation fundamentally dictates our emotional and behavioral response, and therefore, our capacity for resilience.

At its core, cognitive reframing is the psychological process of altering the way we perceive and interpret events, challenges, or our own thoughts. It moves beyond mere observation to active intervention, challenging the validity and usefulness of our default thought patterns. The power of this technique lies in understanding the fundamental principle that it is not the event itself that causes distress, but our interpretation of that event. As the Stoic philosopher Epictetus wisely noted, "Men are disturbed not by things, but by the view which they take of them." This ancient wisdom is the bedrock of modern cognitive behavioral therapy (CBT) and its powerful tool of reframing. Our beliefs, assumptions, and the cognitive schemas we operate from act as lenses through which we view the world. When these lenses are distorted by negativity, pessimism, or rigid thinking, they can lead to a cascade of unhelpful emotions and maladaptive behaviors, significantly hindering our ability to cope with adversity.

The psychological mechanisms at play are profound. Our brains are wired to seek patterns and meaning. When faced with uncertainty or difficulty, our minds often default to familiar, sometimes negative, explanations based on past experiences or ingrained beliefs. This can manifest as all-or-nothing thinking (e.g., "This failure means I'm a complete disaster"), catastrophizing (e.g., "This setback will ruin my career"), or personalization (e.g., "This happened because I'm not good enough"). These types of cognitive distortions act like faulty wiring, leading to an overreaction to stimuli, draining our emotional and mental resources, and diminishing our capacity for effective problem-solving. Cognitive reframing aims to rewire this faulty wiring by identifying these distortions and consciously replacing them with more balanced, realistic, and constructive interpretations. It's about shifting from a victim mentality to a proactive, empowered stance, recognizing that while we may not always control the circumstances we face, we invariably control how we choose to perceive and respond to them.

To effectively implement cognitive reframing, the first critical step is **identifying negative or limiting thought patterns**. This requires a degree of self-awareness, which, as we discussed with mindfulness, is cultivated through diligent practice. We need to become detectives of our own minds, tuning into the internal monologue that accompanies challenging situations. When faced with a setback – perhaps a project deadline missed, a critical review at work, or a personal disappointment – what are the immediate thoughts that arise? Are they accusatory? Do they focus on blame? Do they predict future failures? Keeping a thought journal can be an invaluable tool here. For example, after a difficult conversation with a colleague, you might record: "I can't believe I said that. I sounded so stupid. They must think I'm incompetent. I'll probably get fired." This written record provides concrete data points for analysis, revealing the patterns of self-criticism and catastrophic thinking at play.

Once these patterns are identified, the next crucial step is to **challenge their validity and usefulness**. This involves questioning the evidence for and against the thought. Is it absolutely true that you sounded stupid? What is the evidence for that? Did the colleague explicitly say you sounded stupid? Or is that an interpretation born from your own insecurity? Is it a certainty that you will get fired? What are the actual consequences of the conversation based on objective reality, rather than future predictions? This critical examination involves distinguishing between objective facts and subjective interpretations. For the colleague example, the facts might be: "I participated in a conversation with a colleague. I expressed my opinion. The colleague responded in a certain way. I felt embarrassed about something I said." The interpretation is: "I sounded stupid, they think I'm incompetent, I'll get fired." The challenge lies in separating the factual observations from the emotionally charged, often exaggerated, interpretations.

Furthermore, we must ask ourselves about the *usefulness* of these thoughts. Does dwelling on the idea that you sounded stupid help you in any way? Does it motivate you to improve? Or does it simply paralyze you with anxiety and shame? Often, negative thought patterns are not only inaccurate but also counterproductive, serving only to exacerbate our distress and undermine our confidence. Recognizing this lack of utility is a powerful motivator for change. Consider the thought: "This is too difficult; I can't do it." Challenging this might involve asking: "Is it *truly* impossible, or just challenging? What skills do I possess that could help me tackle this? Have I overcome difficult tasks before?" By dissecting the absolute language ("can't," "impossible") and exploring alternative perspectives, we begin to dismantle the limiting belief.

The third and most active phase is **replacing them with more constructive and empowering ones**. This is where the rewiring truly happens. The goal is not to adopt Pollyanna-ish positivity, which can feel inauthentic and dismissive of genuine challenges, but rather to cultivate more balanced, realistic, and growth-oriented perspectives. This involves actively constructing alternative interpretations that are more helpful and accurate. For the colleague example, instead of "I sounded stupid, they think I'm incompetent, I'll get fired," a reframed thought might be: "I said something I regret, but it's just one comment. I can learn from this and be more mindful of my wording next time. Most people focus more on their own performance than on dissecting others' minor missteps. My job is not in jeopardy over this." This reframed thought acknowledges the experience, accepts a degree of imperfection, focuses on learning and future action, and grounds the interpretation in a more realistic assessment of consequences.

This process is not a one-time fix; it is a skill that requires consistent practice, much like honing a tactical maneuver. The more we engage in identifying, challenging, and reframing our thoughts, the stronger these new neural pathways become, and the more readily our minds will default to more resilient interpretations. Think of it as building a new habit of mind. Each time you successfully reframe a negative thought, you are strengthening your cognitive flexibility and reinforcing your capacity to bounce back from adversity. For instance, when faced with a perceived failure in a physical training exercise, an initial thought might be, "I'm so weak; I'll never be able to do this." A reframed thought, grounded in progress and effort, could be: "This is a challenging exercise, and I'm still developing the strength and technique. Each attempt, even if not perfect, is a step forward. I will focus on proper form and gradual improvement." This shifts the focus from an absolute judgment of capability to a process-oriented perspective that emphasizes progress and learning.

Research in cognitive psychology consistently demonstrates the efficacy of cognitive reframing in enhancing resilience. Studies show that individuals who regularly employ reframing techniques exhibit lower levels of stress, anxiety, and depression, and are better able to cope with difficult life events, such as job loss, illness, or relationship breakdowns. This technique taps into our inherent capacity for psychological adaptation, allowing us to find meaning even in adversity and to emerge from challenging experiences stronger and more capable. It aligns with the principles of post-traumatic growth, where individuals not only recover from trauma but also experience positive psychological change as a result.

Consider the concept of **attributional style**, which refers to the way we explain the causes of events. Those with a more pessimistic attributional style tend to explain negative events as personal ("It's my fault"), permanent ("It will always be this way"), and pervasive ("It affects everything in my life"). Conversely, those with a more optimistic attributional style tend to explain negative events as external ("It was a combination of factors"), temporary ("This is a temporary setback"), and specific ("This only affects this one area of my life"). Cognitive reframing is essentially the active cultivation of an optimistic, or more accurately, a realistic and flexible, attributional style. By consciously choosing to attribute negative events in more external, temporary, and specific ways, we reduce their perceived impact and increase our sense of agency. For example, if a business deal falls through, an unhelpful attribution might be: "I am a terrible negotiator, and this failure proves I'll never succeed in sales." A reframed attribution, however, might be: "This particular deal had complex market factors, and while my negotiation could have been stronger in certain areas, it doesn't define my overall ability. I will analyze what went wrong and apply those learnings to the next opportunity."

The application of reframing extends beyond personal challenges to professional and strategic contexts. In leadership, for instance, a leader who views a team's poor performance as a personal failing of the team members is likely to foster demotivation and resentment. However, a leader who reframes this situation as an opportunity to identify systemic issues, provide better training, or clarify expectations can foster a more positive and productive environment. The "failure" becomes a catalyst for improvement. Similarly, in strategic planning, encountering an unexpected obstacle can be framed as an insurmountable barrier, leading to abandonment of the plan, or it can be framed as a challenge to innovate, adapt, and find alternative routes to the objective. This latter approach is characteristic of resilient and effective leadership.

To further enhance the practice of cognitive reframing, several practical methods can be employed. One effective technique is the **"What's another way to look at this?"** exercise. Whenever you find yourself stuck in a negative interpretation, consciously ask yourself this question. This simple prompt encourages you to generate alternative perspectives. If you believe a colleague is deliberately trying to undermine you, ask: "What's another way to look at their behavior? Could they be stressed? Are they simply communicating differently? Are they focused on their own goals?" This broadens your mental bandwidth and reduces the likelihood of jumping to the most negative conclusion.

Another powerful method is the **"So what?"** technique. This involves systematically questioning the perceived negative consequences of an event or thought. If you made a mistake, you might think, "This is terrible." The "So what?" question then probes: "So what if I made a mistake? What is the actual consequence of this mistake? Will it truly be disastrous?" Repeatedly asking "So what?" can often deflate the perceived magnitude of a negative event, bringing it back into realistic proportions. It helps to identify when we are catastrophizing or exaggerating the impact of a particular situation. For example, if you get a parking ticket, a common unhelpful reaction might be: "This is awful! This will ruin my budget for the month!" Asking "So what?" might reveal: "So what? It's an inconvenience and an expense, but I can adjust my spending in other areas. It doesn't derail my entire financial plan."

The practice of **"finding the opportunity"** within challenges is also a cornerstone of reframing. This involves actively looking for the potential benefits or learning experiences that a difficult situation might offer. For instance, if a planned outdoor event is cancelled due to bad weather, the unhelpful frame is disappointment and lost opportunity. A reframed perspective might be: "This cancellation is an opportunity to shift our focus indoors, perhaps leading to a more intimate gathering or a chance to explore a different type of activity we wouldn't have considered otherwise." In a business context, a competitor's success could be viewed with envy and a sense of personal failure, or it could be reframed as a valuable case study, offering insights into market trends and effective strategies. This perspective-seeking mindset turns obstacles into stepping stones for growth and innovation.

Furthermore, developing **cognitive flexibility** is key. This refers to the ability to shift from one way of thinking to another, to adapt our mental strategies as circumstances change. It's the opposite of rigid, dogmatic thinking. Practicing mindfulness, as discussed previously, significantly enhances cognitive flexibility by allowing us to observe our habitual thought patterns without being rigidly attached to them. When we can observe a thought, we gain the capacity to consciously choose whether or not to adopt it. This ability to detach and re-evaluate is the engine of effective reframing.

It is also important to acknowledge that cognitive reframing is not about denying reality or suppressing genuine negative emotions. Instead, it is about *managing* our interpretations of reality and choosing how we engage with our emotions. Acknowledging feelings of sadness or frustration is valid. The reframing aspect comes in when we ask: "What can I learn from this feeling? What is this emotion telling me? How can I respond constructively to this situation, acknowledging my feelings but not being defined by them?" This approach allows for emotional honesty while maintaining a focus on resilience and forward momentum.

In summary, cognitive reframing is a powerful strategic tool for rewiring thought patterns, enhancing resilience, and fostering effective problem-solving. By consciously identifying limiting interpretations, challenging their validity, and actively replacing them with more balanced and constructive perspectives, we can fundamentally alter our response to adversity. This process, akin to adapting battle plans based on evolving intelligence, empowers us to navigate challenges with greater psychological agility, emotional stability, and a proactive mindset, transforming potential setbacks into opportunities for growth and strength. It is an active engagement with our internal narrative, a deliberate choice to shape our perception in ways that support our objectives and our well-being, building an unshakeable foundation for navigating the complexities of life and leadership.

The capacity for sustained, focused attention is a cornerstone of cognitive fortification. In the crucible of military operations, where split-second decisions can mean the difference between success and failure, the ability to filter out noise and zero in on critical information is paramount. This is not an innate talent possessed by a select few, but a skill that can be systematically developed and honed, much like a sharpshooter refines their aim through rigorous practice. We are, in essence, training our cognitive apparatus to perform under pressure, to lock onto objectives with unwavering clarity, and to resist the insidious creep of distraction that can derail even the most meticulously laid plans.

One of the most potent methods for cultivating this focused attention is through **dedicated concentration practices**. These are not merely abstract exercises but practical drills designed to build the mental stamina required for deep work and sustained engagement. Imagine a forward observer calling in artillery fire. They must maintain their focus on the target, communicating precise coordinates and observing the impact, all while potentially under fire themselves. Their attention is a laser beam, cutting through the chaos. We can cultivate a similar laser-like focus in our daily lives.

A foundational practice is **focused attention meditation**. This involves selecting an object of attention – most commonly the breath – and gently directing your awareness to it. When the mind inevitably wanders, as it will, the practice is not to become frustrated or discouraged, but to simply notice the distraction, acknowledge it without judgment, and then gently, with kindness, guide your attention back to the chosen object. This act of noticing and returning, repeated over and over, is the core of strengthening your attentional 'muscle.' Each return is a rep, building neural pathways that support sustained concentration.

Consider the simple act of observing your breath. Start by bringing your awareness to the physical sensations of breathing: the rise and fall of your chest or abdomen, the feeling of air passing through your nostrils. For a minute, two minutes, or even longer, simply rest your attention on this sensation. You will likely find your mind drifting – perhaps to what you need to do next, a conversation you had earlier, or a worry about the future. The key is not to fight these thoughts or push them away forcefully. Instead, observe them as passing clouds. Notice the thought arise: "I need to email John about the report." Then, without getting caught in the narrative of that thought, gently redirect your attention back to the sensation of your breath. This repeated, gentle redirection is the training.

It is crucial to approach this practice with patience and an understanding of gradual progression. Expecting to achieve hours of uninterrupted focus immediately is unrealistic and counterproductive. The initial stages are often characterized by frequent mind-wandering. This is normal and a sign that the training is actually working. Each time you notice your mind has strayed and bring it back, you are strengthening your capacity for concentration. Think of it like training a new recruit. You wouldn't expect them to execute complex maneuvers perfectly on day one. You start with the basics, drill them consistently, and gradually introduce more challenging tasks.

Another highly effective technique is **body scanning**, which, while often associated with mindfulness, also serves as a powerful concentration exercise. This involves systematically bringing your attention to different parts of your body, from the tips of your toes to the crown of your head, or vice versa. As you move your attention through your body, notice any sensations present: warmth, coolness, tingling, pressure, throbbing, or even the absence of sensation. The directive here is to maintain a steady, focused awareness on each area you are attending to, without rushing or becoming distracted by tangential thoughts.

When practicing body scanning, imagine you are a diagnostician meticulously examining a complex piece of equipment. You need to detect even the subtlest anomaly or characteristic. Your attention is the probe, moving methodically across each component. As you bring your awareness to your feet, for instance, you might notice a slight ache or a feeling of warmth. The practice is to simply observe that sensation with sustained attention, without immediately analyzing it, judging it, or trying to change it. You hold your focus on that particular sensation for a few moments before moving to the soles of your feet, then your ankles, and so on. This sustained focus on a single sensory experience trains the mind to remain present and attentive, resisting the urge to jump ahead or get lost in interpretation.

The beauty of these practices lies in their accessibility. You don't need special equipment or a designated retreat space. A few minutes each day, dedicated to focused attention, can yield significant improvements over time. Consistency is more important than duration. A daily 10-minute session will build more robust concentration skills than an occasional hour-long session. It's about building a habit, integrating mental discipline into the fabric of your daily routine, much like soldiers adhere to rigorous training schedules to maintain peak physical and mental readiness.

Beyond formal meditation, the principle of **single-tasking** is equally vital in strengthening our ability to concentrate. In today's hyper-connected world, multitasking is often lauded as a sign of efficiency. However, research increasingly suggests that multitasking is largely a myth. What we perceive as multitasking is often rapid task-switching, a process that incurs a cognitive cost, leading to decreased efficiency, increased errors, and mental fatigue. Each switch requires our brains to disengage from one task, reorient to another, and then re-engage. This constant shifting fragments our attention and depletes our mental resources.

To counter this, actively embrace single-tasking. When you sit down to work on a report, commit to working *only* on that report. Close unnecessary tabs on your computer, silence notifications on your phone, and inform others that you need uninterrupted time. This creates an environment conducive to deep work. If a thought arises related to another task, jot it down quickly on a notepad to address later, and then immediately return your focus to the primary task. This conscious act of dedicating your full attention to one thing at a time is a direct exercise in building sustained concentration.

Consider the analogy of a sniper. They cannot afford to be distracted by the rustling of leaves or a distant bird call when their target is in their sights. Their entire focus is on the mission, on the precise execution of their role. Similarly, when you are engaged in a task, whether it's writing, problem-solving, or engaging in a conversation, aim to bring that same level of singular focus. When reading a book for learning, immerse yourself in the text, resisting the urge to scroll through social media or check emails. When having a conversation, listen attentively to the speaker, truly hearing their words and intent, rather than formulating your response while they are still speaking.

The benefits of this cultivated focus are profound and far-reaching. It directly enhances our capacity for **deep work**, a term popularized by author Cal Newport, referring to professional activities performed in a state of distraction-free concentration that push your cognitive capabilities to their limit. Deep work is what allows us to create new value, improve our skills, and produce high-quality output. By strengthening our attentional muscle, we become more capable of engaging in these cognitively demanding tasks, leading to greater productivity and more meaningful accomplishments.

Furthermore, improved concentration is critical for **effective learning**. When we are able to focus deeply on new information, we are more likely to encode it into long-term memory. Distraction acts as a barrier to this process. If your mind is constantly wandering during a lecture or while reading an instructional text, you are only passively absorbing a fraction of the material. By practicing focused attention, you create the optimal mental conditions for absorbing, understanding, and retaining new knowledge. This is invaluable in any field that requires continuous learning and skill development.

This ability to concentrate also translates to greater **mindful engagement** in all aspects of life. When we are truly present and focused, we experience activities more richly. A meal becomes more flavorful, a walk in nature more vivid, and interactions with loved ones more meaningful. It's about being fully where you are, rather than being mentally dispersed across multiple thoughts and concerns. This heightened engagement not only enriches our experiences but also contributes to overall well-being and reduces feelings of being overwhelmed or disconnected.

To illustrate the importance of gradual progression, consider learning to play a musical instrument. A beginner doesn't start by playing complex concertos. They begin with scales, simple melodies, and basic finger exercises. The focus is on accuracy, rhythm, and developing muscle memory. Gradually, as their proficiency increases, they can tackle more challenging pieces. Similarly, when building concentration, start with shorter periods of focused attention and gradually increase the duration. If you find yourself unable to focus for 10 minutes, start with 5. The key is consistent, manageable practice.

The process of building concentration is analogous to strength training for the mind. Each focused moment, each return of attention from distraction, is a repetition that strengthens the neural pathways responsible for attention control. Over time, this leads to a more robust and resilient ability to concentrate, even in the face of significant internal or external challenges. It's about developing the mental discipline to direct your cognitive resources where you intend them to be, rather than being passively pulled by whatever captures your attention.

One practical way to implement this is through **time-blocking**. Dedicate specific blocks of time in your schedule for focused work on particular tasks. During these blocks, adhere strictly to the principle of single-tasking and minimize all potential distractions. For example, you might schedule a "Deep Work Block" from 9:00 AM to 10:30 AM for writing your project proposal, and during that time, resist all urges to check email or browse the web. This structured approach helps to externalize the discipline and creates accountability for focused effort.

Another technique that reinforces concentration is **active recall**. After engaging with new information, such as reading a chapter or attending a meeting, pause and try to recall the key points without looking at your notes. This process forces your brain to actively retrieve the information, strengthening the neural connections associated with it. It's a more demanding form of engagement than simply re-reading, and it directly enhances both concentration and retention. Imagine being interrogated after a reconnaissance mission; your ability to recall details under pressure is critical. Active recall is your mental preparation for such scenarios.

Furthermore, understanding the environmental factors that influence attention is crucial. Create a physical environment that supports concentration. This might mean decluttering your workspace, ensuring good lighting, and minimizing noise. If a completely silent environment is not possible, consider using noise-canceling headphones or listening to instrumental music that is known to aid focus. Your surroundings play a significant role in how easily your attention is captured by external stimuli.

It is also important to recognize the role of **physical well-being** in cognitive function. Adequate sleep, proper nutrition, and regular physical activity are not merely supportive of concentration; they are foundational. A tired, undernourished, or sedentary brain will struggle to maintain focus, regardless of the techniques employed. Prioritizing these basic aspects of health creates the optimal physiological conditions for peak cognitive performance, including sustained attention. Just as a soldier needs proper rest and sustenance to perform on the battlefield, your mind requires them to function effectively.

The journey of sharpening your mind through concentrated attention is a continuous one. It requires commitment, patience, and a willingness to practice diligently. By incorporating focused attention meditation, body scanning, single-tasking, and other concentration-building techniques into your routine, you are systematically fortifying your cognitive capabilities. This enhanced ability to focus will not only boost your productivity and learning but will also allow you to engage more fully and meaningfully with every aspect of your life, transforming your capacity for achievement and your overall quality of experience. The ability to focus deeply is not just a cognitive skill; it is a strategic advantage in an increasingly distracted world. It is the quiet power that allows for mastery, for insight, and for the execution of complex tasks with precision and unwavering intent.

Chapter 3: Emotional Fortitude: Mastering the Inner Landscape

Emotional intelligence (EI) stands as a paramount strategic asset, particularly when navigating the complexities of leadership and personal effectiveness. Just as a seasoned commander must understand the morale and motivations of their troops to achieve mission objectives, so too must an individual understand and manage their own inner landscape and their interactions with others. In essence, emotional intelligence is the capacity to recognize, understand, and manage our own emotions, and to recognize, understand, and influence the emotions of others. It is not a mystical aura or an innate, unchangeable trait, but a set of skills that can be cultivated and refined, offering a distinct advantage in both personal and professional arenas. This is not a departure from the rigorous mental discipline we have been exploring, but rather a complementary dimension that amplifies its effectiveness. The ability to maintain focus and execute tasks under pressure is significantly bolstered by a robust understanding and management of one's emotional state, and by extension, the emotional states of those around us.

The foundation of emotional intelligence rests upon several interconnected pillars. At its core is **self-awareness**, the ability to recognize and understand our own emotions, moods, drives, as well as their effect on others. This involves an honest appraisal of one's strengths and weaknesses, a keen awareness of one's values and goals, and a clear understanding of how one's emotional state impacts their thoughts and behaviors. Without this fundamental self-knowledge, any attempt to manage oneself or others will be built on shaky ground. Consider the critical incident response in a high-stakes environment. A leader who is acutely self-aware will recognize the adrenaline surge, the potential for fear or panic, and will be able to acknowledge these feelings without letting them dictate their actions. They understand that their outward composure, or lack thereof, will be observed and emulated by their team. This self-awareness is not about dwelling on negative emotions, but about observing them objectively, like a detached scientist studying a phenomenon.

Building upon self-awareness is **self-regulation**, the ability to control or redirect disruptive impulses and moods. This involves the capacity to think before acting, to manage emotional reactivity, and to maintain composure even when faced with provocation or adversity. It's about choosing your response rather than being controlled by your initial emotional reaction. In military terms, this is the discipline to not engage in a rash retaliatory action, but to adhere to established protocols and de-escalation strategies. Psychologically, it's about developing an internal governor that prevents emotional over-reactions. This doesn't mean suppressing emotions, but rather channeling them constructively. For instance, frustration can be a powerful motivator for problem-solving if it's managed, rather than allowed to devolve into anger that clouds judgment. Research has consistently shown that individuals with high self-regulation exhibit greater patience, are more adaptable to change, and are less prone to impulsive decision-making, all of which are invaluable in leadership and navigating complex challenges. The ability to delay gratification, a hallmark of self-regulation, is directly linked to long-term success across numerous domains, from academic achievement to career progression.

The third pillar is **social awareness**, which encompasses empathy and organizational awareness. Empathy is the ability to understand the emotional makeup of other people, to treat them according to their emotional reactions. This means being able to put yourself in another person's shoes, to grasp their perspectives, and to appreciate their feelings. It is the bedrock of effective communication and strong relationships. In a team setting, an empathetic leader can anticipate how a particular decision might affect individuals, leading to more considered and supportive communication. Organizational awareness, on the other hand, is the ability to understand the currents of emotions and political forces in an organization, and to discern the best way to influence those forces. It's about understanding the unspoken dynamics, the unwritten rules, and the informal networks that shape organizational life. This allows for more strategic and effective engagement with colleagues, superiors, and subordinates. Leaders with high social awareness are better equipped to build cohesive teams, resolve conflicts constructively, and foster a positive and productive environment. They can read a room, understand the underlying sentiments of a group, and tailor their approach accordingly, much like a diplomat understanding the nuances of international relations.

Finally, **relationship management** is the ability to build and maintain relationships, to inspire and influence others, to manage conflict, and to work effectively in teams. It is the culmination of the other three components. When individuals are self-aware, can regulate their own emotions, and are socially aware, they are well-equipped to build strong, positive relationships. This involves clear communication, active listening, providing constructive feedback, and fostering a sense of trust and collaboration. In leadership, effective relationship management is crucial for motivating teams, driving change, and achieving collective goals. It's about orchestrating positive interactions, building bridges between individuals and groups, and creating an environment where people feel valued and understood. This translates into greater team cohesion, higher morale, and improved performance. Consider a situation where a critical project is behind schedule. A leader with strong relationship management skills will not resort to blame but will work with the team to identify the root causes, brainstorm solutions collaboratively, and motivate everyone to get back on track, ensuring that individual contributions are recognized and supported.

The physiological and psychological benefits of cultivating emotional intelligence are substantial and well-documented. From a physiological perspective, higher EI is associated with reduced stress levels and better physical health. When we are emotionally regulated, our bodies are less likely to be in a constant state of fight-or-flight, which can lead to chronic stress-related conditions. Research published in journals such as the *Journal of Personality and Social Psychology* has indicated that individuals with higher EI tend to have lower blood pressure and cortisol levels, key indicators of stress. This improved physiological regulation translates into greater resilience, a better ability to bounce back from setbacks, and a more robust immune system. The capacity to manage anxiety and to approach challenging situations with a sense of calm allows the body's systems to function more optimally, leading to sustained physical well-being.

Psychologically, the benefits are equally profound. High EI contributes to improved mental health, reduced symptoms of depression and anxiety, and greater overall life satisfaction. By understanding and managing our emotions, we are less likely to be overwhelmed by negative feelings. This emotional resilience allows us to cope more effectively with life's inevitable difficulties. Furthermore, strong interpersonal relationships, a direct outcome of effective relationship management, are a significant predictor of happiness and well-being. People with high EI are better at resolving conflicts, collaborating with others, and building supportive social networks, which in turn buffer against stress and promote a sense of belonging. Scientific studies, such as those exploring the link between EI and academic or professional success, often highlight improved decision-making as a key outcome. When emotions are not hijacking our rational thought processes, we can approach decisions with greater clarity and objectivity, leading to more effective and beneficial choices. The ability to consider the emotional impact of decisions on oneself and others also leads to more holistic and sustainable outcomes.

The concept of emotional intelligence is not merely theoretical; it has tangible implications for leadership effectiveness, particularly in environments that demand high levels of coordination, resilience, and adaptability. Military leadership, by its very nature, requires individuals to operate under immense pressure, make critical decisions with incomplete information, and inspire trust and confidence in their teams. A leader who lacks emotional intelligence might inadvertently create a climate of fear or resentment, undermining morale and operational effectiveness. Conversely, a leader with high EI can foster a sense of psychological safety, where team members feel empowered to voice concerns, contribute ideas, and support one another. This creates a more cohesive and high-performing unit. For instance, a commanding officer who can empathize with the anxieties of soldiers deployed in a combat zone, while also maintaining a clear focus on the mission, can provide the necessary guidance and support to ensure that the team functions effectively. This blend of understanding and decisiveness is a hallmark of emotionally intelligent leadership.

Consider the critical role of emotional intelligence in conflict resolution within a unit. A commander who is self-aware will recognize their own biases and triggers, preventing them from escalating a dispute. Their self-regulation will allow them to remain calm and objective when mediating between team members. Their social awareness will enable them to understand the perspectives and underlying emotions of all parties involved. And their relationship management skills will guide them in facilitating a resolution that is fair, constructive, and preserves the integrity of the team. This approach is far more effective than a command-and-control style that relies solely on authority, as it fosters a sense of ownership and mutual respect.

The scientific underpinnings of EI further validate its importance. Neuroscientific research, for example, has illuminated the intricate connections between the limbic system (responsible for emotions) and the prefrontal cortex (responsible for executive functions like decision-making and impulse control). Emotional intelligence, in this context, can be understood as the effective functioning and integration of these brain regions. Individuals with higher EI often exhibit more efficient communication between these areas, allowing for more balanced processing of emotional information and more reasoned responses. Studies utilizing fMRI scans have shown that individuals who are skilled at emotional regulation can more effectively dampen the amygdala's fear response when presented with emotionally charged stimuli. This biological basis underscores that EI is not just a psychological construct but is rooted in our neural architecture, and importantly, is malleable through practice and experience.

Furthermore, the concept of EI aligns with, and is arguably a necessary component of, what psychologists call **grit**, the perseverance and passion for long-term goals. While grit focuses on endurance and commitment, emotional intelligence provides the internal scaffolding to sustain that commitment through emotional turbulence. The ability to manage disappointment, to maintain motivation in the face of setbacks, and to draw strength from supportive relationships are all facets of EI that contribute to the development and expression of grit. Without emotional resilience, even the most determined individual can falter when confronted with prolonged adversity.

In practice, developing emotional intelligence is an ongoing journey. It begins with a conscious commitment to self-reflection. Regularly asking oneself questions like: "What emotions am I feeling right now?", "What triggered this emotion?", "How is this emotion affecting my thoughts and actions?", and "How might my behavior be affecting others?" can be incredibly illuminating. Journaling can be a powerful tool for this process, providing a private space to explore one's emotional landscape without judgment. Mindfulness practices, as previously discussed, are also instrumental in cultivating self-awareness and self-regulation. By observing thoughts and feelings without immediate reaction, we create space for more considered responses.

For social awareness and relationship management, active listening is paramount. This means not just hearing words, but truly understanding the speaker's message, including their non-verbal cues and underlying emotions. Practicing active listening involves giving undivided attention, asking clarifying questions, paraphrasing to ensure understanding, and responding with empathy. Seeking feedback from trusted colleagues or mentors about one's interpersonal style can also provide invaluable insights. Understanding how others perceive our communication and emotional expressions is a crucial step in refining our approach.

In conclusion, emotional intelligence is not a secondary skill but a fundamental asset that enhances cognitive abilities, strengthens leadership capacity, and fosters overall well-being. By understanding and cultivating self-awareness, self-regulation, social awareness, and relationship management, we equip ourselves with the tools to navigate the complexities of both our inner lives and our interactions with the world. This emotional fortitude, intertwined with cognitive discipline, creates a potent synergy, enabling us to lead ourselves and others with greater wisdom, resilience, and effectiveness. It is the essential bridge that connects our capacity for focused thought and action with our ability to connect meaningfully and influence positively, making it an indispensable element of true mastery.

The ability to precisely identify and articulate our emotional state is the foundational bedrock upon which all subsequent emotional mastery is built. Without this clarity, we are akin to a navigator without a compass, adrift in a sea of feeling, unable to chart a course or even understand our current position. Just as a skilled military strategist must meticulously survey the terrain, identify enemy positions, and assess troop morale to formulate an effective plan, so too must we become adept at surveying our internal landscape, recognizing the distinct contours of our emotions, and understanding their impact on our capacity to act. This process of emotional labeling is not merely an academic exercise; it is a vital skill that directly informs our ability to regulate, understand, and ultimately influence our emotional responses and those of others.

Consider the common experience of feeling "bad." This is a vast and unhelpful generalization. Are we feeling frustrated because a plan has been thwarted? Are we experiencing disappointment from a missed opportunity? Perhaps it is a sense of loneliness or a pang of envy. Each of these distinct feelings carries a different energetic signature, triggers different physiological responses, and calls for different coping mechanisms. If we lump them all under the umbrella of "bad," we miss the opportunity to address the specific underlying cause. This is where a rich emotional vocabulary becomes indispensable. Developing this vocabulary is akin to acquiring the specialized terminology of a particular field; it allows for precision, nuance, and a deeper understanding of the subject matter – in this case, our own inner world.

The journey into precise emotional labeling often begins with a deliberate effort to expand our lexicon. We may be accustomed to a limited range of descriptors, perhaps focusing on broad categories like happy, sad, angry, or scared. While these are certainly valid starting points, a more granular understanding unlocks greater potential for self-management. Consider the subtle distinctions within the broad category of "sadness." There is grief, a profound sorrow often associated with loss; melancholy, a pensive and gentle sadness; despair, a complete loss of hope; and dejection, a state of low spirits due to failure or disappointment. Each of these carries a unique quality and demands a different approach to processing and moving through.

Similarly, "anger" can manifest in various forms. There is righteous indignation, a justified anger stemming from perceived injustice. There is irritation, a milder form of annoyance. There is rage, an intense and often uncontrolled fury. And there is resentment, a persistent bitterness or ill will felt towards someone. Recognizing these differences allows us to respond more appropriately. If we label an instance of mild irritation as "anger," we might overreact. Conversely, if we dismiss a surge of genuine frustration as mere "annoyance," we may fail to address a legitimate problem that is hindering our progress.

The process of labeling emotions is inherently linked to mindfulness. It requires a conscious turning inward, a focused observation of our internal state without immediate judgment or the impulse to change it. This is a skill that can be cultivated through practice. When you notice a feeling arise, pause. Take a breath. Ask yourself: "What am I feeling right now?" Resist the urge to immediately label it as "good" or "bad." Instead, focus on the sensation itself. Where do you feel it in your body? Is it a tightness in your chest, a knot in your stomach, a warmth in your face? What is the intensity of this feeling on a scale of one to ten? What thoughts are accompanying this feeling?

This deliberate slowing down, this act of mindful observation, creates a crucial space between the experience of an emotion and our reaction to it. It allows us to move from being solely *in* the emotion to being an observer *of* the emotion. This is a powerful shift in perspective, enabling a more objective assessment. Think of a doctor examining a patient. They don't simply say, "The patient is ill." They conduct a detailed examination, identify specific symptoms, and arrive at a precise diagnosis. Our emotional lives require a similar level of detailed inquiry.

To facilitate this process, it can be incredibly beneficial to utilize an emotional vocabulary list or an "emotion wheel." These tools, often developed by psychologists, provide a comprehensive range of emotion words, organized in a way that highlights nuances and relationships between feelings. For example, an emotion wheel might show that "joy" is a primary emotion, with secondary emotions like "excitement," "contentment," and "elation" branching off from it. Similarly, "fear" might lead to "anxiety," "nervousness," and "terror." By consulting these resources, you can begin to identify words that more accurately capture your internal experience.

A practical exercise to develop this skill is to dedicate a few minutes each day, perhaps during a quiet period or a walk, to an internal "emotional scan." During this scan, systematically check in with yourself. Start with your body: What sensations are present? Are there any areas of tension, warmth, or lightness? Then, move to your thoughts: What is the dominant theme of your thinking? Finally, and most importantly, attempt to assign a precise emotional label to what you are experiencing. If you find yourself struggling to pinpoint a specific feeling, try thinking about what triggered it. Did a particular interaction leave you feeling a certain way? Did a piece of news evoke a particular response? The trigger can often provide clues to the underlying emotion.

It is vital to approach this labeling process without judgment. Emotions are simply data; they are signals from our internal system. A feeling of anger, for instance, might be signaling that a boundary has been crossed. A feeling of sadness might indicate a loss or a need for connection. Our goal is not to eliminate or suppress any particular emotion, but to understand it. Therefore, when you label an emotion, do so neutrally. "I am feeling frustrated," rather than "I am bad for feeling frustrated." "I am experiencing anxiety," rather than "I shouldn't be feeling this anxious." This non-judgmental stance is crucial for fostering a safe internal environment where emotions can be explored honestly.

Another powerful technique involves journaling specifically about your emotional experiences. When you notice a significant feeling, take a moment to write it down. Describe the feeling as precisely as possible, using your expanded vocabulary. Note when it began, what you believe initiated it, how intense it was, and how it affected your thoughts and behaviors. Over time, reviewing these journal entries can reveal patterns in your emotional responses, helping you to understand your triggers and develop more effective strategies for managing challenging emotions. For example, you might notice that you consistently feel a sense of inadequacy after certain types of social interactions, or that a particular recurring thought pattern invariably leads to a feeling of dread.

The distinction between similar emotions is also worth exploring. For instance, the difference between embarrassment and shame. Embarrassment is often a fleeting feeling triggered by a social blunder or a moment of awkwardness, typically focused on how others perceive us in that specific instance. Shame, on the other hand, is a deeper, more pervasive feeling of being fundamentally flawed or bad. Recognizing this distinction is important because shame can be highly corrosive to self-esteem and can lead to self-defeating behaviors, whereas embarrassment is generally a more manageable social emotion.

Similarly, understanding the difference between anxiety and excitement can be illuminating. Both can manifest with similar physiological symptoms – a racing heart, butterflies in the stomach, a sense of anticipation. The key difference often lies in the interpretation of the situation. Anxiety is typically associated with a perceived threat or negative outcome, while excitement is linked to a positive or challenging opportunity. By accurately labeling whether a racing heart is due to apprehension or eagerness, we can begin to manage the situation more effectively. If it's anxiety, we might employ calming techniques. If it's excitement, we can channel that energy productively.

The practice of naming our emotions also has a tangible effect on the intensity of those emotions. Research in neurobiology has shown that when we verbally label an emotional experience, we engage the prefrontal cortex, the part of the brain responsible for rational thought and executive function. This engagement can help to dampen the activity in the amygdala, the brain's emotional processing center, which is responsible for generating initial emotional responses, particularly fear and anger. This "affect labeling" process can, therefore, help to de-escalate intense emotional states, bringing a greater sense of calm and control.

Consider a scenario where you are preparing for a significant presentation. You might feel a knot of unease in your stomach and a heightened sense of alertness. If you label this as "anxiety," you might begin to focus on all the things that could go wrong, potentially amplifying the feeling. However, if you recognize that this physical and mental state is also indicative of preparedness and anticipation, you can label it as "focused readiness" or even "excitement" about the opportunity to share your work. This subtle shift in labeling can change the entire experience, transforming a potentially debilitating feeling into a source of energy and drive.

To further refine this skill, it can be beneficial to engage in reflective exercises after emotionally charged events. Whether it was a challenging conversation, a moment of unexpected success, or a frustrating setback, take time afterward to process what occurred on an emotional level. Ask yourself: What emotions did I experience during this event? How did they manifest in my body? What specific words best describe these feelings? Were there multiple emotions present simultaneously? How did my emotional state influence my actions and decisions? By dissecting these experiences retrospectively, you build a stronger internal framework for recognizing and labeling emotions as they arise in real-time.

The ultimate aim is not to become overly analytical or to intellectualize every feeling to the point of detachment. Rather, it is to develop a fluent and accurate inner language that allows for a more nuanced and effective engagement with our emotional lives. It is about cultivating an awareness that transforms raw emotional data into actionable insights. This precision in labeling is the first, and perhaps most critical, step in building emotional fortitude, enabling us to navigate the complexities of our inner landscape with clarity, intention, and a growing sense of mastery. It is the essential first move in understanding the terrain before planning the campaign.

The ability to precisely identify and articulate our emotional state is the foundational bedrock upon which all subsequent emotional mastery is built. Without this clarity, we are akin to a navigator without a compass, adrift in a sea of feeling, unable to chart a course or even understand our current position. Just as a skilled military strategist must meticulously survey the terrain, identify enemy positions, and assess troop morale to formulate an effective plan, so too must we become adept at surveying our internal landscape, recognizing the distinct contours of our emotions, and understanding their impact on our capacity to act. This process of emotional labeling is not merely an academic exercise; it is a vital skill that directly informs our ability to regulate, understand, and ultimately influence our emotional responses and those of others.

Consider the common experience of feeling "bad." This is a vast and unhelpful generalization. Are we feeling frustrated because a plan has been thwarted? Are we experiencing disappointment from a missed opportunity? Perhaps it is a sense of loneliness or a pang of envy. Each of these distinct feelings carries a different energetic signature, triggers different physiological responses, and calls for different coping mechanisms. If we lump them all under the umbrella of "bad," we miss the opportunity to address the specific underlying cause. This is where a rich emotional vocabulary becomes indispensable. Developing this vocabulary is akin to acquiring the specialized terminology of a particular field; it allows for precision, nuance, and a deeper understanding of the subject matter – in this case, our own inner world.

The journey into precise emotional labeling often begins with a deliberate effort to expand our lexicon. We may be accustomed to a limited range of descriptors, perhaps focusing on broad categories like happy, sad, angry, or scared. While these are certainly valid starting points, a more granular understanding unlocks greater potential for self-management. Consider the subtle distinctions within the broad category of "sadness." There is grief, a profound sorrow often associated with loss; melancholy, a pensive and gentle sadness; despair, a complete loss of hope; and dejection, a state of low spirits due to failure or disappointment. Each of these carries a unique quality and demands a different approach to processing and moving through.

Similarly, "anger" can manifest in various forms. There is righteous indignation, a justified anger stemming from perceived injustice. There is irritation, a milder form of annoyance. There is rage, an intense and often uncontrolled fury. And there is resentment, a persistent bitterness or ill will felt towards someone. Recognizing these differences allows us to respond more appropriately. If we label an instance of mild irritation as "anger," we might overreact. Conversely, if we dismiss a surge of genuine frustration as mere "annoyance," we may fail to address a legitimate problem that is hindering our progress.

The practice of naming our emotions also has a tangible effect on the intensity of those emotions. Research in neurobiology has shown that when we verbally label an emotional experience, we engage the prefrontal cortex, the part of the brain responsible for rational thought and executive function. This engagement can help to dampen the activity in the amygdala, the brain's emotional processing center, which is responsible for generating initial emotional responses, particularly fear and anger. This "affect labeling" process can, therefore, help to de-escalate intense emotional states, bringing a greater sense of calm and control.

Consider a scenario where you are preparing for a significant presentation. You might feel a knot of unease in your stomach and a heightened sense of alertness. If you label this as "anxiety," you might begin to focus on all the things that could go wrong, potentially amplifying the feeling. However, if you recognize that this physical and mental state is also indicative of preparedness and anticipation, you can label it as "focused readiness" or even "excitement" about the opportunity to share your work. This subtle shift in labeling can change the entire experience, transforming a potentially debilitating feeling into a source of energy and drive.

To further refine this skill, it can be beneficial to engage in reflective exercises after emotionally charged events. Whether it was a challenging conversation, a moment of unexpected success, or a frustrating setback, take time afterward to process what occurred on an emotional level. Ask yourself: What emotions did I experience during this event? How did they manifest in my body? What specific words best describe these feelings? Were there multiple emotions present simultaneously? How did my emotional state influence my actions and decisions? By dissecting these experiences retrospectively, you build a stronger internal framework for recognizing and labeling emotions as they arise in real-time.

The ultimate aim is not to become overly analytical or to intellectualize every feeling to the point of detachment. Rather, it is to develop a fluent and accurate inner language that allows for a more nuanced and effective engagement with our emotional lives. It is about cultivating an awareness that transforms raw emotional data into actionable insights. This precision in labeling is the first, and perhaps most critical, step in building emotional fortitude, enabling us to navigate the complexities of our inner landscape with clarity, intention, and a growing sense of mastery. It is the essential first move in understanding the terrain before planning the campaign.

Stoic Resilience: Cultivating Inner Calm Amidst Adversity

In the crucible of life, where challenges invariably arise, the cultivation of resilience is not merely advantageous; it is essential for sustained well-being and effective action. Drawing profound inspiration from the ancient philosophical tradition of Stoicism, we can forge an unshakeable inner core capable of weathering any storm. Stoicism, far from being a doctrine of emotional suppression, is a practical philosophy designed to equip individuals with the mental fortitude to navigate the inevitable vicissitudes of existence with equanimity and purpose. At its heart lies a powerful, actionable principle: the dichotomy of control. This fundamental tenet asserts that while much in life remains outside our direct influence – external events, the actions of others, the circumstances we are born into – a significant domain lies squarely within our purview: our judgments, our desires, our aversions, and our actions.

This distinction is not an academic abstraction; it is a tactical imperative for developing resilience. Consider the mindset of a seasoned military commander. Their success hinges not on controlling the unpredictable nature of the battlefield, which is inherently chaotic and fraught with variables, but on precisely managing their own responses and decisions. They cannot command the weather, nor can they dictate the enemy's movements with absolute certainty. What they *can* control is their strategic planning, the training and morale of their troops, their own tactical execution, and their interpretation of unfolding events. This rigorous focus on the controllable, coupled with a clear-eyed acceptance of the uncontrollable, forms the bedrock of effective leadership and successful outcomes in high-stakes environments.

Stoicism champions this very same disciplined approach to life. Epictetus, a former slave who rose to become one of Rome's most influential philosophers, famously articulated this principle: "Some things are in our control and others are not. Things in our control are opinion, impulse, desire, aversion, and, in a word, whatever are our own actions. Things not in our control are body, property, reputation, command, and, in one word, whatever are not our own actions." This simple yet profound division offers a powerful lens through which to view adversity. When faced with a setback – a job loss, a health crisis, a strained relationship – our natural inclination might be to lament what has been lost or to rail against the unfairness of the situation. These reactions, however, are directed towards the uncontrollable.

The Stoic approach redirects our energy inward. Instead of asking, "Why did this happen to me?" the Stoic asks, "Given that this has happened, what is the most virtuous and effective way for me to respond?" This subtle shift in questioning is transformative. It moves us from a position of passive victimhood to one of active agency. If a project you poured your heart into is canceled, you cannot control the decision that was made. You

can, however, control your reaction to that decision. Will you succumb to despair and inaction, or will you analyze what you can learn from the experience, perhaps seek new opportunities, and maintain your commitment to excellence in your future endeavors?

The Stoic virtue of *apatheia*, often misunderstood as apathy, actually signifies a state of undisturbed equanimity. It is not the absence of feeling, but the absence of being overwhelmed by destructive emotions. It is the ability to experience emotions like fear, anger, or sadness without letting them dictate our actions or compromise our inner peace. This is cultivated through a rigorous practice of examining our judgments. As Marcus Aurelius, Roman Emperor and Stoic philosopher, noted in his *Meditations*, "You have power over your mind – not outside events. Realize this, and you will find strength." Our suffering often arises not from the events themselves, but from our interpretations and judgments about those events.

For instance, if you are stuck in traffic and perceive it as a personal affront designed to ruin your day, you are likely to experience frustration, anger, and anxiety. If, however, you reframe the situation – acknowledging that traffic is a common reality, that you cannot control it, and that you can use this time productively, perhaps by listening to an informative podcast or simply practicing mindful breathing – you transform the experience. The external circumstance remains the same, but your internal response, guided by your judgment, changes entirely. This is the essence of Stoic resilience: the conscious choice to manage our perceptions and maintain our inner citadel, regardless of external circumstances.

This practice of framing and reframing is crucial. Psychological research on resilience consistently highlights the importance of cognitive reappraisal – the ability to reinterpret challenging situations in a less threatening or more manageable way. Stoicism provides a philosophical framework and a set of mental exercises to develop this very skill. One such exercise involves *premeditatio malorum*, or the premeditation of evils. This is not about dwelling morbidly on negative possibilities, but about mentally preparing for potential difficulties. By contemplating what might go wrong, and how we would respond to it virtuously, we reduce the shock and emotional impact when such events inevitably occur.

Imagine preparing for a challenging negotiation. A Stoic approach would involve anticipating potential objections, considering how your counterparts might behave, and deciding in advance how you will respond calmly and rationally, focusing on your objectives and ethical principles, rather than becoming entangled in emotional reactions to their tactics. This mental rehearsal inoculates you against the emotional volatility that often derails negotiations. It builds a reservoir of mental strength, enabling you to remain focused and composed when the pressure is on.

Furthermore, Stoicism emphasizes the importance of virtue as the sole good. External things – wealth, health, reputation – are considered "indifferents." They are not inherently good or bad, but can be used virtuously or viciously. This perspective liberates us from the anxiety of accumulating or protecting external possessions. Our true wealth lies in our character, our integrity, and our capacity for rational and virtuous action. When faced with loss, a Stoic understands that while the loss of property or status is regrettable, it does not diminish their inherent worth as a human being, nor does it impede their ability to live a virtuous life.

This detachment from external outcomes fosters a profound sense of inner freedom. It allows us to pursue our goals with vigor, but without the desperate clinging that breeds fear of failure. We strive for success, but we are not devastated by setbacks. This is a form of emotional invulnerability, not by shielding ourselves from feeling, but by anchoring our sense of self-worth in something unshakeable: our own moral compass and our capacity for rational thought.

To cultivate this Stoic resilience, several practical strategies can be employed. Firstly, consistent journaling is invaluable. Regularly reflecting on your day, identifying situations where you felt disturbed, and examining your judgments about those situations can illuminate patterns of unhelpful thinking. Ask yourself: "What was within my control? What was not? How did my judgments contribute to my emotional distress? How could I have responded more virtuously?" This self-inquiry, akin to a soldier debriefing after a mission to identify lessons learned, sharpens our ability to apply Stoic principles in real-time.

Secondly, practice mindfulness and present-moment awareness. Stoicism, much like modern mindfulness practices, encourages us to be fully present in our experiences, observing our thoughts and feelings without immediate judgment or reaction. By grounding yourself in the present moment, you reduce the power of anxieties about the future or regrets about the past, both of which are rooted in judgments about things beyond your control. A simple breathing exercise, focusing on the sensation of air entering and leaving your lungs, can serve as an anchor, drawing you back to the present when your mind wanders into unproductive emotional territory.

Thirdly, actively seek opportunities to practice virtue, even in small ways. Acts of kindness, honesty, and diligence, performed without expectation of external reward, strengthen your inner resolve. These are exercises for the character, building the muscles of self-control and moral integrity. Each virtuous action reinforces the understanding that your true power lies in your choices and your actions, not in external validation or outcomes.

Fourthly, engage in what is sometimes called "negative visualization" or *premeditatio malorum*. This involves contemplating the impermanence of good things and the possibility of future hardships. For example, before a pleasant meal, briefly consider the possibility that you might not always have access to such food. Before a meeting with loved ones, reflect on the fact that life is finite and relationships can change. This is not about cultivating pessimism, but about fostering gratitude for what you have and preparing your mind to accept potential loss with greater equanimity. It is a form of psychological inoculation, making you more resilient when adversity strikes.

Consider the warrior preparing for battle. They don't simply hope for victory; they train rigorously, study the terrain, anticipate enemy tactics, and condition their bodies and minds for the rigors of combat. They focus on what they can control: their preparation, their discipline, their courage. Similarly, in the arena of life, we must meticulously prepare our minds. We must identify our own "enemy" – irrational judgments, destructive emotions, unhelpful habits – and develop strategies to overcome them.

The Stoic ideal is not to become an unfeeling automaton, but a person of profound inner strength and unwavering character, capable of facing life's challenges with clarity, courage, and compassion. It is about building an internal resilience that is not dependent on external circumstances. By consistently applying the principles of the dichotomy of control, the examination of judgments, and the pursuit of virtue, we can cultivate an inner calm that remains unshaken, even amidst the most turbulent storms of life. This is the essence of Stoic resilience: mastering your inner landscape to navigate the outer world with grace and fortitude.

The capacity to observe our internal and external worlds without being ensnared by them is a cornerstone of emotional fortitude. This is not to advocate for a passive disengagement, but rather for a skilled form of involvement, one that allows us to participate fully in life's unfolding drama without being swept away by its currents. This nuanced approach is deeply resonant with the Buddhist concept of non-attachment. At its core, non-attachment is not about becoming indifferent or apathetic; rather, it is about developing the wisdom to engage with experiences, outcomes, and even our own thoughts and emotions in a way that fosters freedom rather than suffering.

Consider the analogy of a highly trained field medic on a chaotic battlefield. Their task is to provide critical care, to act with precision and urgency, and to make life-saving decisions under immense pressure. They are deeply invested in the well-being of their patients, yet they cannot afford to be paralyzed by the individual suffering they witness. If they were to become consumed by the pain of each casualty, their ability to help others would be severely compromised. Instead, they cultivate a focused professionalism, an emotional discipline that allows them to be present and effective, attending to the immediate needs while maintaining an objective perspective. This is the essence of non-attachment in action: full engagement, tempered by a clear-eyed recognition of what is within our control and what is not.

Attachment, in this context, refers to an excessive clinging or a demand for things to be a certain way. This can manifest in numerous forms: attachment to specific outcomes, to material possessions, to particular relationships, to our own ideas, or even to our emotional states. When we become overly attached, we create a vulnerability within ourselves. We place our peace of mind and our sense of well-being in the hands of external factors that are, by their very nature, impermanent and often unpredictable. This is where the seeds of suffering are sown.

For example, consider the intense disappointment that can arise when a meticulously planned project fails to achieve its intended outcome. If we have become deeply attached to the success of that specific project – perhaps seeing it as a validation of our worth or a critical step towards a desired future – its failure can feel like a personal catastrophe. This attachment magnifies the negative impact, leading to feelings of despair, self-recrimination, and a sense of lost potential. Conversely, if we approach the project with a commitment to doing our best, understanding that success is not guaranteed, and accepting that unforeseen obstacles may arise, we can still be disappointed, but the suffering is significantly mitigated. We can acknowledge the setback, learn from the experience, and redirect our energy without being crushed by the weight of unmet expectations.

This principle extends to our possessions. While it is natural to appreciate and care for our belongings, an excessive attachment can lead to anxiety about their security, distress over their potential loss, or an unhealthy identification of our self-worth with the accumulation of material things. If our sense of identity is tied to our possessions, then any threat to those possessions becomes a threat to our very being. Detachment, in this instance, means valuing possessions for their utility or aesthetic pleasure, but recognizing that they are external to our core self and that true wealth lies in our inner resources.

Even our thoughts and beliefs can become objects of attachment. We may develop strong opinions or deeply held convictions, and the prospect of having them challenged can trigger defensiveness and emotional discomfort. When we are attached to our perspectives, we may find it difficult to consider alternative viewpoints, to learn from new information, or to adapt our thinking in light of changing circumstances. This rigid adherence to our current mental models can stifle growth and lead to unnecessary conflict. Practicing detachment from our thoughts involves recognizing them as mental events, observing their content without necessarily accepting them as absolute truths, and being willing to revise our understanding when presented with compelling evidence or new insights.

The practice of detachment is cultivated through mindful observation and the intentional reframing of our relationship with the transient nature of life. It involves developing an inner space, a capacity for equanimity, that allows us to experience the full spectrum of human emotion and circumstance without being consumed by them. This is akin to a sailor skillfully navigating choppy waters. They do not attempt to calm the waves or change the direction of the wind; instead, they adjust the sails, steer the rudder, and remain focused on reaching their destination, respecting the power of the sea while maintaining control over their vessel.

One practical approach to cultivating detachment is through regular reflection and self-inquiry. When faced with a challenging situation or a strong emotional reaction, take a moment to pause and ask yourself:

What is truly happening? Separate the objective facts of the situation from your interpretations and emotional responses.

What am I attached to in this moment? Is it a particular outcome, a certain perception of myself, or the way things "should" be?

How is this attachment contributing to my suffering or hindering my effectiveness?

What would it look like to engage with this situation with less clinging and more open awareness?

What is within my control, and what is not? (Echoing the Stoic principle, this remains vital.)

This process of inquiry helps to loosen the grip of attachment by bringing it into conscious awareness. When we see our attachments clearly, they lose some of their power over us. We begin to recognize that our suffering is often self-imposed, stemming from our resistance to reality as it is, rather than from the reality itself.

Another powerful tool is the practice of "letting go," not as a passive surrender, but as an active choice to release the burden of clinging. This can be practiced through various forms of meditation. For instance, during a mindfulness meditation, when a particular thought or feeling arises and begins to pull you in, acknowledge its presence, observe it without judgment, and then gently release your attention from it, returning your focus to your anchor, such as your breath. With each iteration, you are strengthening your capacity to observe without needing to grasp or resist. It is like watching clouds drift across the sky; you notice them, appreciate their form, but you do not try to hold onto them or alter their course.

The benefits of cultivating non-attachment are profound. Firstly, it leads to a significant reduction in suffering. By loosening our grip on desired outcomes and external circumstances, we diminish the potential for disappointment and despair. When things do not go as planned, we can still feel sadness or regret, but these emotions are less likely to spiral into prolonged distress.

Secondly, non-attachment enhances objectivity and clarity. When we are not emotionally invested in a particular outcome or perspective, we are better able to assess situations realistically, to make sound judgments, and to consider a wider range of options. This is invaluable in decision-making, problem-solving, and interpersonal interactions. Imagine a negotiation where one party is rigidly attached to a specific concession. Their perspective will likely be narrow, and their ability to find a mutually beneficial solution will be hampered by their inflexibility. A detached negotiator, while still advocating for their interests, remains open to creative solutions and understanding the other party's position.

Thirdly, detachment fosters greater freedom and spontaneity. When we are not bound by rigid expectations or fears of loss, we are more liberated to explore new possibilities, to take calculated risks, and to adapt to changing circumstances. This freedom allows for a more dynamic and fulfilling engagement with life. We are less constrained by the need for things to be a certain way, opening us up to the unexpected joys and lessons that life invariably offers.

Fourthly, it cultivates a deeper sense of inner peace. By recognizing the impermanent nature of all things and by anchoring our sense of self-worth in our inner qualities rather than external achievements or possessions, we build a resilient foundation of contentment. This peace is not contingent on the absence of challenges, but on our capacity to navigate them with equanimity and wisdom.

Consider the disciplined approach of a seasoned strategist. They meticulously analyze the battlefield, understand the strengths and weaknesses of their forces and the enemy, and formulate plans with precision. Yet, they also understand that no plan is foolproof, and that the fog of war can obscure even the clearest intelligence. Therefore, they build flexibility into their strategies, and they prepare themselves mentally for the unexpected. They are attached to their mission and the well-being of their troops, but they are not rigidly attached to a single, predetermined path to victory. This ability to observe the unfolding situation with clear eyes, to adapt their tactics as needed, and to accept that some elements are beyond their direct control is a powerful demonstration of strategic detachment. They are fully engaged in the fight, but they are not prisoners of their own projections or desires for a specific outcome.

To integrate this practice into your daily life, consider these steps:

Identify areas of strong attachment: Begin by noticing where you tend to cling most tightly. Is it to your reputation, your career goals, your relationships, your comfort, or your ideas? Keep a journal for a week to track instances where you feel significant emotional resistance or distress related to something external.

Practice mindful observation of thoughts and feelings: When you notice a strong emotion or a persistent thought, simply observe it without labeling it as good or bad. See it as a temporary phenomenon. Try to notice its qualities – its intensity, its physical sensations, its duration.

Reframe expectations: Instead of demanding that things unfold in a particular way, practice setting intentions and committing to your best effort, while remaining open to the possibility that the outcome may differ from your initial vision. Phrase your aspirations as possibilities rather than certainties. For example, instead of "I must get this promotion," try "I am working towards this promotion and will do my best, open to whatever opportunities arise."

Engage in "sacred letting go" rituals: At the end of the day, or at a designated time, consciously practice releasing any attachments that have arisen. This could involve a simple mental acknowledgment of the day's experiences and a gentle release of any lingering hopes, fears, or disappointments.

Cultivate gratitude: Regularly express gratitude for what you have, rather than focusing on what you lack or what you fear losing. Gratitude shifts the focus from acquisition and possession to appreciation and contentment, naturally loosening the grip of attachment.

The journey of cultivating non-attachment is an ongoing practice, not a destination. It is about developing a more skillful, resilient, and peaceful way of being in the world, allowing us to engage fully with life's richness while preserving our inner equilibrium. By observing without attachment, we gain the freedom to act with clarity, to love with openness, and to live with a profound sense of peace, regardless of the ever-changing circumstances that life presents. This art of detachment is not about disconnecting from life, but about connecting with it more wisely, more freely, and more effectively. It is the quiet strength that allows us to witness the storms without becoming the storm itself.

Empathy, often described as the capacity to understand and share the feelings of another, is far more than a mere emotional response; it is a potent force multiplier for connection and collaboration. In the intricate dance of human interaction, particularly within the demanding environments where personal fortitude is tested, the ability to truly connect with others on an emotional and cognitive level can elevate individual efforts into collective triumphs. Think of a highly trained military unit. Each member possesses specialized skills, discipline, and courage. Yet, it is the unspoken understanding, the shared commitment, and the intuitive grasp of a comrade's situation that transforms a collection of individuals into an cohesive and effective fighting force. Empathy fuels this cohesion, enabling team members to anticipate needs, offer support without being asked, and function with a synchronized purpose that far exceeds the sum of their individual capabilities.

It is crucial to distinguish empathy from its often-confused cousin, sympathy. While sympathy involves feeling *for* someone – an expression of pity or sorrow for their misfortune – empathy is about feeling *with* them. Sympathy can create a distance, a sense of separation between the observer and the observed, often implying a hierarchical position of the observer who is outside the experience. Empathy, conversely, bridges that gap. It requires stepping into another's shoes, even if only for a moment, to perceive the world from their vantage point, to understand the emotional landscape they inhabit. This distinction is vital. To offer sympathy without empathy can sometimes feel patronizing or dismissive, inadvertently invalidating the other person's experience. Empathy, however, validates. It communicates, "I may not have walked your exact path, but I can grasp the weight of your burden and the texture of your emotions." This validation is the bedrock upon which genuine trust and rapport are built, essential ingredients for any high-functioning team or enduring personal relationship.

Developing this capacity for empathy is not an innate, fixed trait; it is a skill that can be cultivated and honed through conscious practice. One of the most direct pathways to deepening our empathy is through active listening. This goes beyond simply hearing words; it involves a focused intention to understand the speaker's message, both explicit and implicit. Active listening demands our full attention, both mental and physical. It means setting aside distractions – silencing the internal monologue that often preoccupies us with our own thoughts, reactions, or upcoming responses – and dedicating our energy to truly absorbing what the other person is conveying. Non-verbal cues are a significant part of this. Maintaining appropriate eye contact, nodding to show engagement, and mirroring subtle body language can all signal to the speaker that they are being heard and understood. More importantly, it requires us to listen for the emotions underlying the words. What is the speaker feeling? Are they expressing frustration, joy, anxiety, or resignation? Learning to detect these emotional undercurrents is key to moving from superficial listening to deep empathetic understanding.

Another powerful technique for cultivating empathy is through perspective-taking. This involves intentionally imagining oneself in another person's situation and attempting to see the world through their eyes. This can be practiced in various ways. When interacting with someone, pause before responding and ask yourself: "What might be going through their mind right now? What pressures are they facing? What are their underlying needs or fears?" This exercise is particularly potent when dealing with individuals whose perspectives differ significantly from your own. Instead of immediately dismissing their viewpoint as incorrect or illogical, make a deliberate effort to understand the reasoning and emotional drivers behind it. Social psychology research consistently highlights the efficacy of this approach. Studies have shown that when individuals are encouraged to take the perspective of others, their levels of prosocial behavior – actions intended to help others – increase significantly. They become more understanding, less judgmental, and more inclined to cooperate.

Consider the strategic planning sessions that are commonplace in both military and civilian leadership contexts. A successful strategy rarely emerges from a single, monolithic viewpoint. Instead, it is forged through the synthesis of diverse perspectives, each informed by different experiences, expertise, and insights. An empathetic leader will actively solicit these varied viewpoints, creating an environment where team members feel safe to express their honest assessments, even if they challenge the prevailing opinion. They will listen not just to the content of the suggestions but also to the underlying concerns and motivations. This inclusive approach not only leads to more robust and well-rounded strategies but also fosters a sense of psychological safety and shared ownership among the team, enhancing morale and commitment. The leader who can empathetically understand the anxieties of a junior officer about an upcoming mission, or the frustrations of a civilian analyst facing bureaucratic hurdles, is far more likely to address those concerns proactively and build a more resilient team.

The benefits of empathetic communication extend profoundly into conflict resolution. Disagreements and friction are inevitable when people work together, especially under pressure. However, the *way* these conflicts are handled can either escalate the situation or lead to constructive resolutions. Empathetic communication shifts the focus from winning an argument to understanding the root causes of the conflict and finding mutually agreeable solutions. When parties in a dispute feel truly heard and understood, their defensiveness often diminishes, creating space for genuine dialogue. Instead of approaching a disagreement with the mindset of proving oneself right and the other person wrong, an empathetic approach involves seeking to understand the other person's needs, fears, and underlying interests that are driving their position. This often reveals common ground that was previously obscured by emotional reactivity. For example, two team members might be clashing over project deadlines. One might be perceived as being overly demanding, while the other is seen as being uncooperative. Through empathetic listening, it might emerge that the "demanding" individual is under immense pressure from senior leadership for timely delivery, while the "uncooperative" individual is grappling with unforeseen technical issues and feeling unheard in their attempts to communicate these challenges. By understanding these underlying factors, a more collaborative solution can be found, such as adjusting timelines, reallocating resources, or providing additional support, rather than resorting to punitive measures or fostering resentment.

Furthermore, empathy is the cornerstone of building trust. Trust is not something that can be commanded; it is earned through consistent actions that demonstrate reliability, integrity, and genuine care for others. When individuals feel that their colleagues and leaders understand and value their perspectives, their willingness to be vulnerable and to rely on others increases dramatically. This creates a positive feedback loop: as trust deepens, collaboration becomes more effective, leading to greater success, which in turn further strengthens trust. In high-stakes environments, this trust is not merely a pleasant interpersonal dynamic; it is a critical operational necessity. A soldier needs to trust that their squad mates have their back, not just in terms of covering fire, but in terms of understanding their limitations and supporting them when they are struggling. Similarly, in any complex project, team members need to trust that their contributions will be understood and appreciated, and that their colleagues will act with consideration for the collective good.

To cultivate a more empathetic approach in daily interactions, consider incorporating specific practices. One effective method is to consciously practice curiosity about others. Approach conversations with a genuine desire to learn about the other person's experiences, motivations, and feelings. Ask open-ended questions that encourage elaboration, such as "Can you tell me more about that?" or "How did that make you feel?" Avoid questions that elicit simple yes/no answers. Another valuable practice is to regularly reflect on your interactions. After a conversation or a meeting, take a few moments to consider: "Did I truly listen to understand, or did I just wait for my turn to speak? Did I make an effort to see the situation from the other person's perspective? How could I have communicated more empathetically?" This form of self-inquiry helps to identify areas for improvement and reinforces empathetic habits.

The principle of "seek first to understand, then to be understood," popularized by Stephen Covey, is a profound guide for empathetic engagement. It suggests that in any communication, especially during potential conflict or disagreement, our primary goal should be to gain a clear and accurate understanding of the other person's point of view before attempting to articulate our own. This requires suspending our own agenda temporarily and immersing ourselves in the other person's narrative. It means listening not just for the facts, but for the feelings, the values, and the underlying needs being expressed. This is particularly challenging when emotions are running high, either on our part or on the part of the other person. However, the rewards are immense. When someone feels truly understood, they are far more likely to be receptive to what you have to say. They are less likely to feel attacked or defensive, and more open to finding common ground and collaborative solutions. This is a fundamental principle that underpins effective negotiation, leadership, and indeed, all meaningful human connection.

Furthermore, the practice of mindfulness, as discussed in the context of non-attachment, also serves as a powerful precursor to empathy. By cultivating greater awareness of our own thoughts, emotions, and bodily sensations, we develop a more nuanced understanding of our internal landscape. This self-awareness is a prerequisite for understanding the internal landscapes of others. When we are more attuned to our own feelings of frustration, disappointment, or joy, we become better equipped to recognize and interpret these emotions in others. Mindfulness meditation, by training the mind to observe without judgment, also helps us to approach others with greater openness and less preconceived notions. It allows us to meet each interaction as a fresh experience, rather than filtering it through a lens of past judgments or biases. This mindful presence is what allows us to truly be "with" another person, to offer genuine support and understanding.

In essence, empathy is not just a soft skill; it is a critical competency that enhances our ability to navigate complex social environments, build robust relationships, and achieve collective goals. It transforms superficial interactions into meaningful connections, disagreements into opportunities for growth, and disparate individuals into cohesive, high-performing teams. By understanding the difference between empathy and sympathy, practicing active listening and perspective-taking, and integrating mindful awareness into our daily interactions, we can cultivate this powerful force multiplier and unlock a deeper level of connection and collaboration in all aspects of our lives. It is the quiet strength that allows us to see beyond ourselves and truly connect with the shared human experience, fostering resilience, trust, and a collective capacity to overcome challenges.

Chapter 4: Strategic Execution: Planning and Implementing for Success

The journey toward any significant achievement, whether in the crucible of military operations or the quiet determination of personal growth, begins with a clear articulation of purpose. This is the bedrock of strategic execution, the foundational element upon which all subsequent planning and action must be built. Without a well-defined mission, efforts become diffused, energy is wasted, and the path forward remains obscured, like navigating treacherous terrain without a map or compass. In military parlance, a mission statement is not merely a declaration of intent; it is a directive, a guiding star that illuminates the objective and provides the necessary context for all operational planning. It answers the fundamental question: "What are we trying to accomplish, and why?" This clarity is paramount, for it imbues the entire endeavor with direction and meaning, transforming a collection of tasks into a cohesive and purposeful undertaking.

The efficacy of a mission definition hinges on its precision and clarity. Vague aspirations, however noble, are insufficient as operational guides. To truly set a course for success, goals must be framed in a manner that leaves no room for ambiguity. This is where the well-established framework of SMART criteria becomes indispensable. SMART, an acronym for Specific, Measurable, Achievable, Relevant, and Time-bound, provides a robust structure for transforming broad ambitions into actionable objectives. Applying the "Specific" element means dissecting a general aim into its constituent parts. Instead of aiming to "improve fitness," a specific goal might be to "increase cardiovascular endurance by running a 5K race without stopping." This level of detail clarifies exactly what needs to be done, eliminating guesswork and providing a clear target.

Following specificity, the "Measurable" aspect introduces the critical element of progress tracking. How will you know if you are succeeding? For the fitness example, measurability could involve tracking running times, distances covered, or heart rate recovery. In a professional context, it might be about quantifiable improvements in sales figures, customer satisfaction scores, or project completion rates. Without a metric, progress remains subjective and difficult to assess, making it impossible to gauge the effectiveness of your strategy. The absence of measurability often leads to a slow drift away from the original objective, as without clear indicators of success, it becomes difficult to identify when adjustments are needed or when momentum is being lost. This principle is fundamental in military planning; a tactical objective must have definable success criteria, such as securing a specific piece of terrain or neutralizing a particular threat, so that commanders can ascertain whether the mission is being accomplished.

The "Achievable" criterion is not about setting the bar low, but about setting it realistically. It requires a candid assessment of resources, capabilities, and constraints. An achievable goal is one that is within reach, given the current circumstances, while still demanding significant effort and stretching one's capabilities. Setting an unattainable goal, while perhaps inspiring in theory, can lead to demoralization and ultimately, failure. Conversely, goals that are too easily met can foster complacency. The art lies in striking a balance, pushing boundaries without exceeding them to the point of impossibility. This often involves a degree of honest self-assessment or team capability assessment. For instance, if a new business aims to capture 50% of a market within its first quarter, and the market is dominated by established players with deep resources, this goal might be deemed unachievable. A more achievable goal might be to secure 5% of the market share by focusing on a specific niche or customer segment. This principle is crucial in military operations, where overestimating capabilities or underestimating enemy strength can have catastrophic consequences. Planning must be grounded in an accurate assessment of available manpower, equipment, intelligence, and the operational environment.

"Relevancy" ensures that the goal is aligned with your broader purpose and values. In the context of personal development, this means connecting your immediate objectives to your long-term aspirations and core beliefs. If your ultimate aim is to lead a more fulfilling life, a goal that distracts from this overarching vision, even if achievable and measurable, might not be truly relevant. It asks: "Does this goal matter? Does it contribute to the larger picture?" For a military unit, relevancy means ensuring that every tactical objective directly supports the strategic operational plan and ultimately, the overarching national interest or political objective. A unit might be highly efficient at a particular maneuver, but if that maneuver does not contribute to the overall campaign, it is a misallocation of valuable resources and effort. This alignment prevents actions that are efficient but ineffective in the grand scheme.

Finally, the "Time-bound" aspect introduces a sense of urgency and accountability. Setting a deadline creates a clear endpoint, providing a framework for planning and execution. It prevents tasks from languishing indefinitely and encourages focused effort. Without a time limit, even the most specific and achievable goal can be perpetually deferred. This element is critical for maintaining momentum and for effective progress management. For example, "Learn to play a musical instrument" is a goal lacking a time constraint. "Learn to play three basic chords on the guitar within one month" is a SMART goal that is specific, measurable, achievable, relevant to the broader desire to play music, and time-bound. In a team setting, deadlines for project milestones or individual tasks ensure that the overall project stays on track. In military operations, mission timelines are meticulously planned, with phased objectives and critical deadlines that dictate the tempo and coordination of the entire operation.

The process of breaking down large, overarching objectives into smaller, more manageable steps is a cornerstone of effective strategic execution. This hierarchical decomposition of tasks ensures that the path forward remains clear and that the sheer magnitude of a significant undertaking does not become a source of paralysis. Imagine a large-scale military campaign; it is not executed as a single, monolithic action, but as a series of coordinated subordinate operations, each with its own specific objectives, resources, and timelines. Similarly, a personal goal of writing a book, for instance, can seem daunting. However, by breaking it down into stages—research, outlining, drafting each chapter, editing, revising—the task becomes far more approachable. Each stage, in turn, can be further segmented into smaller actions, such as "conduct research for chapter one" or "write the introduction to chapter two." This methodical approach provides clarity at every level, allowing for focused effort on immediate tasks while keeping the ultimate objective in sight.

This process of defining clear and achievable goals is not merely an exercise in organizational efficiency; it is deeply intertwined with maintaining motivation and fostering a sense of progress. When individuals can see tangible steps being completed, and when the progress towards the ultimate goal is measurable, it fuels a positive feedback loop. Each accomplished sub-goal serves as a mini-victory, reinforcing commitment and building momentum. This is particularly important in long-term endeavors, where the ultimate reward may be distant. The ability to celebrate interim successes, however small, can be critical for sustaining the necessary drive and resilience. In military operations, successful completion of a patrol, the securing of a forward operating base, or the neutralization of a localized threat are all critical achievements that build morale and demonstrate progress toward the larger campaign objective, even amidst ongoing danger and uncertainty.

Furthermore, the act of defining these goals must be intrinsically linked to one's core values and overarching aspirations. A goal that is merely specific, measurable, achievable, relevant, and time-bound, but which clashes with one's fundamental beliefs or life purpose, is unlikely to lead to genuine satisfaction or sustained commitment. For instance, pursuing a highly lucrative career in a field that one finds morally objectionable would likely create internal conflict, undermining long-term well-being and eroding motivation. Therefore, the "R" in SMART – Relevance – must encompass not only the strategic importance of the goal within a given context but also its alignment with personal values and deeper life aspirations. This connection imbues the pursuit with meaning, transforming a task-oriented objective into a purposeful endeavor. It is about ensuring that the destination is not only reachable but also a place where one genuinely wants to be.

Consider the process of strategic planning in any complex organization. Before any operational plan is formulated, the leadership must first establish a clear mission statement. This statement articulates the organization's purpose, its core objectives, and its desired future state. This is not a static document but a dynamic guide that informs all subsequent decisions. For example, a technology company might define its mission as "to empower individuals and businesses through innovative and accessible software solutions." From this overarching mission, specific goals can be derived for different departments: the research and development team might have a goal to launch a new product with specific features by a certain date, the marketing team might aim to increase brand awareness by a quantifiable percentage, and the customer support team might strive to reduce average response times. Each of these departmental goals, when broken down further into individual or team tasks, must ultimately contribute to the realization of the company's core mission. Without this clear hierarchical alignment, departments might pursue objectives that are efficient in isolation but ultimately contradictory or unhelpful to the overall organizational purpose.

The discipline of setting clear and achievable goals also fosters a crucial element of strategic thinking: foresight. By defining specific objectives and timelines, one is compelled to anticipate potential obstacles, identify necessary resources, and map out a sequence of actions. This proactive approach stands in stark contrast to reactive problem-solving, which often arises when goals are ill-defined or absent altogether. When a mission is clearly articulated, potential challenges can be identified early, allowing for contingency planning and the development of mitigation strategies. This anticipatory mindset is a hallmark of effective leadership and is essential for navigating the inherent uncertainties of any complex undertaking. For a military commander, this means not only planning the initial assault but also anticipating the enemy's likely responses, planning for resupply, and considering potential egress routes. For an individual pursuing a personal development goal, it might involve identifying potential time constraints due to work or family commitments and proactively scheduling dedicated time for their pursuits.

The translation of abstract aspirations into concrete, actionable goals is a critical step in bridging the gap between intention and realization. It requires a disciplined approach to self-reflection and planning. It is about translating the "what" and the "why" into a precise "how" and "when." This foundational work of mission definition sets the stage for everything that follows. Without it, strategic execution risks becoming a series of disjointed efforts, lacking the coherence and direction necessary for sustained success. It is the first, indispensable step in transforming vision into tangible reality, providing the clarity, focus, and motivation required to navigate the complexities of execution and ultimately, to achieve meaningful outcomes. This deliberate and structured approach to goal setting is not merely a bureaucratic formality; it is the very engine that drives progress and ensures that efforts are consistently aligned with the desired end state, whether that end state is a battlefield victory or a personal transformation.

The efficacy of any strategic plan, whether devised on the battlefield or in the quiet contemplation of personal aspiration, is inextricably linked to the quality of intelligence that underpins it. Before a single soldier advances or a single step is taken towards a personal objective, a comprehensive understanding of the operational landscape—the terrain, the adversary, the resources available, and the prevailing conditions—must be established. This crucial phase, often referred to as intelligence gathering, is not a mere preliminary exercise but a continuous, dynamic process that informs every subsequent decision and action. It is the bedrock of informed execution, transforming potential chaos into calculated progress. Neglecting this vital step is akin to embarking on a perilous journey without a map, a compass, or even a basic understanding of the destination. The consequences of such oversight can range from wasted effort and missed opportunities to catastrophic failure.

In the realm of strategic planning, thorough research and effective information gathering serve as the functional equivalent of military reconnaissance. Just as a commander dispatches scouts and analysts to assess enemy dispositions, terrain features, and potential hazards, an individual or organization aiming for success must diligently collect and analyze relevant data. This involves identifying what information is critical to achieving the objective and then devising methods to acquire it. The breadth of this research will vary depending dynamically with the nature of the goal. For a military operation, this might involve satellite imagery, signals intelligence, human intelligence sources, and meteorological reports. For a personal goal, such as learning a new skill or starting a business, it could encompass academic studies, industry reports, market analyses, expert interviews, and the experiences of those who have trod a similar path before. The common thread is the pursuit of knowledge to reduce uncertainty and enhance the probability of success.

The initial, and perhaps most critical, aspect of this phase is the identification of reliable sources. In an age saturated with information, discerning truth from falsehood, and signal from noise, is a paramount challenge. For military operations, strict protocols govern the vetting of intelligence sources, ensuring that information is not only accurate but also actionable and its origins understood. Similarly, in strategic planning for any endeavor, one must develop a discerning eye for credible sources. This means looking beyond superficial appearances and delving into the provenance and methodology behind the information presented.

Academic journals, peer-reviewed studies, established industry publications, government data, and interviews with recognized experts generally carry a higher degree of reliability than anonymous online forums, biased opinion pieces, or unsubstantiated claims. It requires a deliberate effort to understand the potential biases of a source, its historical accuracy, and its vested interests. A well-researched plan is built on a foundation of vetted information, not on the shifting sands of misinformation.

Furthermore, the sheer volume of data available necessitates an organized approach to information acquisition. Simply collecting a mass of documents or data points is insufficient. A strategic approach requires a clear understanding of what questions need to be answered and what information is required to answer them. This involves framing specific research queries that directly relate to the objectives and potential challenges of the strategic plan. For instance, if the goal is to launch a new product, research might focus on market demand for similar products, competitor pricing strategies, potential manufacturing partners, regulatory requirements, and customer demographics. Each of these areas represents a distinct line of inquiry, requiring different sources and methodologies. This systematic approach prevents research from becoming a meandering, unfocused activity and ensures that the effort is directed towards gathering intelligence that is truly relevant and useful.

Once information has been gathered, the next crucial step is its critical evaluation. This is where the intellectual rigor of the strategist comes into play. Information, even from seemingly reliable sources, must be subjected to a process of scrutiny. This involves questioning assumptions, identifying logical fallacies, assessing the validity of evidence, and considering alternative interpretations. For instance, a market research report, while valuable, may contain inherent assumptions about consumer behavior or future economic trends. A critical evaluator will not accept these assumptions at face value but will seek to understand the basis for them and consider the potential impact if those assumptions prove incorrect. This analytical process is vital for uncovering potential weaknesses in the gathered intelligence and for identifying areas where further research may be needed. It is about moving beyond passive consumption of information to active, discerning engagement.

In military contexts, this critical evaluation often involves cross-referencing intelligence from multiple sources to corroborate findings. If several independent intelligence streams point to the same conclusion, the confidence in that conclusion increases significantly. Conversely, if reports conflict, it signals a need for further investigation to resolve the discrepancies. This principle of triangulation is equally applicable to strategic planning in any domain. Comparing information from different sources, evaluating conflicting data points, and seeking explanations for discrepancies strengthen the overall understanding and lead to more robust decision-making. It is through this process of questioning, comparing, and verifying that the raw data begins to transform into actionable intelligence.

The synthesis of this evaluated information is where raw data coalesces into a comprehensive understanding of the situation. This is not a linear process of simply compiling facts, but rather an interpretive and analytical endeavor. It involves identifying patterns, drawing connections between seemingly disparate pieces of information, and constructing a coherent narrative or model of the operating environment. For a military planner, this might involve creating a comprehensive threat assessment that analyzes enemy capabilities, intentions, and likely courses of action, layered onto a detailed understanding of the terrain and weather. For a business strategist, it might involve synthesizing market data, competitor analysis, and internal capabilities to identify opportunities and threats, leading to a strategic positioning statement. This synthesis phase is where the raw intelligence is transformed into insights that can directly inform the planning and execution of the strategic objective.

This synthesis requires an ability to see the forest for the trees. It means stepping back from the minutiae of individual data points to discern the broader implications and strategic significance. It is about connecting the dots to reveal the underlying dynamics at play. This often involves developing conceptual frameworks or mental models that help to organize and interpret the information. For example, frameworks such as SWOT analysis (Strengths, Weaknesses, Opportunities, Threats), Porter's Five Forces, or scenario planning can be invaluable tools for synthesizing complex information and identifying strategic leverage points. These frameworks provide a structure for thinking about the gathered data and for deriving meaningful conclusions.

The output of this synthesis is a clear, comprehensive understanding of the operational environment. This understanding should provide answers to critical questions: What are the key opportunities and threats? What are the strengths and weaknesses of the actors involved (including oneself)? What are the likely future trajectories of the situation? What are the critical success factors and potential pitfalls? Possessing this informed awareness is what allows for the development of strategies that are not based on guesswork or wishful thinking, but on a realistic assessment of the situation. It is the foundation upon which sound objectives are set, resources are allocated, and action plans are formulated.

Moreover, the intelligence gathering and synthesis process is not a one-time event. The operational landscape is rarely static. Conditions change, adversaries adapt, and new information constantly emerges. Therefore, effective intelligence gathering must be an ongoing, iterative process. This means establishing mechanisms for continuous monitoring of the environment, updating gathered intelligence, and reassessing the strategic plan as circumstances evolve. A military unit does not cease its intelligence gathering upon entering the operational theater; it intensifies it, constantly seeking to maintain situational awareness and adapt to changing enemy tactics or environmental conditions. Similarly, any strategic endeavor requires a commitment to ongoing learning and adaptation. Regularly revisiting assumptions, seeking new information, and being willing to adjust the plan based on evolving intelligence is crucial for sustained success. This adaptability is a hallmark of resilient strategies.

The insights gained from thorough research and synthesis directly inform the goal-setting process, which was discussed previously. A clear understanding of the environment, the available resources, and potential obstacles allows for the formulation of SMART goals that are not only specific, measurable, achievable, relevant, and time-bound, but also strategically sound. For instance, knowing the competitive landscape might inform the "Achievable" and "Relevant" aspects of a business goal, while understanding potential logistical challenges might influence the "Time-bound" element. Without this informational foundation, goal setting can become an exercise in abstract idealism, detached from the realities of implementation.

The ability to synthesize information effectively is also a critical skill that can be cultivated. It requires practice in analytical thinking, pattern recognition, and critical evaluation. Developing this skill involves actively engaging with information, asking probing questions, and seeking to understand the underlying connections and implications. It is about moving from a passive recipient of information to an active architect of understanding. This process of building a coherent and insightful picture from fragmented data is what empowers strategic decision-making. It allows one to anticipate challenges, identify opportunities, and navigate complex situations with confidence and clarity. Without this crucial step, the most brilliant intentions can falter, undone by a lack of foresight and a failure to grasp the nuances of the operating environment. The investment in thorough research and diligent synthesis is, therefore, not merely an optional preliminary step, but the very engine that drives the entire strategic execution process, ensuring that actions are not only well-intentioned but also exceptionally well-informed and strategically aligned. This deep dive into the facts, critically examined and artfully synthesized, provides the necessary clarity to move forward with purpose, resilience, and a significantly enhanced probability of achieving desired outcomes.

Having established a robust understanding of the operating environment through meticulous intelligence gathering and synthesis, the next critical phase in strategic execution is the development of the operational plan. This is where foresight and analysis translate into a tangible roadmap for action, a blueprint that guides the journey from aspiration to achievement. An operational plan is not merely a list of tasks; it is a dynamic framework that articulates the 'how'—the specific methods and sequences of actions—to achieve the overarching mission and objectives. It bridges the gap between conceptual strategy and practical implementation, akin to how a military commander translates a strategic directive into a detailed battle plan.

At its core, developing an operational plan requires a disciplined approach to strategic thinking. Strategy, in this context, refers to the overarching approach or method chosen to achieve a particular objective. It is the high-level concept, the grand design, that dictates the general direction of effort. Tactics, conversely, are the specific actions or maneuvers employed to execute the strategy. They are the smaller, concrete steps taken in pursuit of the broader strategic goals. For instance, if a business strategy is to capture market share through superior customer service, the tactics might include implementing a 24/7 customer support hotline, offering personalized follow-up calls, and establishing a comprehensive customer feedback system. The interplay between strategy and tactics is crucial; a brilliant strategy can be undermined by poor tactics, and conversely, exceptionally executed tactics might not salvage a fundamentally flawed strategy.

The process of devising strategy begins with revisiting the mission and objectives. These serve as the north star, ensuring that every element of the operational plan remains aligned with the ultimate purpose. Given the intelligence gathered, the strategist must then identify the most viable and effective pathways to achieve these objectives. This often involves a critical evaluation of potential courses of action, weighing the advantages and disadvantages of each in light of the environmental conditions, resource availability, and the nature of any opposition or challenges. In military planning, this would involve analyzing enemy capabilities, terrain advantages, and logistical considerations to determine the optimal offensive or defensive posture. For personal or organizational goals, it might mean evaluating different market entry strategies, varying approaches to skill acquisition, or diverse methods for resource mobilization.

A key component of strategic development is risk assessment. Every plan, by its very nature, involves navigating uncertainty. Identifying potential risks—events or conditions that could negatively impact the plan's execution or outcome—is paramount. This isn't about succumbing to pessimism, but about embracing realism. Risks can be internal, stemming from a lack of resources, skill deficits, or organizational inertia, or external, arising from market volatility, competitor actions, regulatory changes, or unforeseen environmental factors. Once identified, each risk needs to be analyzed in terms of its likelihood of occurrence and its potential impact. This analysis allows for prioritization, focusing attention on the most significant threats.

Following risk identification and analysis, the next logical step is the development of mitigation strategies and contingency plans. Mitigation strategies are proactive measures designed to reduce the likelihood or impact of identified risks. For example, if a risk is a key supplier going out of business, a mitigation strategy might involve diversifying the supplier base or establishing a partnership with an alternative provider. Contingency plans, often referred to as "Plan B," are reactive measures designed to be implemented if a specific risk materializes. These plans pre-define the actions to be taken to manage the situation, minimize damage, and bring the operation back onto a successful trajectory. In military terms, this is like having pre-arranged rendezvous points or alternative routes if the primary path is blocked. For a business, it could be a crisis communication plan or a system for rapidly reallocating staff if a critical project faces unexpected delays.

The construction of the tactical elements of the operational plan involves breaking down the chosen strategy into a series of sequential, actionable steps. This requires meticulous planning regarding the 'who,' 'what,' 'when,' and 'how' of each task. For each objective or phase of the strategy, specific tasks must be defined. These tasks should be clear, unambiguous, and assigned to responsible individuals or teams. The sequencing of these tasks is critical; some actions may be dependent on the completion of others, creating a logical flow that prevents bottlenecks and ensures efficiency. This is where the concept of a timeline or schedule becomes essential, mapping out the expected duration of each task and establishing deadlines.

Resource allocation is another fundamental aspect of operational planning. This involves identifying all the resources required for each task—personnel, time, budget, equipment, information, and expertise—and ensuring that they are available and allocated appropriately. Overestimating or underestimating resource needs can have significant consequences. Insufficient resources can lead to delays, compromised quality, or outright failure, while excessive allocation can be wasteful and inefficient. A thorough resource assessment helps to ensure that the plan is not only theoretically sound but also practically feasible within the given constraints. This often involves creating detailed budgets, staffing plans, and equipment requisitions.

Moreover, the operational plan must also account for the potential for adaptation. While a well-constructed plan provides a clear direction, the reality of execution often involves unforeseen circumstances and evolving conditions. Therefore, the plan should incorporate mechanisms for monitoring progress, gathering feedback, and making necessary adjustments. This is where the iterative nature of strategic execution comes into play. Regular reviews, performance metrics, and feedback loops are essential for identifying deviations from the plan and for making informed decisions about modifications. The ability to adapt without losing sight of the ultimate objective is a hallmark of effective operational planning.

Consider the strategic objective of launching a new software product. The overarching strategy might be to penetrate a specific market segment by offering a superior user experience and robust functionality. The gathered intelligence might reveal that the target audience values ease of use and quick access to support. Based on this, the tactical plan would detail specific actions:

Phase 1: Product Development & Refinement

Task 1.1: Finalize core feature set based on user feedback. (Responsibility: Development Team Lead. Timeline: 2 weeks.)

Task 1.2: Conduct extensive beta testing with a representative user group. (Responsibility: QA Manager. Timeline: 4 weeks.)

Task 1.3: Address critical bugs identified during beta testing. (Responsibility: Development Team. Timeline: 2 weeks.)

Resource Allocation: 5 developers, 2 QA testers, 1 project manager, beta tester stipends.

Risk Assessment: Beta testers may not provide sufficient feedback; critical bugs may emerge late.

Mitigation/Contingency: Recruit a larger beta group; allocate buffer time for bug fixing.

Phase 2: Marketing & Pre-Launch

Task 2.1: Develop marketing collateral (website, brochures, social media content). (Responsibility: Marketing Manager. Timeline: 3 weeks.)

Task 2.2: Execute pre-launch marketing campaign to build awareness. (Responsibility: Marketing Team. Timeline: 6 weeks, ongoing.)

Task 2.3: Train customer support staff on product features and troubleshooting. (Responsibility: Support Manager. Timeline: 2 weeks.)

Resource Allocation: Marketing budget, graphic designers, copywriters, customer support team.

Risk Assessment: Low market awareness; negative initial reviews.

Mitigation/Contingency: Increase ad spend; prepare response strategies for negative feedback.

Phase 3: Launch & Post-Launch Support

Task 3.1: Officially launch the software product. (Responsibility: Project Manager. Timeline: Day 1.)

Task 3.2: Monitor sales and user acquisition closely. (Responsibility: Sales & Marketing Teams. Timeline: Ongoing.)

Task 3.3: Provide prompt customer support and address emerging issues. (Responsibility: Support Team. Timeline: Ongoing.)

Task 3.4: Collect post-launch user feedback for future iterations. (Responsibility: Product Manager. Timeline: Ongoing.)

Resource Allocation: Sales team, marketing budget for ongoing campaigns, customer support infrastructure.

Risk Assessment: Server overload on launch day; critical security vulnerability discovered.

Mitigation/Contingency: Scalable server infrastructure; robust security auditing process; incident response team on standby.

This detailed breakdown illustrates how a broad strategy is translated into concrete, manageable actions. Each task has a clear owner, a defined timeline, and associated resource requirements. The risks are identified, and plans are in place to address them. This structured approach ensures that no critical element is overlooked and that the entire effort is coordinated and purposeful.

Furthermore, the development of the operational plan should also consider the optimal sequencing of different strategic thrusts. For instance, in a military context, intelligence gathering might precede troop deployment, which then precedes the commencement of offensive operations. Similarly, in a business context, market research might precede product development, which then precedes marketing and sales efforts. The plan must reflect these logical dependencies. Introducing a product before thorough market research has been completed, or before the product itself is fully ready, significantly increases the risk of failure. The plan should map out these interdependencies, ensuring that each stage builds effectively upon the previous one.

The level of detail in an operational plan will vary depending on the complexity and scale of the objective. A simple personal goal might require a relatively straightforward plan, while a large-scale organizational project or military campaign would necessitate a far more intricate and comprehensive document. However, the underlying principles remain the same: clarity of objectives, a well-defined strategy, actionable tactics, realistic resource allocation, thorough risk assessment, and a capacity for adaptation.

The process of creating this plan is not merely an intellectual exercise; it is a crucial step in building confidence and commitment. When individuals or teams understand the strategy, the tactics, and their specific roles within the plan, they are more likely to be engaged and motivated. A well-communicated operational plan fosters a sense of shared purpose and provides a clear framework for collective action. It ensures that everyone is working towards the same goals, using coordinated efforts.

In essence, the operational plan is the bridge between strategic intent and tangible results. It demands rigor, foresight, and a practical understanding of how to marshal resources and navigate challenges. By meticulously crafting this plan, drawing upon the intelligence gathered and the strategic principles discussed, individuals and organizations significantly enhance their capacity to execute their objectives effectively and achieve success. It transforms vague intentions into a concrete, executable pathway, providing both direction and the necessary foresight to overcome the inevitable obstacles that lie ahead. The plan is not static; it is a living document that, when combined with diligent execution and continuous monitoring, becomes the engine of progress. The clarity it provides is indispensable, turning potential confusion into focused action, and aspiration into tangible accomplishment. The development of this plan is, therefore, not just a step, but a fundamental pillar upon which all successful strategic execution rests, ensuring that every action taken is deliberate, informed, and contributes directly to the overarching mission. It is the practical embodiment of strategic thinking, meticulously translated into a sequence of achievable actions.

The most meticulously crafted strategy, the most insightful intelligence, and the most comprehensive operational plan are ultimately constrained by the availability and effective deployment of resources. In any endeavor, whether it's a military campaign, a complex business venture, or a personal pursuit of ambitious goals, the ability to optimize what is available is often the decisive factor between success and failure. This crucial aspect of strategic execution hinges on the judicious management of three primary, interconnected resources: time, energy, and tools. Neglecting any one of these can create significant bottlenecks, derail progress, and ultimately lead to the dissolution of well-laid plans.

Time, often perceived as an abstract concept, is in reality a finite and precious commodity. In the context of strategic execution, time is not merely a measure of duration but a fundamental dimension within which actions must unfold. The efficiency with which we utilize our temporal capital directly correlates with our ability to achieve objectives within the planned parameters. This necessitates a disciplined approach to prioritization. Just as a military commander must allocate time for reconnaissance, troop movement, and offensive action based on strategic imperatives, individuals and organizations must learn to distinguish between urgent and important tasks. The Eisenhower Matrix, a venerable tool for time management, categorizes tasks into four quadrants: urgent and important (do first), important but not urgent (schedule), urgent but not important (delegate), and neither urgent nor important (eliminate). Focusing disproportionately on the urgent, particularly tasks that are not important, is a common pitfall that saps productivity and diverts attention from activities that truly drive progress toward strategic goals.

Furthermore, effective time management involves a critical examination of how time is currently being spent. This often begins with a simple, yet profound, exercise: time tracking. By meticulously recording how hours are allocated across various activities over a period, one can uncover hidden inefficiencies and time sinks. Are there recurring meetings that could be shortened or eliminated? Are there administrative tasks that consume disproportionate amounts of time relative to their strategic value? Are there habitual interruptions—digital notifications, unscheduled drop-ins, or excessive email checking—that fragment focus and necessitate costly context switching? Identifying these "time bandits" is the first step; the subsequent step is to implement strategies to mitigate their impact. This might involve batching similar tasks together, establishing dedicated "focus blocks" free from interruption, setting strict time limits for certain activities, or proactively communicating availability to colleagues. The principle here mirrors the logistical planning in military operations: identifying choke points and optimizing the flow of movement to ensure maximum operational tempo. For instance, if a marketing campaign requires coordinated efforts across design, content creation, and social media posting, understanding the dependencies and allocating sufficient, uninterrupted time for each phase is critical to meeting launch deadlines.

Energy optimization is the equally vital, yet often overlooked, counterpart to time management. Time can be managed, but energy must be replenished. Our capacity to perform at a high level, to think critically, to solve complex problems, and to maintain focus is directly tied to our physical, mental, and emotional energy levels. Just as a military unit requires rest and recuperation to maintain combat effectiveness, individuals and teams need to proactively manage their energy reserves. This goes beyond simply "getting enough sleep," though that is foundational. It involves understanding one's own personal rhythms and peaks of cognitive function. Are you most productive in the morning, afternoon, or evening? Aligning demanding tasks with periods of peak energy is a strategic advantage. This might mean scheduling complex problem-solving or creative work during your most alert hours and reserving administrative or less cognitively demanding tasks for periods when your energy naturally dips.

Moreover, energy is not a static quantity; it is influenced by a myriad of factors, including nutrition, exercise, stress management, and even the quality of our work environment. A sedentary lifestyle, poor dietary choices, and chronic stress can all deplete energy reserves, making it difficult to sustain effort on strategic objectives. Conversely, regular physical activity, a balanced diet, mindfulness practices, and taking regular breaks can significantly enhance mental clarity and stamina. The concept of "energy management" is akin to managing the readiness and morale of troops; neglecting the well-being of personnel leads to reduced performance and increased susceptibility to error or burnout. For example, a team working on a critical project might schedule short, energizing breaks, encourage walking meetings, or provide healthy snacks to help maintain focus and motivation throughout a demanding period. This proactive approach to energy ensures that the "human capital" remains at its optimal operational capacity, ready to engage with the challenges of execution. It's not about working longer hours, but about working smarter and more effectively during the hours one is engaged.

The third critical pillar of resource optimization lies in the strategic use of tools and technology. In the modern landscape, the right tools can amplify both time and energy, acting as force multipliers in the execution of plans. These range from sophisticated project management software that facilitates task tracking, collaboration, and progress monitoring, to simple yet effective communication platforms that streamline information flow. The key is not to simply adopt every new piece of technology, but to identify and leverage those tools that demonstrably enhance efficiency, improve accuracy, or reduce friction in the execution process. This requires a careful assessment of current workflows and a clear understanding of the specific challenges that tools can address. For instance, if a team struggles with coordinating multiple project dependencies and tracking deadlines, a robust project management system can provide a centralized dashboard, automated reminders, and clear visibility into each team member's contributions, thereby preventing delays and misunderstandings that could derail the plan.

However, it is crucial to recognize that tools are only as effective as the strategy behind their deployment and the skill with which they are used. A powerful software package that is poorly implemented or whose features are underutilized becomes a liability rather than an asset. This echoes the military principle of proper equipment maintenance and operator training; advanced weaponry is useless if it is not properly maintained or if the personnel operating it are not adequately trained. Therefore, investing time in learning how to effectively use chosen tools, establishing clear protocols for their use, and regularly reviewing their efficacy is essential. Furthermore, one must be vigilant against the allure of "tool overload" – the tendency to adopt too many disparate systems that create more complexity than they solve. The aim is to integrate tools seamlessly into workflows, not to add layers of unnecessary complexity. This might involve standardizing on a few core platforms for communication, project management, and data analysis, ensuring that everyone on the team is proficient in their use and understands how they contribute to the overall strategic execution.

Applying these principles to a strategic objective, such as launching a new product line, provides a concrete illustration. The plan dictates a timeline of six months, with distinct phases for market research, product development, marketing, and sales.

Time Optimization:

Prioritization: The marketing team identifies that creating compelling digital content is crucial for pre-launch awareness. Instead of engaging in low-priority tasks like extensive social media browsing, they dedicate their peak morning hours to content creation, blocking out specific times for drafting blog posts, shooting short promotional videos, and designing social media graphics.

Efficiency: The product development team, facing a tight deadline, realizes that daily stand-up meetings have become overly long. They implement a stricter 15-minute format, ensuring each member briefly reports on progress, obstacles, and planned actions, thereby maintaining momentum without excessive time expenditure.

Elimination: A recurring weekly report that requires significant manual data compilation is identified as time-consuming and rarely consulted. The team leader, after analysis, decides to automate the report generation using a data analytics tool and makes it accessible on a shared drive, eliminating the need for manual creation and distribution.

Energy Optimization:

Rhythm Alignment: The lead designer, knowing her cognitive energy is highest in the late morning, schedules intensive design sessions for the product packaging during this period. For less demanding tasks like responding to emails or reviewing minor design revisions, she utilizes the afternoon when her energy levels are typically lower.

Replenishment: Recognizing that a long stretch of uninterrupted work leads to fatigue and reduced creativity, the sales team implements a "pomodoro technique" approach, working in focused 25-minute intervals followed by 5-minute breaks. During these breaks, team members are encouraged to stand up, stretch, or briefly step away from their screens, which helps to refresh their focus and prevent burnout.

Environment: The customer support team, anticipating a surge in inquiries post-launch, proactively reorganizes their workspace to minimize distractions, ensuring comfortable seating and access to necessary information to reduce physical and mental strain.

Tools and Technology:

Project Management: A central project management platform is adopted to map out all tasks, assign responsibilities, set deadlines, and track progress across all departments involved in the product launch. This ensures transparency and allows for real-time monitoring of how each element is contributing to the overall timeline. For instance, the marketing team can see when the product development team has finalized key features, enabling them to align their content creation accordingly.

Communication: Instead of relying on fragmented email chains, a dedicated team communication tool is implemented, allowing for instant messaging, group discussions on specific project aspects, and file sharing, which significantly speeds up information exchange and decision-making.

Automation: The sales team integrates a Customer Relationship Management (CRM) system that automates lead tracking, follow-up reminders, and sales pipeline analysis. This frees up valuable time that would have otherwise been spent on manual data entry and allows sales representatives to focus on building relationships with potential customers.

By systematically addressing how time is spent, how energy is managed, and how tools are leveraged, individuals and organizations can unlock unprecedented levels of productivity and efficiency. This disciplined approach to resource allocation transforms strategic intent into tangible progress, ensuring that the execution of the plan is not hampered by avoidable inefficiencies or depleted capacity. It is about making every moment count, channeling every ounce of available energy effectively, and harnessing technology as a powerful enabler, much like a well-equipped and well-positioned military force leverages its assets for maximum impact. The synergy between these three elements—time, energy, and tools—forms the bedrock of successful execution, enabling the translation of strategic vision into concrete achievements. It is a continuous process of assessment, adjustment, and optimization, ensuring that resources are always aligned with the demands of the strategic objective, much like a conductor precisely guiding an orchestra to produce a harmonious and powerful performance.

The strategic blueprint, once finalized, represents a carefully considered pathway, but its true value is only realized through its diligent execution. This phase is where vision coalesces into tangible action, where the abstract ideals of planning are tested against the dynamic realities of the operational environment. It is the crucible where well-intentioned strategies are either forged into successes or dissolved into unrealized potential. The transition from planning to execution is not merely a change in tempo; it is a fundamental shift in focus, demanding a particular mindset and a disciplined approach to the challenges that inevitably arise.

At its core, successful execution is predicated on the principle of **disciplined action**. This means adhering to the established plan, not out of blind obedience, but out of a clear understanding of its rationale and the interconnectedness of its components. In military operations, this translates to units executing their assigned tasks with precision, understanding that their individual actions contribute to the larger operational picture. For any strategic endeavor, this requires breaking down the overarching plan into manageable, actionable steps, each with clear objectives, timelines, and assigned responsibilities. It involves cultivating a culture where commitment to these steps is paramount, and where deviations are not arbitrary but are the result of informed decisions to adapt. This discipline ensures that the momentum generated during the planning phase is not lost to indecision or wavering resolve. It's about ensuring that the energy invested in strategy formulation is effectively channeled into productive activity, rather than dissipating into a lack of clear direction.

A critical element in maintaining this disciplined action is the concept of **overcoming inertia**. Plans, no matter how robust, can face the formidable barrier of procrastination, the comfort of the status quo, or the sheer psychological weight of initiating complex undertakings. This inertia can manifest as delayed decision-making, a tendency to dwell on potential obstacles rather than progress, or an over-reliance on incremental steps that fail to build significant momentum. Drawing a parallel from military experience, overcoming inertia is akin to initiating an offensive operation. It requires a decisive push, a clear signal to commence, and the immediate engagement of forces to gain advantageous ground. In strategic execution, this often means establishing clear launch points for key initiatives, setting firm deadlines for initial actions, and fostering an environment where taking the first step, even a small one, is encouraged and celebrated. It's about recognizing that the most difficult part of any journey is often the beginning, and equipping oneself with the psychological fortitude to push past initial resistance. This might involve employing techniques such as the "two-minute rule" – if a task takes less than two minutes, do it immediately – or the "eat the frog" method, tackling the most daunting task first thing in the day to clear mental bandwidth and build momentum. The objective is to create a cascade of small wins that build confidence and propel the execution forward, transforming the abstract plan into a series of concrete achievements.

Furthermore, the execution phase demands a commitment to **maintaining momentum**. Once initiated, the strategic plan must be driven forward with consistent effort. This isn't about a single burst of activity, but about sustained application of energy and resources. In a military context, maintaining momentum is crucial to prevent an adversary from regrouping or exploiting any lull in activity. Similarly, in strategic execution, periods of stagnation can allow competitors to gain an advantage, or internal challenges to fester and grow. This requires vigilant monitoring of progress against established milestones and proactive intervention when momentum begins to wane. It involves fostering a sense of urgency, celebrating intermediate successes to keep morale high, and continuously reinforcing the value and purpose of the ongoing efforts. Think of a complex construction project; each completed phase, from laying the foundation to erecting the framework, builds upon the last, and delays in one area can have a cascading effect. Effective momentum management ensures that each phase is completed on time and to standard, allowing subsequent phases to begin without impediment. This can be facilitated by employing regular progress reviews, such as weekly team check-ins or monthly strategy review meetings, where progress is assessed, roadblocks are identified, and corrective actions are swiftly implemented.

However, the operational environment is rarely static. Unforeseen challenges, shifts in market dynamics, or new intelligence can necessitate adjustments to the original plan. This leads to the critical principle of **adapting to evolving circumstances**. The ability to remain flexible without compromising the core strategic intent is a hallmark of effective execution. A rigid adherence to a plan that has become obsolete can be as detrimental as a complete lack of planning. Military forces are trained to adapt their tactics and operations in response to enemy actions, terrain changes, or intelligence updates. This adaptation is not a sign of weakness, but of intelligent response. In strategic execution, this requires cultivating an agile mindset within the organization or individual. It means establishing mechanisms for continuous environmental scanning, encouraging open communication about emerging challenges and opportunities, and empowering decision-makers to make necessary adjustments. This might involve building contingency plans into the original strategy, or establishing clear protocols for how and when the plan can be modified. For instance, a company launching a new software product might encounter unexpected bugs during beta testing. Instead of pushing forward with a flawed product, a flexible strategy would allow for a delay in the public launch to address these issues, thereby safeguarding the product's reputation and long-term success. This is not about abandoning the plan, but about refining the path to achieve the ultimate objective. It's about being able to pivot when necessary, learning from setbacks and incorporating new information to enhance the likelihood of success.

The transition from planning to execution, therefore, is not a passive handover, but an active, dynamic process. It requires a deliberate shift from ideation to implementation, from forecasting to action. The disciplined commitment to planned actions, the proactive effort to overcome initial hesitation, the sustained drive to maintain progress, and the intelligent adaptability to changing conditions are the pillars upon which successful strategic execution is built. This phase demands clarity of purpose, resilience in the face of adversity, and a relentless focus on moving the objective forward, much like a seasoned military commander marshaling their forces to achieve a critical mission objective. It is in this crucible of action that strategies are truly validated, and where the seeds of success are sown through consistent, purposeful effort. The planning phase provides the 'what' and the 'why'; the execution phase delivers the 'how', transforming strategic intent into tangible results.

The successful translation of a strategic plan into actionable outcomes hinges on a clear understanding and implementation of the **Concept of Operations (CONOPS)**. The CONOPS is not merely a detailed task list; it is the overarching narrative of how the plan will be executed, providing a common understanding of the overall approach, sequence of actions, and synchronization required to achieve the desired end state. It paints a picture of the mission in motion, detailing the phases of operation, the key activities within each phase, and the relationships between different elements involved. Think of it as the operational script that guides the entire performance, ensuring that all actors are aligned and moving in concert.

In a military context, a CONOPS would outline the maneuver, fire support, intelligence, logistics, and command and control elements, describing how they will interact to achieve battlefield objectives. For civilian strategic endeavors, this translates to detailing how different departments, teams, or even individuals will contribute to the overall goal. It clarifies who does what, when, and how their actions are integrated. For example, a company aiming to launch a new product line would have a CONOPS that details the synchronized efforts of marketing, sales, product development, and customer support. It would specify the sequence of activities: the marketing team initiating pre-launch campaigns, the sales team being trained on the new product, the product development team providing final technical specifications, and customer support preparing for initial inquiries. Each element needs to understand its role and its dependencies on other elements.

A critical aspect of the CONOPS is defining the **sequence of events and their synchronization**. Plans often involve a series of interconnected actions, and the order in which these actions occur, and how they are timed together, is crucial. Misplaced timing or a lack of synchronization can lead to significant inefficiencies or outright failure. For instance, if a sales team is ready to promote a product but the manufacturing or delivery process is not yet operational, valuable market opportunities can be lost, or customer dissatisfaction can arise. The CONOPS must clearly map out these dependencies and establish triggers or milestones that signal the readiness for subsequent actions. This involves identifying critical path activities – those that, if delayed, will directly impact the overall timeline – and ensuring they are meticulously managed. This meticulous sequencing is akin to coordinating an artillery barrage with an infantry assault; both must be timed perfectly to achieve maximum effectiveness.

Furthermore, the CONOPS must address the **allocation of resources across operational phases**. While previous sections may have discussed resource optimization in general, the CONOPS details how these resources—personnel, equipment, budget, and time—will be deployed and reallocated as the execution unfolds. As operations progress, the demands on certain resources may shift. For example, during a product launch, the marketing team might require significant resources in the early stages, while the customer support and operations teams might see increased resource needs post-launch. The CONOPS provides the framework for anticipating these shifts and making necessary adjustments to ensure that resources are available where and when they are most needed, preventing bottlenecks and ensuring a smooth transition between phases. This requires not just planning for initial resource allocation but also building in flexibility and mechanisms for re-tasking or augmenting resources as circumstances dictate.

The CONOPS also serves as a vital tool for **communication and shared understanding**. By articulating the execution strategy in a clear, coherent manner, it ensures that all stakeholders, from senior leadership to front-line personnel, have a common picture of the operational landscape. This shared understanding is fundamental to effective teamwork and coordinated action. When everyone understands the overall mission, their individual role within it, and how their efforts contribute to the collective objective, it fosters a sense of unity and purpose. This is particularly important in complex projects involving multiple teams or departments, where disparate efforts can easily become fragmented without a unifying operational concept. The CONOPS acts as a unifying narrative, ensuring that everyone is working towards the same goal with the same understanding of the path forward. It provides a common language and a shared vision that can guide decision-making at all levels.

An essential element within the CONOPS is the articulation of **decision points and command and control mechanisms**. Execution is rarely a linear process, and there will be moments when critical decisions must be made, often with incomplete information. The CONOPS should identify these key decision points, define the criteria for making those decisions, and specify who has the authority to make them. It also outlines the command and control structure, clarifying lines of authority and communication channels. This ensures that decisions are made promptly and decisively, and that information flows efficiently to those who need it. Without clear decision-making authority and communication protocols, operations can falter, bogged down by indecision or miscommunication. For instance, if a critical supplier fails to deliver components on time, the CONOPS might stipulate that the Head of Operations, in consultation with the project manager, has the authority to approve an alternative, more expensive supplier to maintain the project timeline, with notification to the CEO. This pre-defined authority prevents paralysis when unexpected issues arise.

Moreover, the CONOPS must incorporate mechanisms for **monitoring, evaluation, and feedback**. The execution of any plan should be an ongoing process of learning and adaptation. The CONOPS should define how progress will be measured, what key performance indicators (KPIs) will be tracked, and how feedback will be collected and integrated. This allows for early detection of deviations from the plan, identification of what is working well and what is not, and the ability to make timely adjustments. This feedback loop is crucial for refining the execution process and for informing future strategic planning. It's about creating a dynamic system that learns and improves as it operates. Regular reporting, performance reviews, and post-action analyses are all components of this feedback mechanism.

Let's consider a real-world example to illustrate the application of the CONOPS in execution. Imagine a large-scale humanitarian aid response to a natural disaster. The strategic objective is to deliver essential supplies and provide medical assistance to affected populations.

Phased Approach: The CONOPS might define three phases: Immediate Relief (first 72 hours), Stabilization (weeks 1-4), and Recovery Support (months 1-6).

Synchronization: Within the Immediate Relief phase, the CONOPS would detail the synchronized deployment of search and rescue teams, the establishment of emergency medical facilities, and the rapid distribution of food, water, and shelter kits. It would specify that the arrival of transportation assets (airlifts, convoys) must be coordinated with the pre-positioning of supplies at staging areas, and that medical teams are deployed concurrently with the assessment of immediate health needs.

Resource Allocation: The CONOPS would outline the initial allocation of personnel (medical staff, logistics coordinators, security teams), equipment (ambulances, communication devices, temporary shelters), and financial resources, anticipating the need to scale up operations and potentially reallocate resources from immediate relief to the stabilization phase (e.g., shifting focus from emergency medical care to longer-term health services and sanitation).

Decision Points: Key decision points might include: when to shift from air-only transport to ground convoys based on road conditions; when to authorize the procurement of additional specialized medical equipment based on evolving patient needs; and who has the authority to declare a phase transition.

Command and Control: The CONOPS would establish a clear command structure, designating a lead agency or overall coordinator, and outlining communication protocols between different operational units, government agencies, and non-governmental organizations. This ensures that information is shared effectively and that decisions are made with a comprehensive understanding of the situation on the ground.

Monitoring and Feedback: It would specify daily operational briefings to assess progress, identify challenges, and gather feedback from field teams regarding the effectiveness of aid distribution and the needs of the affected population. This feedback would inform adjustments to the distribution routes, types of supplies, or medical interventions.

By meticulously detailing the CONOPS, the humanitarian organization ensures that its response is organized, efficient, and impactful, transforming the strategic intent into a coordinated, life-saving operation. This comprehensive operational framework is what bridges the gap between a well-conceived plan and its successful realization on the ground, ensuring that the mission is not just attempted, but effectively carried out. It transforms a static document into a dynamic guide, empowering action and fostering clarity in the midst of chaos.

Chapter 5: Adaptive Warfare: Navigating Change and Overcoming Obstacles

Situational awareness is not a passive state of being; it is an active, perpetual engagement with the surrounding environment. Just as a seasoned commander on the battlefield must constantly scan the horizon, analyze troop movements, decipher enemy intentions, and understand the terrain, so too must any strategist navigating the complexities of modern challenges maintain an equally vigilant and discerning awareness. This capacity to "read the battlefield," whether it be a corporate boardroom, a competitive market, or the intricate landscape of personal growth, is foundational to adaptive warfare and, by extension, to the successful execution of any strategic endeavor. Without a clear, unvarnished perception of the present reality, even the most meticulously crafted plan can become an anchor, dragging its proponents into obsolescence or failure.

At its core, situational awareness is about perceiving and understanding the elements that constitute your operational environment. This involves more than just seeing what is directly in front of you; it requires an active process of observation, assessment, and comprehension. It's about gathering information from multiple sources, both overt and subtle, and synthesizing it into a coherent picture of the current state. In a military context, this might involve analyzing satellite imagery, intercepting enemy communications, debriefing patrols, and understanding weather patterns. For a business leader, it means monitoring market trends, analyzing competitor strategies, understanding customer feedback, and staying abreast of technological advancements. For an individual pursuing personal development, it translates to self-reflection, understanding one's own strengths and weaknesses, recognizing external pressures, and discerning the opportunities and threats presented by one's immediate circumstances and broader societal shifts. The critical differentiator lies in the *active* nature of this process. It is not enough to simply exist within an environment; one must engage with it, probe its depths, and seek to understand its underlying currents.

Developing robust situational awareness is a learned discipline, cultivated through consistent practice and a conscious effort to sharpen one's observational faculties. One of the most effective ways to foster this is through **deliberate environmental scanning**. This involves setting aside dedicated time to actively look outwards, to seek out information and patterns that might otherwise remain hidden. For individuals, this could mean establishing a routine of reading industry news, listening to podcasts, attending webinars, or engaging in conversations with mentors and peers. It's about creating a structured approach to information gathering, ensuring that no critical data points are missed. For example, a marketing executive might dedicate thirty minutes each morning to reviewing competitor social media activity, industry news feeds, and relevant market research reports. This regular scan provides a baseline understanding of the competitive landscape, allowing for the early detection of shifts or emerging trends that could impact their own strategy. This is not a passive consumption of information; it is an active interrogation of the environment. The goal is to move beyond simply being aware that change is happening to understanding *what* is changing, *why* it is changing, and *what the implications* of that change might be.

Beyond simply gathering data, situational awareness demands the ability to **interpret subtle cues and discern underlying patterns**. The battlefield is rarely a clear-cut display of intentions; rather, it is often characterized by ambiguity, deception, and the fog of war. Similarly, strategic environments are rife with signals that, when properly interpreted, can provide invaluable foresight. These cues can be explicit, such as a competitor's product announcement, or they can be far more nuanced, like a change in customer purchasing behavior, a subtle shift in public discourse, or even a change in the demeanor of a key stakeholder. The ability to recognize these subtle indicators and connect them to a broader narrative is a hallmark of advanced situational awareness. This often requires stepping back from the immediate data and considering the context. For instance, a sudden increase in online searches for a particular product feature, even if not yet translated into sales, might signal a nascent customer demand that a competitor could exploit. Similarly, a period of unusual quiet from a typically vocal competitor might not indicate a lack of activity, but rather the preparation for a significant, disruptive move. The skill lies in not just seeing the individual pieces of information but in recognizing how they fit together to form a larger, more meaningful picture.

A key component of this interpretation is understanding the **interconnectedness of variables**. No element of an operational environment exists in isolation. Market forces influence consumer behavior, technological advancements shape competitive strategies, political shifts can alter regulatory landscapes, and societal trends impact consumer preferences. Effective situational awareness requires recognizing these complex interdependencies. It's about understanding that a change in one area can have ripple effects throughout the entire system. For example, a new government regulation impacting data privacy might not only affect how a company collects customer information but also influence its marketing strategies, product development roadmap, and even its supply chain logistics. A leader with strong situational awareness will anticipate these cascading effects, rather than reacting only to the immediate impact. This requires a systems-thinking approach, viewing the environment not as a collection of discrete components but as an integrated whole. This holistic perspective allows for the anticipation of secondary and tertiary consequences, enabling more proactive and resilient strategic planning.

Furthermore, cultivating situational awareness involves actively **challenging assumptions and seeking disconfirming evidence**. Our perceptions are often filtered through our existing beliefs, biases, and past experiences. This can lead to confirmation bias, where we tend to seek out and interpret information that supports our pre-existing notions, while ignoring or downplaying evidence that contradicts them. In the context of strategic decision-making, this can be a fatal flaw. A soldier who believes the enemy is retreating might fail to spot a hidden ambush. A business leader who is convinced of their product's superiority might overlook critical flaws identified by early adopters. To counter this, it is essential to cultivate a habit of intellectual humility and a rigorous approach to evidence. This means actively seeking out dissenting opinions, exploring alternative hypotheses, and deliberately looking for data that might disprove one's current understanding. It's about asking oneself: "What evidence would convince me that my current assessment is wrong?" This willingness to be proven wrong is not a weakness; it is a critical strength that allows for continuous refinement of one's understanding and a more accurate perception of reality.

Another crucial aspect of situational awareness is the **recognition of one's own cognitive limitations and biases**. We are all prone to errors in judgment, influenced by factors such as stress, fatigue, and emotional state. Understanding these limitations is the first step toward mitigating their impact. This might involve developing structured decision-making processes, employing checklists, or establishing a "red team" function within an organization to challenge prevailing assumptions. For individuals, it could mean implementing mindfulness practices to enhance self-awareness and emotional regulation, or seeking feedback from trusted advisors who can offer an objective perspective. For instance, during a high-pressure negotiation, a negotiator might be more prone to making concessions due to stress. Recognizing this tendency, they might agree with their team beforehand on a predefined set of acceptable compromises, ensuring that their decisions remain rational and aligned with the strategic objectives, even under duress. This self-awareness allows for the implementation of internal checks and balances, ensuring that situational understanding is as clear and objective as possible.

The act of **continuous learning and adaptation** is intrinsically linked to situational awareness. The environment is not static; it is in a constant state of flux. What was true yesterday may not be true today. Therefore, situational awareness must be a dynamic, ongoing process, not a one-time assessment. This requires a commitment to lifelong learning and a willingness to adjust one's understanding as new information emerges. Military doctrine often emphasizes "lesson learned" exercises after operations, not merely to document successes and failures, but to refine future strategies and tactics based on real-world experience. Similarly, in any strategic domain, it is vital to build feedback loops into the process, regularly reviewing and updating one's understanding of the environment. This might involve periodic strategy reviews, post-project debriefs, or simply maintaining an open channel for new information and insights. The ability to learn from both successes and failures, and to integrate that learning into an evolving understanding of the situation, is what allows for true adaptability and resilience.

Consider the metaphor of navigating a ship through uncharted waters. The captain must not only understand the currents, the wind, and the stars but also constantly monitor the ship's own condition, the crew's morale, and the integrity of the navigational instruments. A deviation in course, a change in weather, or a malfunction in equipment all require immediate assessment and adjustment. If the captain relies solely on an initial map and ignores the changing sea state, they risk running aground or becoming lost. The same applies to strategic execution. The "uncharted waters" represent the dynamic and often unpredictable nature of any endeavor. Situational awareness is the continuous process of using all available instruments – data analysis, market intelligence, team feedback, self-reflection – to understand where you are, where you are going, and what obstacles or opportunities lie ahead.

The practice of **observational discipline** is another vital technique. This involves consciously training oneself to notice details that are easily overlooked. It's about cultivating a habit of active looking, rather than passive seeing. This could be as simple as paying attention to the body language of people in a meeting, noting the types of vehicles passing on a street, or observing the subtle shifts in tone during a conversation. For instance, a sales professional might develop situational awareness by not just listening to a client's stated needs, but also by observing their environment, noting personal effects that might reveal interests or priorities, or even the condition of their office, which might hint at their company's financial health. These are not necessarily direct indicators of business needs, but they contribute to a richer, more nuanced understanding of the individual and their context. It's about building a mental library of observations that can be drawn upon when interpreting larger strategic patterns. This discipline requires slowing down, being present, and engaging all senses in the process of information gathering.

Moreover, **understanding the "why" behind observed phenomena** is critical. Situational awareness is not merely about cataloging events; it is about understanding their causes and potential consequences. Why did that competitor launch a new product at this specific time? Why is that particular market segment showing increased demand? Why is employee morale declining? Asking "why" repeatedly, in the manner of the "five whys" technique, can help peel back layers of superficiality to reveal underlying drivers and root causes. This deeper understanding is essential for developing effective responses. A leader who simply notes a drop in sales might implement a broad discount strategy. However, a leader with strong situational awareness who asks "why" might discover that the decline is due to a specific feature deficiency or a new competitor offering superior value, leading to a more targeted and effective solution, such as product development or a strategic partnership.

The process of building situational awareness also necessitates the **establishment of clear communication channels and feedback mechanisms**. In any complex operation, information needs to flow freely and accurately between different levels and functions. This means creating an environment where individuals feel empowered to report what they see, even if it contradicts prevailing wisdom or management expectations. In a military unit, this might be the sergeant reporting enemy troop movements to the company commander, or the forward observer relaying artillery spotting corrections. In a business, it could be a frontline employee flagging a customer service issue to management, or a data analyst highlighting an unexpected trend in sales figures. Without these open channels, critical pieces of the situational picture can remain obscured. Furthermore, it is vital to have mechanisms for synthesizing this incoming information, ensuring that it reaches the right people in a timely and actionable manner. This might involve regular briefings, shared dashboards, or dedicated intelligence analysis teams. The ability to aggregate and interpret diverse inputs is crucial for maintaining a coherent and accurate understanding of the overall situation.

Ultimately, situational awareness is the bedrock upon which adaptive strategy is built. It is the continuous process of perceiving, understanding, and anticipating the dynamics of one's operating environment. It requires an active, disciplined approach to observation, a keen ability to interpret subtle cues, a systems-thinking mindset that recognizes interconnectedness, and a commitment to challenging one's own assumptions. By honing these skills, individuals and organizations can move beyond simply reacting to change, to proactively shaping their future, much like a skilled navigator who, by constantly reading the sea and the sky, can chart a course through even the most turbulent conditions, ensuring that the journey remains purposeful and the destination attainable. This vigilant awareness transforms the battlefield of challenges from a source of constant surprise into a landscape that can be understood, navigated, and ultimately, mastered.

The strategic landscape is a theater of perpetual motion, where the only constant is change itself. Even the most meticulously crafted operational plan, born from rigorous analysis and informed by the sharpest situational awareness, is but a hypothesis, a best guess about how events will unfold. History, both in military campaigns and in the annals of business and personal endeavor, is replete with examples of well-laid plans being shattered by the sheer recalcitrance of reality. It is here, in the shadow of the unexpected, that the true mettle of a strategist is tested. This is not a call to embrace fatalism, but rather a pragmatic acknowledgment of the inherent uncertainties that define any pursuit of significant objectives. To acknowledge this reality is to embrace the discipline of contingency planning – the proactive, deliberate preparation for when things, inevitably, do not go according to the initial script.

Contingency planning is not merely an exercise in pessimism; it is an act of strategic foresight, an investment in resilience. It is the martial equivalent of building a sturdy foundation before constructing a skyscraper, or a sailor ensuring their vessel is seaworthy before venturing into open waters. At its core, it involves a critical self-assessment of the primary plan, identifying its vulnerabilities, its choke points, and the potential external factors that could render it obsolete or ineffective. This process demands a rigorous interrogation of assumptions. What if the intelligence was flawed? What if the adversary reacts in a way we did not anticipate? What if a key resource becomes unavailable, or a technological breakthrough by a competitor disrupts our market position? Answering these questions is not about dwelling on potential failures, but about building the capacity to navigate them should they arise.

The genesis of effective contingency planning lies in the thorough analysis of potential failure points within the primary strategy. This requires stepping back from the enthusiasm of the initial plan and adopting a critical, almost adversarial, perspective. Imagine yourself as an opponent, tasked with derailing the very objective you are trying to achieve. Where are the weakest links? What are the most plausible scenarios that could undermine success? For a military operation, this might involve analyzing enemy counter-attack capabilities, the terrain's susceptibility to adverse weather, or the potential for logistical disruption. In a business context, it could mean scrutinizing market volatility, the threat of new entrants, regulatory changes, or the fragility of supply chains. For an individual, it might involve considering the impact of personal health issues, unexpected financial setbacks, or shifts in family priorities. This identification process is not about listing every conceivable problem, but about prioritizing those that are both plausible and potentially catastrophic to the mission's success.

Once potential failure points are identified, the next crucial step is to develop alternative courses of action – often referred to as "Plan B," "Plan C," and so on. These contingencies are not meant to be complete rewrites of the original strategy, but rather pre-defined, adaptive responses designed to mitigate the impact of specific disruptions and, if possible, to pivot towards achieving the objective through a different route. For instance, if a primary marketing campaign relies heavily on a particular social media platform, a contingency might involve shifting resources to other channels if that platform experiences a significant outage or a drastic change in its algorithm. In a military maneuver, if the planned ingress route is blocked by unexpected enemy resistance, a contingency might involve utilizing a secondary, less direct, but safer approach. The key is to have these alternatives pre-thought and, where possible, pre-resourced, so that the decision to pivot can be made rapidly and efficiently, rather than being improvised under duress.

The development of these alternative plans requires a deep understanding of the mission's core objectives and the resources available. A contingency plan should ideally be flexible enough to adapt to a range of potential disruptions, or specific enough to address a particular high-probability, high-impact threat. For example, a company launching a new product might have a primary plan that focuses on direct sales through its own e-commerce platform. A contingency plan could involve establishing partnerships with key retailers or distributors if the direct-to-consumer model encounters unforeseen logistical challenges or lower-than-expected consumer adoption. This dual approach ensures that the product still reaches the market and achieves its sales targets, even if the initial pathway is blocked. Similarly, an individual training for a marathon might have a primary training schedule. If an injury occurs, a contingency plan could involve focusing on cross-training activities, such as swimming or cycling, to maintain cardiovascular fitness and prevent muscle atrophy, thus preserving the ability to resume running when recovery permits.

Beyond simply identifying alternative actions, robust contingency planning also necessitates the preparation of contingency resources. This could involve setting aside specific funds, acquiring or maintaining reserve equipment, cultivating alternative supplier relationships, or developing additional skill sets within a team. These resources are the tangible enablers of the alternative plans. Without them, a well-conceived Plan B remains merely a theoretical construct. For a military unit, this might mean maintaining a cache of essential supplies separate from the main logistical train, or ensuring that key personnel have cross-trained in critical functions. In a business setting, it could involve having a backup server infrastructure, maintaining relationships with multiple raw material suppliers, or investing in ongoing training for employees to broaden their skill sets. For an individual, it might mean building an emergency fund to cover unexpected expenses, or ensuring they have a diverse network of contacts who can offer support or advice during challenging times. These contingency resources act as a buffer, absorbing the shock of disruption and providing the means to execute alternative strategies.

The process of contingency planning is not a one-time event; it is a continuous cycle that must be integrated into the broader strategic management framework. As the operational environment evolves, and as new information is gathered through ongoing situational awareness, existing contingency plans must be reviewed, updated, and potentially revised. A scenario that was once considered improbable might become a more significant threat, or a new opportunity might emerge that warrants the development of entirely new contingency options. This iterative approach ensures that the organization or individual remains prepared for a dynamic set of potential challenges, rather than being locked into a static set of pre-planned responses. Regularly revisiting assumptions, reassessing risks, and refining alternative actions are critical to maintaining a state of proactive preparedness.

The psychological aspect of contingency planning is also profound. Knowing that alternatives exist and that preparatory steps have been taken can significantly reduce anxiety and enhance decision-making under pressure. When faced with a deviation from the original plan, the presence of pre-defined contingencies provides a framework for action, preventing the panic or indecision that can often paralyze individuals and teams during crises. It fosters a sense of control and agency, even when external circumstances are chaotic. This is akin to a pilot who has trained extensively for emergency landings; while the situation is inherently stressful, the ingrained procedures and practiced responses allow them to execute the necessary actions with a degree of calm competence. This psychological resilience, built upon the foundation of thorough preparation, is a critical differentiator in navigating adversity.

To illustrate the practical application of this discipline, consider a project manager tasked with delivering a complex software system. The primary plan involves a phased rollout, with intensive testing at each stage. However, several potential disruptions exist: key developers might leave the project, a critical third-party component might prove unreliable, or the client might request significant scope changes late in the development cycle. Robust contingency planning would involve several layers. Firstly, identifying these risks: developer attrition, third-party dependency, and scope creep. Secondly, developing alternative actions: cross-training junior developers to take over critical roles if senior staff depart, identifying alternative third-party suppliers or developing in-house modules as a backup, and establishing a strict change control process with clear guidelines for evaluating and implementing client requests. Thirdly, preparing contingency resources: building a knowledge-sharing repository for project documentation to facilitate faster onboarding of new team members, pre-negotiating terms with alternative suppliers, and allocating a portion of the project budget and timeline as a buffer for approved change requests. By proactively addressing these potential roadblocks, the project manager significantly increases the likelihood of successful delivery, even when unforeseen challenges arise. The project doesn't grind to a halt; it adapts, leveraging the pre-prepared alternatives to maintain momentum towards its ultimate goal.

Another crucial element of contingency planning is the establishment of clear triggers for activating these alternative plans. Simply having a Plan B is insufficient; there must be a defined set of circumstances or metrics that signal when that plan should be put into motion. This prevents premature activation, which can be wasteful, and also avoids delaying the pivot until it is too late. For example, if a marketing campaign's success is measured by daily lead generation, a trigger might be set: if the average daily leads fall below a certain threshold for three consecutive days, the contingency plan involving a shift in advertising spend or a revised creative approach is automatically initiated. In a military context, a "go/no-go" decision point before an operation might have pre-defined conditions that, if met, would necessitate executing a contingency plan instead of the primary one. These triggers provide objective criteria for decision-making, removing ambiguity and ensuring a timely response to changing circumstances.

Furthermore, the communication strategy surrounding contingency plans is paramount. While these plans are often developed in confidence by a core strategic team, it is vital to ensure that relevant individuals understand their roles and responsibilities should a contingency be activated. This might involve selective briefing of key personnel, ensuring that individuals understand the alternative courses of action and their part in executing them. Transparency, within appropriate bounds, can foster greater agility and reduce confusion during periods of disruption. It allows individuals to be mentally prepared for potential shifts in strategy and to understand the rationale behind them. This preparation can transform a potential crisis into a controlled adaptation.

Ultimately, contingency planning is a testament to the principle of adaptive warfare – the ability to not just react to change, but to anticipate it, prepare for it, and leverage it as an opportunity. It is about building redundancy and flexibility into the strategic framework, ensuring that the pursuit of objectives is resilient to the inevitable turbulence of reality. By embracing the discipline of developing and resourcing alternative courses of action, individuals and organizations can transform potential setbacks into strategic pivots, ensuring that the journey towards their goals remains purposeful and their ultimate success is not contingent on the absence of adversity, but on their preparedness to navigate it. It is the strategic art of having multiple paths to victory, ensuring that the loss of one route does not signal the end of the campaign, but merely the initiation of a different, equally viable, approach.

The dynamism inherent in any significant undertaking necessitates a deliberate, structured approach to ongoing refinement. Simply setting a course and rigidly adhering to it, regardless of emergent realities, is a recipe for stagnation, if not outright failure. This is where the principle of iterative improvement comes into play, offering a robust framework for continuous learning and adaptation. At its core, iterative improvement is a cyclical process: taking action, gathering feedback, reflecting on that feedback, and then adjusting future actions based on the insights gained. This is not a one-time fix, but a perpetual motion machine of progress, designed to ensure that strategies remain relevant, processes are optimized, and objectives are pursued with increasing efficacy.

This iterative cycle draws a powerful parallel to the military concept of the "After Action Review" (AAR). Following any mission, operation, or significant training exercise, military units engage in a systematic process of reviewing what happened, comparing it against what was planned, and identifying lessons learned. The AAR is not about assigning blame; rather, it is a dispassionate inquiry into performance. It asks fundamental questions: What was supposed to happen? What actually happened? Why were there differences? What went well, and what could be improved? This structured introspection serves as the engine of operational learning. It ensures that successes are understood and repeatable, and that failures are dissected to prevent their recurrence.

Translating this military discipline into the broader context of personal and professional development, the first stage of the iterative improvement cycle is, naturally, **action**. This is the execution of the plan, the implementation of the strategy, the doing of the work. Whether it's launching a new product, training for a marathon, or implementing a new sales process, action is the catalyst for learning. Without taking action, there is no real-world data to analyze, no empirical evidence to inform the next steps. It is the engagement with the environment, the putting of theory into practice, that creates the conditions for genuine insight. This phase requires courage and commitment, the willingness to step forward and make things happen, even in the face of uncertainty. It's about initiating the process, committing to the chosen path, and setting the wheels of progress in motion.

Following the action, the crucial next step is to **gather feedback**. This is the process of collecting information about the results of the action. Feedback can come in many forms. In a business context, it might be sales figures, customer reviews, website analytics, or market share data. For an individual athlete, it could be performance metrics, coach's observations, or physiological data from wearable devices. In the realm of personal development, feedback might manifest as the outcomes of a new habit, the results of a communication approach, or the impact of a learning strategy. The key is to be open to all forms of feedback, both positive and negative, and to recognize that even seemingly minor data points can hold significant clues. This phase requires diligent observation and the establishment of clear metrics by which success or deviation can be measured. It is about actively seeking out and absorbing the signals from the environment that indicate how the action is performing against its intended outcome.

Once feedback has been gathered, the process moves into the vital stage of **reflection**. This is where the real learning takes place, where the data is transformed into actionable insights. Reflection involves critically examining the feedback in light of the initial plan and objectives. It's about asking: What does this feedback tell us? Were our assumptions correct? Did the action produce the intended results? Where did we exceed expectations, and where did we fall short? This stage mirrors the structured debriefing of an AAR, encouraging a deep dive into the "why" behind the observed outcomes. It's not enough to simply observe that sales were lower than expected; reflection requires understanding *why*. Was it a flaw in the marketing message? Was the pricing too high? Was the target audience incorrectly identified? This process of critical self-assessment, free from emotional bias, is essential for unlocking the learning embedded within the feedback. It's a moment to pause, to synthesize, and to begin formulating hypotheses for improvement.

The final, and perhaps most critical, stage of the iterative loop is **adjustment**. Based on the insights gained during reflection, specific changes are made to the action plan for the next cycle. This might involve refining the strategy, altering the tactics, reallocating resources, or even revisiting the initial objectives if the feedback suggests they are unattainable or no longer relevant. Adjustment is about translating learning into tangible action. If reflection reveals that a particular marketing channel is underperforming, the adjustment might be to shift budget to more effective channels. If an athlete's performance data indicates a weakness in a specific muscle group, the adjustment might be to incorporate targeted strengthening exercises. If a personal development effort is not yielding the desired results, the adjustment might involve trying a different approach or seeking expert guidance. This stage is the culmination of the cycle, closing the loop and preparing for the next round of action. It is the embodiment of adaptive thinking, turning insights into improvements that propel progress forward.

This cyclical nature of action, feedback, reflection, and adjustment fosters a culture of continuous improvement. It moves organizations and individuals away from a static, plan-centric mindset towards a dynamic, learning-oriented approach. This is particularly potent in environments characterized by rapid change or high levels of uncertainty, where the ability to adapt quickly is paramount. The iterative process allows for incremental gains, reducing the risk associated with large, unproven strategic shifts. Each cycle builds upon the last, creating a compounding effect on performance over time. It's akin to a sculptor carefully chipping away at a block of marble; each stroke, informed by the observation of the stone's grain and form, brings the envisioned masterpiece closer to reality.

Moreover, embracing iterative improvement cultivates a valuable psychological resilience. By engaging in regular cycles of action and learning, individuals and teams become more comfortable with experimentation and less fearful of setbacks. They learn that "failure" is often just data, an opportunity to recalibrate rather than a definitive end. This mindset shift is crucial for innovation and for sustained effort in the face of challenges. It democratizes learning, making it an ongoing, integrated part of the operational fabric, rather than a theoretical exercise confined to annual reviews.

Consider, for example, the development of a new software application. The initial "action" might be to build a Minimum Viable Product (MVP) with core features. The "feedback" would come from early user testing and adoption rates. The "reflection" would involve analyzing user comments, identifying bugs, and understanding which features are most used and which are ignored. The "adjustment" could lead to a revised roadmap, prioritizing features based on user demand, fixing critical bugs, and perhaps even pivoting the product's core functionality if the initial assumptions about user needs prove incorrect. This iterative cycle—build, measure, learn—is fundamental to agile software development and has proven incredibly effective in bringing successful products to market in a constantly evolving technological landscape.

Similarly, an individual seeking to improve their public speaking skills can apply this iterative model. The initial **action** might be to prepare and deliver a short presentation to a small group of friends. The **feedback** could be direct commentary from the audience on clarity, confidence, and engagement, as well as self-observation of nervousness or delivery stumbles. The **reflection** would involve analyzing this feedback: "My friends said I spoke too quickly, and I noticed myself fidgeting when I discussed the statistics." The **adjustment** for the next presentation might be to practice pacing, incorporate intentional pauses, and consciously focus on standing still during key points. Each subsequent presentation, informed by these cycles, leads to progressively better performance.

The power of iterative improvement also lies in its ability to manage complexity. Large, ambitious goals can often feel overwhelming. By breaking them down into a series of smaller, manageable actions within iterative cycles, the path forward becomes clearer and less daunting. Each cycle represents a tangible step, a demonstrable progress, which can be highly motivating. This incremental approach also allows for course correction without derailing the entire endeavor. If a particular iteration doesn't yield the expected results, the impact of the necessary adjustments is usually contained, making it easier to get back on track.

To ensure that the iterative improvement cycle is truly effective, several key elements must be in place. Firstly, clear objectives and measurable outcomes are essential. Without a defined target and a way to measure progress towards it, it's difficult to assess whether an action has been successful or if adjustments are needed. These objectives should be SMART: Specific, Measurable, Achievable, Relevant, and Time-bound. Secondly, a commitment to honest and open feedback is critical. This requires creating an environment where constructive criticism is welcomed and where individuals feel safe to share their observations without fear of reprisal. In a team setting, this often necessitates fostering psychological safety. Thirdly, the capacity to act on the feedback is paramount. Identifying areas for improvement is useless if there isn't the will or the ability to implement the necessary changes. This might involve allocating resources, empowering individuals, or redesigning processes. Finally, the discipline to consistently engage in the cycle is crucial. Iterative improvement is not a sporadic activity; it is an ongoing discipline that must be integrated into the routine operations.

The integration of contemplative practices can significantly enhance the effectiveness of the reflection stage. Practices such as mindfulness meditation can cultivate greater self-awareness, allowing individuals to observe their thoughts and emotions more objectively during the reflection process. This can lead to a deeper understanding of the subtle factors that influenced performance and a more nuanced interpretation of feedback. Similarly, journaling can provide a structured space for processing experiences and identifying patterns that might otherwise remain hidden. By bringing a calm, focused awareness to the reflection process, one can move beyond surface-level analysis to uncover more profound insights, leading to more impactful adjustments in subsequent actions. This mindful approach transforms reflection from a mere review into a profound opportunity for self-discovery and strategic refinement.

Ultimately, iterative improvement is more than just a process; it is a mindset. It is the understanding that mastery is not achieved through a single, perfect execution, but through a sustained, deliberate journey of learning and adaptation. It's about embracing the reality that the path to success is rarely a straight line, and that the ability to learn from experience, to adjust course, and to continuously refine one's approach is the hallmark of true strategic acumen and enduring achievement. It transforms challenges into learning opportunities, and setbacks into stepping stones, fostering a dynamic and resilient pursuit of goals.

The strategic landscape is rarely static. It is a fluid, dynamic environment where unforeseen challenges can emerge with startling rapidity, rendering even the most meticulously crafted plans obsolete overnight. In such contexts, the ability to not merely adapt, but to *pivot* strategically, becomes the ultimate differentiator between perseverance and obsolescence. A pivot is not a minor adjustment; it is a fundamental shift in direction, a decisive change in strategy driven by the recognition that the current course is no longer tenable or optimal. It requires a keen awareness of the surrounding environment, an honest assessment of one's own trajectory, and the courage to embrace change when it is most difficult.

Recognizing the imperative for a pivot is the first, and often most challenging, step. This discernment doesn't arise from a vague sense of unease, but from rigorous analysis and a clear understanding of key performance indicators and external trends. It means actively monitoring the battlefield—whether that battlefield is a competitive market, a complex personal endeavor, or a geopolitical arena. This involves not just looking at internal data, which can sometimes offer a distorted or overly optimistic view, but also actively seeking external validation and identifying signals of disruption. Are competitors introducing disruptive technologies? Has customer sentiment shifted dramatically? Are regulatory environments changing in ways that undermine the existing strategy? Are personal circumstances or capabilities evolving in a manner that makes the current path untenable? These are the critical questions that prompt a strategic re-evaluation.

The process of assessing the need for a pivot often involves a disciplined "red teaming" of one's own strategy. This means proactively imagining worst-case scenarios and exploring how the current plan would fare. It's about asking, "What could go wrong, and how would we respond?" It also involves seeking out dissenting opinions and encouraging critical feedback from trusted advisors or team members. Often, those closest to a strategy can become blind to its nascent flaws, so cultivating an environment where constructive dissent is not only tolerated but actively encouraged is vital. This allows potential weaknesses to be identified and addressed before they become catastrophic failures. Moreover, understanding the opportunity cost of sticking with a failing strategy is paramount. Every resource—time, capital, effort—invested in a direction that is no longer viable is a resource that cannot be redirected to a more promising alternative.

Once the necessity for a pivot has been identified, the next crucial phase is analyzing the available adaptation options. This is not a brainstorming session devoid of reality, but a structured exploration of potential new directions. It requires understanding the core strengths and capabilities that can be leveraged in a new context. A pivot is rarely about abandoning everything and starting from scratch; it is more often about redeploying existing assets and expertise in a novel way to address a new set of challenges or opportunities. For instance, a company that built its success on a particular technology might pivot by applying that same core technology to a different industry or a related problem. Similarly, an individual who has developed strong analytical skills might pivot from one career path to another where those skills are equally valuable but applied to a different domain.

This analysis must also consider the feasibility and potential impact of each adaptation option. What resources are required to implement a new direction? What is the projected timeline? What are the potential risks associated with each alternative? What is the likelihood of success? A thorough risk-reward analysis, informed by market research, competitive intelligence, and expert consultation, is essential. This is where strategic foresight plays a critical role. It involves not just reacting to current circumstances but anticipating future trends and positioning the organization or oneself to capitalize on emerging opportunities. A well-executed pivot anticipates the next shift, rather than merely reacting to the last one.

The implementation of a pivot is where strategic thinking meets decisive action. It requires clear communication, strong leadership, and the ability to rally support for the new direction. When a significant change in strategy is undertaken, there will invariably be inertia, resistance, and uncertainty. Leaders must articulate a compelling vision for the new path, explaining *why* the pivot is necessary and *what* the anticipated benefits are. This communication needs to be transparent, consistent, and empathetic, acknowledging the challenges and anxieties that such a change might engender.

In a business context, this might involve retraining employees, reallocating budgets, or even rebranding. For example, Netflix's pivot from DVD-by-mail rentals to streaming video was a monumental shift that required significant investment in technology, content acquisition, and a complete reorientation of the company's business model. The success of this pivot, executed under the leadership of Reed Hastings, transformed the entertainment industry and cemented Netflix's position as a global media giant. The initial resistance and skepticism within the company and from the market were overcome by a clear, unwavering commitment to the new vision and a willingness to invest heavily in making it a reality.

On a personal level, a pivot might involve a career change, a fundamental shift in lifestyle, or a redefinition of personal goals. Consider the story of individuals who, after years in a demanding corporate career, pivot to pursue a passion such as art, writing, or entrepreneurship. This often involves a period of lower income, increased uncertainty, and a steep learning curve. However, for those who have carefully assessed their motivations, identified transferable skills, and developed a viable plan, this pivot can lead to greater fulfillment and long-term success. The courage to step away from a known, albeit unsatisfactory, path to embrace an unknown, but potentially more rewarding, future is the essence of personal strategic adaptation.

The execution of a pivot is not a single event, but a process that requires ongoing monitoring and adjustment. Just as in the iterative cycles discussed previously, the newly adopted course must be subject to continuous feedback and refinement. The market conditions may evolve, new competitors may emerge, or unforeseen challenges may arise that necessitate further adaptation. The key is to maintain the agility and responsiveness that characterized the decision to pivot in the first place. This means embedding a culture of continuous learning and adaptation into the very fabric of the organization or one's personal approach.

One of the most powerful illustrations of strategic adaptation through pivoting can be found in the history of technological innovation. Companies that have successfully navigated market shifts often do so by recognizing the limitations of their existing business models and boldly venturing into new territory. Consider IBM's transition from a hardware-centric company to a services and software powerhouse. Faced with the commoditization of hardware and the rise of personal computing, IBM made a strategic pivot, investing heavily in software development, IT consulting, and business solutions. This was not an easy transition; it involved significant restructuring, divestitures, and a cultural shift away from its hardware legacy. However, by embracing this strategic adaptation, IBM was able to reinvent itself and remain a dominant force in the technology sector for decades.

Another compelling example can be seen in the airline industry. Airlines are constantly battling razor-thin margins, volatile fuel prices, and intense competition. Many have had to pivot their business models to survive.

Low-cost carriers, for instance, pivoted away from the traditional hub-and-spoke model with full-service offerings, focusing instead on point-to-point routes, reduced amenities, and optimized aircraft utilization. This strategic shift fundamentally altered the economics of air travel and forced established carriers to adapt or risk becoming irrelevant. The success of airlines like Southwest in the United States or Ryanair in Europe demonstrates the power of a decisive pivot when market conditions demand it. They identified a segment of the market underserved by incumbents and built a business model tailored to their specific needs, effectively pivoting the industry's trajectory.

The act of pivoting also has significant psychological implications. For leaders, it requires immense conviction to steer the ship in a new direction, especially when facing internal dissent or external skepticism. For teams, it can be unsettling, demanding a willingness to learn new skills, adopt new processes, and embrace a new organizational identity. Contemplative practices can be particularly valuable during these times of transition. Mindfulness, for instance, can help individuals remain grounded and focused amidst the uncertainty of a pivot. By cultivating present-moment awareness, leaders and team members can better manage stress, avoid reactive decision-making, and maintain clarity of purpose. A regular meditation practice can enhance emotional regulation, allowing individuals to respond to challenges with equanimity rather than succumbing to anxiety or frustration.

Furthermore, practices like mindful listening and empathetic communication are crucial for navigating the interpersonal dynamics of a pivot. When a significant change is underway, open and honest dialogue is essential for building trust and fostering buy-in. Leaders who can listen deeply to the concerns of their teams, acknowledge their feelings, and communicate the rationale behind the pivot with clarity and compassion are far more likely to achieve successful adaptation. This fosters a sense of shared purpose and resilience, enabling the collective to weather the storm of transition. The ability to see the pivot not as an ending but as a new beginning, infused with possibility, is a mindset that can be cultivated through consistent contemplative practice.

The decision to pivot is often born out of necessity, but its success hinges on strategic foresight and a willingness to embrace calculated risk. It is about understanding that rigidity in the face of change is a form of strategic paralysis. The ability to analyze the environment, identify a more promising path, and commit resources to that new direction is the hallmark of adaptive leadership. This involves a profound understanding of one's own capabilities and limitations, as well as a clear-eyed assessment of the external landscape.

Consider the retail industry's response to the rise of e-commerce. Many traditional brick-and-mortar retailers initially resisted or underinvested in online channels, clinging to their established business models. However, those that recognized the irreversible shift in consumer behavior and executed a strategic pivot towards omnichannel retail—integrating their physical stores with their online presence—have been able to thrive. Companies like Best Buy, which once faced existential threats from online competitors, successfully pivoted by leveraging its physical stores as service centers, distribution hubs, and experience showrooms, complementing its growing e-commerce operations. This pivot was driven by a data-informed understanding of customer needs and a willingness to fundamentally reconfigure the retail experience.

Personal development, too, offers countless examples of the power of the pivot. An individual might dedicate years to mastering a particular skill or pursuing a specific career path, only to discover that their passions or the demands of the market have shifted. Rather than rigidly adhering to the original plan, a strategic pivot involves recognizing this divergence and charting a new course. This might mean acquiring new skills, changing industries, or even redefining what success looks like. For instance, a scientist who finds their research yielding unexpected results might pivot their focus to explore those new avenues, even if it means departing from their original research questions. This intellectual agility and willingness to follow the evidence, even when it leads to unexpected destinations, is a powerful form of strategic adaptation.

The pivot is not about reacting impulsively to every fluctuation in the environment. It is about discerning when a change is fundamental and requires a significant alteration of course. This requires a deep understanding of the underlying forces at play, not just the superficial symptoms. It also demands the courage to make difficult choices, to potentially abandon strategies that were once considered sound, and to invest in an unproven future. The rewards for successful pivots can be immense, leading to renewed growth, increased resilience, and the achievement of objectives that might have otherwise remained out of reach. It is a testament to the fact that in a dynamic world, the ability to adapt is not just an advantage, but a necessity for sustained success. The strategic pivot, therefore, is not merely a maneuver; it is a mindset, a commitment to intelligent evolution in the face of an ever-changing reality. It is the embodiment of adaptive warfare in its most nuanced and impactful form.

The strategic landscape, whether on the battlefield or in the arena of personal and professional endeavor, is a crucible where resilience is forged. While the preceding discussions have focused on anticipating change and executing strategic pivots, equally vital is the disciplined process of extracting wisdom from those moments when plans falter and objectives are not met. These are not mere obstacles to be overcome or forgotten, but rather potent instructors, offering profound lessons for future campaigns. The art of transforming setbacks into a catalyst for growth lies in a deliberate and systematic approach to post-action review and analysis. This practice, deeply ingrained in military doctrine, is the bedrock upon which adaptive warfare is built, ensuring that each misstep becomes a stepping stone, not a stumbling block.

At its core, the post-action review (PAR) is an exercise in honest self-appraisal and objective analysis. It demands a shift in perspective, moving away from the emotional aftermath of disappointment or frustration towards a detached, analytical examination of what transpired. The objective is not to assign blame, but to understand causality. This requires creating an environment where open communication is paramount, and individuals feel safe to articulate their experiences, observations, and reflections without fear of recrimination. In a military context, this often takes the form of a formal debriefing session immediately following an operation or engagement. Participants, from the highest-ranking officer to the most junior soldier, are encouraged to share their accounts, contributing to a comprehensive picture of the event. This collaborative approach ensures that diverse perspectives are captured, revealing nuances that might otherwise be overlooked.

The process typically begins with a chronological recounting of the events. What was the initial plan? What actions were taken? What were the immediate consequences? This narrative framework provides context for the subsequent analysis. It is crucial to establish a shared understanding of the timeline and the sequence of actions, ensuring that all participants are operating from the same factual basis. This stage is not about judgment; it is about establishing the factual record. Detailed notes are taken, audio recordings might be made, and visual aids such as maps or diagrams can be employed to reconstruct the scenario as accurately as possible. The goal is to create an objective account, free from the distortions that memory can sometimes introduce.

Following the reconstruction of events, the focus shifts to identifying deviations from the plan and analyzing the reasons for these divergences. This is where the critical work of root cause analysis begins. It's not enough to say, "We failed because X happened." The question must be, "Why did X happen?" and "What underlying factors contributed to X?" This might involve examining a range of contributing elements: Was the intelligence flawed? Were the assumptions made during the planning phase incorrect? Was the execution flawed due to a lack of training, poor communication, or insufficient resources? Were external factors, such as unforeseen environmental conditions or enemy actions, the primary drivers of the setback?

For instance, imagine a small unit tasked with securing a particular objective. The mission plan, based on available intelligence, indicated minimal enemy presence. However, upon reaching the objective, the unit encountered unexpectedly heavy resistance. The post-action review would not simply conclude that "the enemy was there." Instead, it would delve deeper. Was the intelligence outdated? Was there a failure to properly scout the area beforehand? Did enemy forces reposition themselves after the intelligence was gathered? Was the unit's approach predictable, allowing the enemy to prepare an ambush? Each of these questions probes a different layer of causality, moving beyond the superficial to uncover the fundamental reasons for the unexpected outcome.

This analytical process is often guided by structured questioning. Techniques like the "Five Whys" can be invaluable. Starting with the observed setback, repeatedly asking "Why?" can help peel back layers of causality until the fundamental root cause is identified. For example:

1. **Setback:** The patrol was ambushed.

2. **Why?** Because the enemy knew our route.

3. **Why?** Because our patrol route was predictable.

4. **Why?** Because we didn't vary our routes sufficiently during reconnaissance.

5. **Why?** Because the team leader prioritized speed over thoroughness in route selection.

The root cause here isn't just "the enemy," but a systemic issue in route selection prioritization.

Another powerful analytical tool is the "Fishbone Diagram" or Ishikawa diagram, which visually maps out potential causes categorised into main branches (e.g., People, Process, Equipment, Environment, Management, and Materials). This encourages a holistic examination, ensuring that no potential contributing factor is overlooked. For example, in a scenario where a critical piece of equipment failed, a Fishbone Diagram might explore causes related to maintenance schedules (Process), operator error (People), inherent design flaws (Equipment), environmental conditions (Environment), or cost-cutting measures impacting quality (Management).

Once the root causes are identified, the crucial next step is to extract actionable insights. These insights are the lessons learned, the specific recommendations for improvement that can be integrated into future plans and practices. They must be concrete, specific, and feasible. Vague statements like "be more careful next time" are not useful. Instead, actionable insights might include: "Implement a mandatory route reconnaissance protocol for all patrols operating in urban environments," or "Invest in advanced predictive maintenance software for critical communication equipment," or "Develop a standardized communication protocol for reporting unexpected enemy contact."

These insights then form the basis for revising standard operating procedures (SOPs), updating training curricula, modifying equipment specifications, or even influencing strategic doctrine. The aim is to ensure that the same mistake is not repeated. The iterative nature of learning is what allows organizations and individuals to become more effective over time. Each cycle of planning, execution, review, and refinement builds a cumulative advantage.

The mental and emotional dimension of processing setbacks is as important as the analytical process itself. For many, acknowledging a failure can be difficult. Ego, pride, and the fear of negative consequences can create resistance to a truly objective assessment. This is where the cultivation of a "growth mindset," as described by Carol Dweck, becomes paramount. A growth mindset views challenges and failures not as indicators of inherent inability, but as opportunities for learning and development. Individuals with this mindset understand that abilities and intelligence can be developed through dedication and hard work.

In the context of adaptive warfare, this translates to approaching every operation, regardless of outcome, with a spirit of curiosity. Instead of asking, "What went wrong?" the more productive question is, "What can we learn from this?" This framing shifts the focus from blame to improvement. It encourages a proactive engagement with the learning process, fostering a culture where setbacks are seen not as endpoints, but as data points that can inform future success.

Contemplative practices can significantly enhance this psychological shift. Mindfulness, for instance, helps individuals observe their thoughts and emotions without judgment. When a setback occurs, the initial reaction might be disappointment, anger, or self-criticism. Mindfulness allows one to acknowledge these feelings, understand their transient nature, and then gently redirect attention to the analytical task at hand. By developing the ability to detach from immediate emotional responses, one can approach the post-action review with greater clarity and objectivity. A regular meditation practice can build this capacity for emotional regulation, enabling individuals to remain calm and focused even when confronting difficult truths about their performance.

Furthermore, practices like self-compassion can be incredibly beneficial. Recognizing that everyone makes mistakes, and that setbacks are an inherent part of any challenging endeavor, can alleviate the pressure of perfectionism and foster a more resilient approach to learning. This doesn't mean excusing poor performance, but rather acknowledging the human element and focusing on constructive action rather than self-recrimination. When individuals feel supported and understood, they are more likely to be open and honest during the review process.

The review process itself should be conducted in a structured and facilitated manner. A skilled facilitator can guide the discussion, ensure that all voices are heard, and keep the group focused on the objectives of the review. The facilitator acts as a neutral party, encouraging participation and managing any potential conflicts that may arise. They are responsible for maintaining a safe space for honest feedback and for ensuring that the review remains productive and forward-looking.

For complex operations involving multiple units or agencies, the post-action review process can become even more intricate. Integrating feedback from various sources requires careful coordination and a commitment to a unified understanding of events. Cross-functional debriefings, where representatives from different branches or disciplines come together, are essential for identifying interdependencies and systemic issues that might not be apparent within a single group. For example, a ground combat unit might have a different perspective on the effectiveness of air support than the aircrew themselves. Bringing these perspectives together in a joint review can highlight communication breakdowns or coordination challenges that need to be addressed.

The output of the post-action review is not just a collection of lessons learned; it is a living document that should inform ongoing strategy and operations. These lessons should be actively disseminated, integrated into training programs, and used to update doctrine, tactics, techniques, and procedures (TTPs). The effectiveness of the review process is ultimately measured by its impact on future performance. If the same mistakes continue to be made, the review process itself is failing.

A critical element in ensuring the impact of these lessons is the follow-through. Once insights are identified, clear action plans must be developed with assigned responsibilities and deadlines. Who will update the SOPs? Who will revise the training materials? Who will champion the adoption of a new technology or procedure? Without this accountability, lessons learned can quickly become lost or ignored. The feedback loop must be closed by demonstrating tangible changes that result from the review process. This builds confidence in the system and reinforces the value of engaging in these reflective practices.

Consider the historical development of military aviation. Early aerial reconnaissance missions were often hampered by poor visibility and inaccurate reporting. Through a rigorous process of post-action reviews, pilots and intelligence officers identified critical shortcomings in camera technology, film processing techniques, and the methods for interpreting aerial imagery. These reviews led to significant advancements in photographic equipment, the development of specialized interpretation training, and new protocols for reporting findings. Each mission, whether successful or not, contributed to a continuous cycle of improvement that transformed aerial reconnaissance from a rudimentary practice into a sophisticated intelligence-gathering discipline.

Similarly, naval warfare has been shaped by countless post-engagement analyses. The lessons learned from the

Battle of Tsushima in 1905, for example, highlighted the devastating effectiveness of accurate long-range gunnery and the importance of effective fire control systems. These insights, derived from a detailed review of the battle's outcomes, profoundly influenced naval design and tactics for decades to come. The Japanese victory, though decisive, was not accidental; it was the product of rigorous analysis and adaptation based on prior experiences and a deep understanding of the technological and tactical advantages gained.

In the realm of cybersecurity, the concept of "lessons learned" is particularly acute. With adversaries constantly evolving their tactics, techniques, and procedures (TTPs), organizations must be adept at analyzing security breaches and near misses. A post-incident review in cybersecurity goes beyond identifying the exploited vulnerability. It seeks to understand the attacker's methodology, the extent of the compromise, the effectiveness of the defensive measures in place, and the response time of the incident response team. This analysis leads to immediate patching of vulnerabilities, updates to security policies, enhanced monitoring capabilities, and refined incident response plans. For example, a review following a phishing attack might reveal weaknesses in employee awareness training, leading to the implementation of more frequent and targeted training modules.

The commitment to learning from setbacks is a hallmark of truly adaptive organizations and individuals. It requires a culture that values reflection, embraces honest feedback, and prioritizes continuous improvement. It means cultivating the intellectual humility to admit when a plan has gone awry and the discipline to rigorously analyze why. By systematically deconstructing failures, identifying root causes, and translating those findings into actionable insights, every setback can be transformed into a powerful engine of growth and resilience. This process ensures that the lessons of experience are not lost, but rather are consciously woven into the fabric of future endeavors, paving the way for more effective strategies and ultimately, greater success. The ability to face challenges, analyze them objectively, and emerge wiser and better prepared is the essence of adaptive warfare, a perpetual cycle of learning and refinement that is crucial for navigating an uncertain world.

Chapter 6: The Mindful Warrior: Integrating Contemplation into Action

The relentless pace of modern life, characterized by a constant barrage of information, demands, and distractions, can leave even the most disciplined individual feeling scattered and overwhelmed. The "mindful warrior" understands that true effectiveness in action stems not solely from external preparation and strategic foresight, but also from an unshakeable inner equilibrium. This inner stillness is not a passive state of idleness, but an active, cultivated quality of mind that serves as the bedrock for clarity, focus, and decisive action. Meditation, in its myriad forms, offers a potent pathway to cultivating this essential internal resource.

At the heart of contemplative traditions, particularly within Buddhism, lies the profound understanding that the mind, left untended, is prone to agitation, rumination, and a constant flux of thoughts and emotions. This mental chatter, often referred to as the "monkey mind," can cloud judgment, diminish our capacity for deep concentration, and ultimately hinder our ability to respond effectively to challenges. Meditation is the discipline that trains the mind to transcend this inherent restlessness, fostering a state of settled awareness that allows for greater insight and sharper focus.

Two fundamental pillars of Buddhist meditation practice, Vipassanā and Samatha, offer distinct yet complementary approaches to achieving this inner stillness. Samatha, often translated as "calm-abiding" or "tranquility" meditation, aims to quiet the mental noise and cultivate a deep sense of peace and stability. The primary object of Samatha practice is typically the breath. By gently bringing attention to the sensation of the breath entering and leaving the body, practitioners learn to anchor their awareness in the present moment. When the mind wanders, as it inevitably will, the practice is to gently, without judgment, guide the attention back to the breath. This repeated act of returning the focus strengthens the mind's ability to concentrate, much like training a muscle. Over time, this consistent redirection builds a reservoir of mental calm, reducing the power of distracting thoughts and fostering a more settled state of being.

The benefits of Samatha meditation extend far beyond a fleeting sense of relaxation. Physiologically, regular practice has been shown to lower heart rate, reduce blood pressure, and decrease the production of stress hormones like cortisol. Psychologically, it leads to a significant reduction in anxiety, a greater ability to manage intrusive thoughts, and an improved sense of emotional regulation. This heightened self-awareness, born from observing the subtle rhythms of the breath, creates a foundation of inner quietude that is essential for clear thinking. Imagine preparing for a critical negotiation or a high-stakes strategic decision. In such moments, a mind agitated by external pressures or internal anxieties is a compromised instrument. A mind trained in Samatha, however, is more likely to remain calm, assess the situation dispassionately, and access its full cognitive capabilities.

Complementing Samatha is Vipassanā, often translated as "insight" or "mindfulness" meditation. While Samatha cultivates stability, Vipassanā focuses on developing a deeper understanding of the nature of reality, particularly the impermanent and interdependent nature of our own experience. In Vipassanā, the object of meditation is not solely the breath, but a broader, more panoramic awareness of whatever arises in consciousness. This can include bodily sensations, thoughts, emotions, and external sounds. The practice involves observing these phenomena with a quality of detached curiosity, noting their arising and passing without judgment or attachment.

The core principle of Vipassanā is to see things as they truly are, free from the filters of our preconceived notions, biases, and emotional reactions. By diligently observing the constant flux of experience, practitioners begin to gain insight into the impermanent nature of all phenomena, including their own thoughts and feelings. This understanding can be profoundly liberating, helping to dismantle the grip of negative thought patterns and emotional reactivity. When faced with a setback or a difficult situation, a Vipassanā practitioner is more likely to observe their initial feelings of frustration or disappointment without being consumed by them. They can recognize these emotions as transient states, understand their origins, and then choose a more considered response, rather than reacting impulsively.

The integration of these two practices creates a powerful synergy. Samatha provides the stable, clear mental platform from which Vipassanā can be effectively applied. A calm and focused mind is better equipped to engage in the subtle observation required for insight meditation. Conversely, the insights gained through Vipassanā can deepen the appreciation for and motivation to cultivate the stillness offered by Samatha. Together, they form a comprehensive approach to mental training that cultivates both inner peace and profound wisdom.

Integrating these contemplative practices into a busy life does not require vast blocks of uninterrupted time. The mindful warrior understands that effectiveness lies in consistency and quality, not necessarily in quantity. Even short, dedicated sessions can yield significant benefits. The key is to establish a regular routine, making meditation a non-negotiable part of the day, much like physical training or strategic planning.

For beginners, starting with just five to ten minutes of meditation per day can be a powerful beginning. This might involve finding a quiet space, sitting comfortably with a straight but not rigid spine, and gently closing the eyes. The initial focus can be solely on the breath. Notice the sensation of the air as it enters the nostrils, fills the lungs, and then leaves the body. Observe the natural rhythm, the subtle pauses between breaths. When the mind inevitably drifts to planning the day, replaying a conversation, or worrying about a future event, simply acknowledge the thought without judgment and gently redirect attention back to the breath. This simple act, repeated consistently, builds the foundational skill of present-moment awareness.

As comfort and familiarity grow, one can gradually extend the duration of these sessions or explore the Vipassanā approach by expanding awareness to include other sensations or mental objects. The critical element is to approach the practice with patience and self-compassion. There is no "perfect" meditation session. Each time the mind wanders and is brought back, that is a moment of successful practice. It is in these moments of gentle redirection that the mind's capacity for focus and resilience is strengthened.

Consider the practice of mindful breathing as a micro-meditation that can be incorporated throughout the day. Before entering a meeting, during a brief pause between tasks, or even while waiting in line, one can take a few conscious breaths. This brief recalibration serves to anchor the mind in the present, clearing away mental clutter and preparing the individual for the next activity with renewed clarity. Similarly, a short walking meditation, where attention is brought to the physical sensations of walking – the lifting of the foot, the swing of the arms, the contact with the ground – can be a powerful way to cultivate mindfulness in motion.

The benefits of such practices are cumulative. Over time, the ability to access a state of calm, focused awareness becomes more readily available. This translates directly into improved performance in all areas of endeavor. For the strategist, it means the ability to analyze complex situations with greater clarity, unburdened by emotional reactivity. For the leader, it fosters a presence that inspires confidence and facilitates effective communication. For the individual striving for mastery, it provides the mental discipline to persevere through challenges and to learn effectively from every experience.

The physiological benefits are also noteworthy. Studies have consistently demonstrated that regular meditation practice can lead to significant reductions in perceived stress, symptoms of anxiety and depression, and even improvements in immune function. By downregulating the sympathetic nervous system's "fight-or-flight" response and activating the parasympathetic nervous system's "rest-and-digest" mode, meditation helps to restore balance within the body and mind. This physiological recalibration is crucial for maintaining optimal cognitive function and emotional resilience, especially in demanding environments.

The development of enhanced cognitive control is another significant outcome of consistent meditation practice. This refers to the mind's ability to regulate thoughts, emotions, and impulses in pursuit of goals. Through practices like Samatha, individuals train their attentional networks, improving their capacity to sustain focus on a chosen object and resist distractions. Vipassanā, in turn, cultivates meta-cognitive awareness – the ability to observe one's own thinking processes without getting entangled in them. This separation between the observer and the observed allows for a more deliberate and less reactive engagement with internal experiences. Imagine a situation where a critical piece of information is unexpectedly revealed, triggering a strong emotional response. Without cognitive control, this response might hijack attention, derailing the ability to process the information objectively. With developed cognitive control, however, the practitioner can acknowledge the emotional reaction, allow it to pass, and then return their focus to the task at hand, ensuring that decisions are made based on reasoned analysis rather than visceral reaction.

The practice of meditation, therefore, is not merely an exercise in relaxation; it is a rigorous form of mental training that builds essential capacities for clarity, focus, and emotional regulation. It equips the individual with the inner tools to navigate complexity with a settled mind, to respond to challenges with considered action, and to maintain a clear perspective amidst the inevitable turbulence of life. By cultivating this stillness within, the mindful warrior is better prepared to face any external storm, operating from a place of grounded awareness and unwavering purpose. The commitment to this inner discipline is as vital as any external preparation, forming the bedrock of a resilient and effective approach to achieving objectives, both in strategic endeavors and in the broader pursuit of a life lived with intention and presence.

The disciplined cultivation of stillness through meditation forms a crucial foundation for the mindful warrior. However, the warrior's path is not one of perpetual quietude; it is a journey of engaging with the world, of action and response. It is within this realm of movement and engagement that the principles of mindfulness can be further deepened and integrated, transforming ordinary physical activity into a profound practice of mind-body synergy. This is the essence of "mindful movement," where the very act of engaging the body becomes an extension of contemplative practice, enhancing not only physical prowess but also mental acuity and presence.

To truly embody the mindful warrior, one must learn to carry the quality of awareness cultivated in seated meditation into the dynamic sphere of action. This is not about performing a specific athletic feat with perfect form, although that can be a byproduct. Rather, it is about infusing intention and conscious awareness into every physical engagement, no matter how mundane or demanding. Think of the seasoned operative who moves with an economy of motion, each step deliberate, each gesture purposeful, a living embodiment of focused energy. This is not merely a matter of physical conditioning; it is a manifestation of a mind fully present and integrated with its physical vessel.

One of the most accessible forms of mindful movement is mindful walking. It's a practice that can be integrated into daily life, whether traversing a busy street or a quiet trail. The essence lies in bringing the same gentle, non-judgmental awareness to the physical sensations of walking that one brings to the breath during meditation. As you walk, pay attention to the subtle interplay of muscles in your legs, the sensation of your feet making contact with the ground – the lifting, the moving forward, the landing. Notice the rhythm of your breath as it naturally aligns with your stride. Observe the movement of your arms, the swing, the subtle tension or relaxation in your shoulders.

The world around you also becomes part of this contemplative experience. Instead of being lost in thought about past events or future plans, allow your senses to engage with your environment. Notice the quality of the light, the sounds that reach your ears – not to analyze them, but simply to register their presence. Observe the textures, the colors, the vastness of the sky or the intricate details of a leaf. This expanded awareness, grounded in the physical act of walking, creates a powerful connection between the internal state of mindfulness and the external reality.

When the mind inevitably wanders, as it will, the practice is to gently acknowledge the distraction and then return your awareness to the sensations of walking, to the rhythm of your breath, to the present moment experience. This continuous, gentle redirection is the very training that strengthens the mind-body connection. It's akin to the focused attention required in a strategic planning session, where extraneous data must be filtered out to focus on critical elements. In mindful walking, the "extraneous data" is the mental chatter, and the "critical element" is the present, embodied experience.

Yoga, in its myriad forms, offers another rich avenue for cultivating mindful movement. While often viewed primarily as a physical discipline, its roots are deeply embedded in contemplative traditions. The practice of yoga, particularly styles that emphasize slow, deliberate transitions between postures (asanas) and conscious breathwork (pranayama), invites a profound integration of mind and body. Each pose becomes an opportunity to explore the limits of one's physical being while maintaining a steady, present-moment awareness.

In a yoga practice, attention is directed to the subtle energetic currents within the body, the alignment of the spine, the engagement of specific muscle groups. The breath is often used as an anchor, guiding the movement and deepening the internal focus. Holding a challenging pose requires not just physical strength but also mental fortitude and the ability to remain present with discomfort without succumbing to it. This mirrors the resilience required in confronting difficult situations, where the ability to maintain composure and focus is paramount.

The transitions between poses are particularly instructive. They are moments of dynamic equilibrium, where the body is in motion, requiring a sophisticated interplay of balance, strength, and awareness. A mindful approach to these transitions ensures that the movement is not jerky or rushed, but fluid and controlled, a seamless flow of energy. This fluidity is a hallmark of highly skilled performers, whether athletes, musicians, or operatives, who can execute complex actions with apparent ease because their minds and bodies are perfectly synchronized.

Even disciplined physical training routines, from martial arts to strategic fitness regimens, can be transformed into practices of mindful movement. The key is to shift the focus from merely achieving a physical outcome – lifting a certain weight, running a certain distance – to the *quality* of the experience. This involves paying attention to the sensations of exertion, the feeling of muscles contracting and releasing, the rhythm of the breath supporting the effort.

In martial arts, for instance, every movement is imbued with intention and precise awareness. The strike is not just a physical act but a culmination of focused energy, rooted in a stable stance and channeled through a clear mind. The defensive maneuver is executed with an understanding of spatial awareness and the opponent's momentum, a dance of precise reaction and calculated action. This level of integration, where the physical and mental are inseparable, is the essence of a warrior's prowess.

The benefit of this integration extends beyond improved physical performance. It enhances proprioception – the body's innate sense of its position in space and the relative position of its parts. By bringing conscious awareness to movement, we sharpen this internal map, leading to better coordination, balance, and a more intuitive understanding of our physical capabilities. This heightened proprioception is invaluable in any situation that demands precision and agility, allowing for more effective and less error-prone actions.

Furthermore, mindful movement can significantly enhance emotional regulation. Physical exertion often brings forth a range of emotions, from frustration to exhilaration. By observing these emotions without judgment as they arise during activity, individuals can learn to manage them more effectively. Instead of being swept away by anger or disappointment, a mindful approach allows one to acknowledge these feelings, understand their somatic components, and respond with greater equanimity. This capacity to remain centered amidst physical and emotional intensity is a critical attribute for anyone operating under pressure.

The principle of "form follows function" takes on a new dimension when infused with mindfulness. It's not just about achieving the correct physical form for efficiency, but about ensuring that the internal state of awareness is aligned with the external action. This means being present to the intent behind the movement, the purpose it serves. Whether it's the precise positioning of a tool, the measured cadence of steps, or the controlled exertion of strength, each action can be an expression of focused presence.

Consider the process of learning a new skill that involves physical coordination, such as a complex operational procedure or even a new sport. A mindful approach to learning accelerates the process by fostering deeper engagement with the sensations and feedback loops involved. Instead of rote repetition, it becomes an exploration of the body's capacity and the mind's ability to guide it. This leads to a more ingrained understanding and a greater ability to adapt the skill to varied circumstances.

The mindful warrior understands that the body is not merely a vehicle for the mind, but an integral part of the self, a sophisticated instrument that must be attuned and responsive. Through mindful movement, the warrior cultivates this attunement, fostering a seamless integration of thought, sensation, and action. This creates a state of dynamic presence, where the individual is not only mentally sharp but also physically fluid, agile, and in command of their being, ready to engage with the world with both clarity and power. It is in this active, embodied state that the true essence of the mindful warrior comes alive, demonstrating that contemplation is not an escape from action, but a preparation for it, and that action, when undertaken mindfully, becomes a continuation of contemplation.

The ability to remain anchored in the present moment is not merely a desirable trait; it is a critical survival mechanism in situations where the stakes are high and the consequences of error can be severe. For the mindful warrior, this is the apex of contemplative practice – the seamless translation of inner stillness into outward effectiveness when faced with intense pressure. It is about cultivating an unwavering capacity to be fully where you are, doing what you are doing, irrespective of the surrounding chaos or the internal storm of stress. This is not about suppressing fear or anxiety, but about acknowledging their presence without allowing them to hijack your cognitive functions or dictate your actions.

Consider the seasoned emergency responder entering a volatile scene. The air crackles with uncertainty, the cacophony of alarms and shouts can overwhelm the senses, and the body's innate fight-or-flight response is triggered. In such moments, the tendency for the mind to race, to jump to catastrophic conclusions, or to become paralyzed by indecision is immense. Yet, it is precisely at this juncture that the mindful warrior's training comes to the fore. The practice is to recognize the surge of adrenaline, the quickening heartbeat, the tightening in the chest, not as signals of imminent doom, but as physiological data to be observed. This observation is done with a dispassionate curiosity, a mental step back that creates a crucial buffer between stimulus and response.

The core of this present moment awareness under duress lies in anchoring oneself to a tangible, immediate reality. This can be as simple as focusing on the breath, allowing its rhythm to become a consistent, grounding force amidst the swirling unpredictability. The inhalation and exhalation are simple, repeatable actions that exist solely in the present. By directing attention to the rise and fall of the chest, the feeling of air entering and leaving the nostrils, one creates an internal anchor. When the mind inevitably skitters towards anxieties about potential outcomes or replays past errors, the gentle, non-judgmental redirection back to the breath acts as a consistent recalibration. This isn't about forcing the breath into an unnatural pattern, but about allowing its natural cadence to become a focal point, a quiet hum beneath the noise of the crisis.

Another powerful anchor is the direct sensory experience of the immediate environment. Instead of getting lost in the abstract implications of a situation, the mindful warrior actively engages their senses. What are the concrete visual cues that demand attention? What are the specific sounds that require identification? What are the tactile sensations that provide information about the physical context? For instance, in a high-stress tactical situation, this might involve noting the precise position of cover, the angle of a door, the feel of the weapon in one's hand, or the specific sounds that indicate a threat versus benign noise. This is not about passively absorbing sensory input, but about actively selecting and focusing on the information that is most relevant to immediate decision-making and action. It is a form of applied observation, where awareness is directed with purpose.

Intrusive thoughts, those sudden, unwelcome mental intrusions that can derail focus, are a common enemy in high-pressure environments. These can range from self-doubt ("I can't do this") to catastrophic imaginings ("What if X happens?"). The mindful approach to such thoughts is not to engage with them, to argue with them, or to suppress them entirely, as this often gives them more power. Instead, the practice is akin to watching clouds drift across the sky. Acknowledge the thought's presence without judgment, label it internally (e.g., "thinking," "worrying," "imagining"), and then gently guide attention back to the chosen anchor – be it the breath, a sensory input, or the immediate task. This creates a mental space where the thought is observed as a transient mental event, rather than an absolute truth or an unavoidable directive. Over time, this practice weakens the grip of intrusive thoughts, allowing for clearer cognition.

The physiological manifestations of stress – the racing heart, the shallow breathing, the muscle tension – are direct feedback loops from the body's threat response system. Mindfulness offers tools to modulate these responses not by eliminating them, but by influencing the parasympathetic nervous system, which counteracts the fight-or-flight response. Deep, diaphragmatic breathing is a cornerstone of this. By consciously slowing the breath and deepening the inhalations and exhalations, one signals to the body that the perceived threat is being managed, allowing for a return to a more balanced physiological state. This can be practiced discreetly, even while engaged in active tasks, by simply taking a slightly longer, deeper breath whenever an opportunity arises.

Furthermore, progressive muscle relaxation, a technique that involves tensing and then releasing different muscle groups, can be adapted for use under pressure. Even a brief, conscious release of tension in the shoulders, jaw, or hands can create a palpable shift in the body's state, reducing the overall physical burden of stress and improving cognitive function. This is about actively disengaging from the physical manifestations of anxiety, breaking the feedback loop that often exacerbates it.

Maintaining focus on the task at hand in a high-pressure situation requires a deliberate and consistent effort to filter out distractions, both external and internal. This is where the discipline honed through seated meditation becomes invaluable. The ability to notice when attention has strayed and to gently bring it back is the essence of sustained focus. In a crisis, the task at hand might be incredibly complex, requiring the synthesis of multiple pieces of information, the rapid assessment of options, and the execution of a precise action. Mindfulness ensures that cognitive resources are directed where they are most needed, rather than being squandered on irrelevant concerns or anxieties.

Consider the analogy of a spotlight. In a dimly lit room, a spotlight can illuminate a specific area, making details visible that would otherwise be lost in shadow. Mindfulness acts as this internal spotlight, allowing the warrior to direct their attention to the critical elements of a situation, enhancing clarity and precision. If the task is to disarm a device, the focus must be on the specific components, the tools, and the sequence of actions, not on the potential explosion or the personal danger. This laser-like focus is achieved through the consistent practice of bringing attention back to the immediate objective, again and again.

The principle of acceptance, central to many contemplative traditions, is particularly potent in high-pressure scenarios. Acceptance does not mean resignation or a passive surrender to circumstances. Instead, it means acknowledging reality as it is, without resistance or denial. If a plan goes awry, or if an unexpected obstacle emerges, the mindful warrior accepts this new reality without wasting precious cognitive energy on wishing it were different. This acceptance frees up mental resources to adapt, to problem-solve, and to formulate a new approach based on the current facts. This is a stark contrast to an unmindful response, where denial or frustration can lead to rigid adherence to a failing plan, or to impulsive, poorly considered actions.

The ability to make effective decisions under pressure is intrinsically linked to present moment awareness. Stress often impairs executive functions, including decision-making. However, by maintaining an anchored, mindful state, the warrior can access a more rational and considered cognitive process. This involves:

1. **Accurate Assessment:** Remaining present allows for a clearer perception of the situation, free from the distortions of fear or wishful thinking. This leads to a more accurate assessment of threats, opportunities, and available resources.

2. **Option Generation:** With a calm and focused mind, the capacity to brainstorm and evaluate multiple options increases. Instead of a single, panic-driven response, a range of potential actions can be considered.

3. **Consequence Evaluation:** Mindfulness enables a more rational appraisal of the potential outcomes of each option, facilitating a choice that aligns with strategic objectives.

4. **Decisive Action:** Once a decision is made, a present-moment focus allows for its confident and precise execution.

The integration of contemplation into action during high-pressure situations is not about achieving an emotionless state. It is about operating with a regulated emotional landscape, where feelings are acknowledged and managed, rather than suppressed or allowed to dictate behavior. This emotional intelligence, cultivated through mindfulness, is what allows the warrior to remain effective when the external environment is chaotic and the internal experience is intense. It is the ability to feel the pressure, to acknowledge the fear, and yet to proceed with clarity, purpose, and unwavering presence. This is the hallmark of the truly mindful warrior, who understands that true strength lies not in the absence of challenge, but in the capacity to meet it fully, with an unshakeable anchor in the here and now.

The journey of the mindful warrior extends beyond mere tactical prowess and emotional regulation; it encompasses the cultivation of a profound and nuanced quality: compassion. This is not the soft, sentimental emotion often misconstrued as weakness, but a robust, action-oriented stance that acknowledges suffering and actively seeks to alleviate it, starting from within. Self-compassion forms the bedrock upon which this outward-facing empathy is built. Without a genuine capacity for kindness and understanding towards oneself, extending that same grace to others becomes a hollow pretense, unsustainable in the face of adversity.

For individuals who operate in demanding, high-stakes environments, the tendency towards harsh self-criticism can be a pervasive and debilitating force. The pressure to perform, the inevitability of mistakes, and the constant evaluation – whether internal or external – can foster a relentless inner monologue of judgment. This self-recrimination, however, is counterproductive. It erodes resilience, dampens motivation, and paradoxically, can lead to a greater susceptibility to errors by impairing cognitive function under stress. Embracing self-compassion, therefore, is not an act of self-indulgence but a strategic imperative for sustained effectiveness and psychological well-being. It involves recognizing that imperfection is an inherent part of the human experience, particularly in challenging roles. When a mission doesn't go as planned, when a tactical decision results in an undesirable outcome, or when personal capabilities fall short of expectations, the default response of many is to blame themselves, often in severe terms. Self-compassion offers an alternative: to meet these moments with the same gentle understanding and encouragement one would offer a trusted comrade who is struggling. This means acknowledging the difficulty, the disappointment, and the pain, without resorting to harsh condemnation.

A key component of self-compassion is the recognition of shared humanity. This perspective helps to dismantle the isolation that often accompanies difficult experiences. When we fail or suffer, it's easy to feel singled out, as if we are the only ones who have ever made such mistakes or experienced such pain. However, by understanding that struggle, error, and vulnerability are universal aspects of being human, we can alleviate much of the personal shame and self-blame. This realization fosters a sense of connection rather than alienation. For the mindful warrior, this translates to understanding that even the most skilled and experienced individuals encounter setbacks. It means seeing one's own imperfections not as character flaws, but as common human experiences that provide opportunities for learning and growth. This mindset shift is crucial for maintaining morale and forward momentum after a difficult engagement or a personal failure.

Developing self-compassion often involves actively challenging negative self-talk. This is where practices like mindful self-inquiry can be particularly beneficial. Instead of allowing critical thoughts to run unchecked, one can learn to observe them with curiosity, to question their validity, and to reframe them with more balanced and compassionate perspectives. For instance, if the internal critic declares, "You're incompetent for missing that detail," a self-compassionate response might be, "This was a high-pressure situation, and it's understandable that not every detail was captured. What can I learn from this for next time, and how can I support myself to do better?" This doesn't negate the importance of accuracy or skill development, but it frames the learning process within a context of kindness rather than condemnation. It acknowledges the effort made and the challenges faced, fostering a spirit of continuous improvement without self-punishment.

One of the most potent tools for cultivating both self-compassion and compassion for others is the practice of loving-kindness meditation, often referred to as *metta* meditation. While rooted in Buddhist tradition, its principles are universally applicable and profoundly effective for anyone seeking to soften their inner critic and open their heart. The practice typically begins by directing feelings of warmth, well-wishes, and acceptance towards oneself. This often involves silently repeating phrases such as, "May I be filled with loving-kindness. May I be well. May I be peaceful and at ease. May I be happy." The intention is to consciously cultivate a sense of genuine affection and care for oneself, acknowledging one's own inherent worthiness. This initial step is paramount. It is difficult to genuinely extend compassion outward if one's inner wellspring is dry, or if it's tainted by self-judgment and resentment. By first nurturing a benevolent inner disposition, the capacity to offer it to others is amplified and made authentic.

The process of extending this loving-kindness outwardly is then systematically broadened. After directing these wishes towards oneself, the practice moves to loved ones, then to neutral acquaintances, then to difficult individuals, and finally, to all beings. This gradual expansion helps to break down barriers and cultivate a sense of interconnectedness. When directing loving-kindness towards someone with whom there is difficulty, the intention is not necessarily to condone their actions or to erase past grievances. Instead, it is to acknowledge their humanity, their own potential suffering, and to wish them freedom from that suffering.

This can be a challenging but transformative aspect of the practice, allowing the mindful warrior to approach interpersonal conflicts with a greater degree of emotional equilibrium and a reduced tendency towards reactive anger or bitterness.

For the warrior who must often interact with a diverse range of individuals, some of whom may be adversaries, victims, or those who have made grave errors, the cultivation of empathy is essential. Empathy is the ability to understand and share the feelings of another. It allows for more effective communication, better conflict resolution, and a deeper understanding of the human dynamics at play in any situation. When combined with compassion, empathy transforms into a powerful force for positive change and de-escalation. By seeking to understand the underlying motivations, fears, and experiences of others, even those whose actions are detrimental, a warrior can develop more nuanced strategies and responses that go beyond simple force or retribution. This doesn't imply a loss of resolve or a compromise of principles; rather, it enhances the ability to engage with complex human situations with greater wisdom and efficacy.

In practical terms, this means actively listening to understand, rather than listening to respond. It involves making a conscious effort to see situations from another person's perspective, even if that perspective is flawed or disagreeable. For instance, in a negotiation or a de-escalation scenario, understanding the fears or frustrations driving the other party can unlock pathways to resolution that might otherwise remain hidden. Similarly, when dealing with individuals who have been subjected to trauma or hardship, a compassionate and empathetic approach can foster trust and facilitate healing or cooperation, which can be critical in a mission's success or in building long-term stability.

The mindful warrior understands that compassion is not an emotion that is passively felt, but a discipline that is actively practiced. It requires conscious effort, particularly when confronted with situations that trigger negative emotions like anger, fear, or disgust. The ability to maintain an open heart and a clear mind, even when faced with hostility or suffering, is a testament to the depth of one's contemplative training. This is where the strength of the mindful warrior truly shines – in their capacity to act with kindness and understanding without compromising their objectives or their ethical compass. It is the recognition that true strength lies not in the absence of feeling, but in the skillful and compassionate management of those feelings, both within oneself and in relation to others.

The practice of self-compassion, in particular, is a vital safeguard against burnout and disillusionment, common afflictions in demanding professions. When individuals are constantly exposed to difficult situations, suffering, and loss, without adequate internal resources for emotional repair, they can become emotionally numb or cynical. Self-compassion provides a mechanism for self-soothing and emotional resilience. It allows individuals to process difficult experiences without becoming overwhelmed, to acknowledge the toll that challenging work takes, and to replenish their inner reserves. This is crucial for maintaining long-term engagement and effectiveness, ensuring that the warrior can continue to contribute without sacrificing their own well-being.

Consider the scenario of a leader who has had to deliver difficult news to their team, or make tough decisions that impact individuals. The weight of such responsibilities can be immense. Without self-compassion, the leader might carry guilt, regret, or self-blame, which can cloud judgment and undermine confidence. With self-compassion, the leader can acknowledge the difficulty of the situation, the weight of the decisions, and the inevitable emotional fallout, while still extending grace to themselves. They can recognize that they acted with the best available information and intentions, and that the outcome, while perhaps unfortunate, does not define their character. This allows them to learn from the experience and move forward with renewed clarity and purpose, rather than being bogged down by self-criticism.

Extending this to interpersonal relationships, compassion acts as a powerful lubricant. In any team or organization, friction is inevitable. Disagreements will arise, misunderstandings will occur, and individuals will bring their own unique challenges and perspectives to the collective effort. A compassionate approach fosters an environment where these differences can be navigated constructively. It encourages open communication, encourages mutual support, and builds trust. When team members feel that their struggles are understood and met with kindness, they are more likely to be open, resilient, and collaborative. This is particularly important in environments where trust and mutual reliance are paramount, such as in military units, emergency services, or high-performance teams.

The mindful warrior, therefore, cultivates compassion not as an optional add-on, but as an integral part of their operational effectiveness. It is the recognition that the human element, with all its vulnerabilities and strengths, is central to any mission. By fostering self-compassion, they build a robust inner foundation of resilience and self-acceptance. By extending compassion to others, they enhance their ability to connect, to understand, and to lead with integrity and wisdom. This dual cultivation creates a balanced warrior, one who is both strong and gentle, effective and humane, capable of navigating the complexities of action with a heart that is as finely tuned as their tactical acumen. The development of these qualities is a continuous journey, requiring consistent practice and a willingness to meet oneself and others with unwavering kindness. It is the recognition that the warrior who can face down fear and adversity is often the same warrior who can offer solace and understanding, demonstrating that true strength is interwoven with the capacity for profound and active compassion.

The battlefield, whether it is a literal zone of conflict, a corporate boardroom, or a complex personal challenge, presents a ceaseless stream of decisions. These decisions, often made under duress, can have far-reaching consequences, impacting not only the immediate situation but also the lives of individuals, the trajectory of organizations, and the broader societal landscape. In the pursuit of becoming a truly effective and ethical agent of change – a mindful warrior – the integration of contemplative practices into the very fabric of decision-making is not merely beneficial; it is essential. This subsection delves into the practice of mindful decision-making, transforming it from a reactive, often flawed, process into an act of profound wisdom born from cultivated awareness.

At its core, mindful decision-making is about fostering a deliberate pause, an intentional space between the stimulus of a situation and the response of a choice. In the heat of the moment, the default is often to react based on ingrained habits, emotional impulses, or incomplete information. This reactive mode, while sometimes necessary for rapid action, can lead to regrettable outcomes. It's the equivalent of firing a weapon without properly sighting your target or assessing the environment. Mindfulness, however, trains the warrior to create that crucial pause. It is the cultivated ability to step back, even for a fleeting moment, from the immediate urgency, to observe the unfolding situation with a clear, non-judgmental gaze. This involves recognizing the onset of a decision point, acknowledging the internal stirrings of emotion or bias, and consciously choosing to engage with the decision from a more centered and aware state.

This pause is not about inaction; it is about **informed action**. It is about moving from a position of being driven by circumstances to one of being a deliberate shaper of them. Consider a commander facing a sudden enemy maneuver. The immediate instinct might be to counter with a pre-planned defensive posture. However, a mindful approach would involve a brief scan: What is the enemy's likely objective? What are the terrain advantages or disadvantages? What are the current troop dispositions and morale? Crucially, what are my own internal reactions – is it fear driving a hasty retreat, or anger pushing for an aggressive, potentially reckless, counterattack? By consciously observing these internal and external factors, the commander can transcend the automatic response and consider a wider array of options, potentially discovering a more advantageous or less costly solution. This reflective space allows for the integration of sensory data, cognitive analysis, and emotional intelligence, leading to a more robust and strategic decision.

The process begins with **situational awareness**, but a deeper, more nuanced form than typically considered. This extends beyond merely knowing the physical layout or the enemy's disposition. It involves an awareness of the *internal landscape* as well. What biases are at play? What assumptions am I making? Am I seeing the situation clearly, or is my perception colored by past experiences, personal desires, or external pressures? This self-awareness is critical because our internal state profoundly influences how we interpret external events and, consequently, the decisions we make. For instance, a leader who is feeling insecure might misinterpret a subordinate's well-intentioned feedback as criticism, leading to a defensive and counterproductive response. Mindfulness practice cultivates the ability to recognize these internal states as they arise, allowing the decision-maker to account for them, much like accounting for windage or atmospheric conditions when aiming a rifle.

This involves developing a skill akin to **inner observation**. When faced with a decision, the mindful warrior learns to observe their own thoughts and feelings without immediate identification or judgment. Instead of thinking, "I am angry, so I must attack," the mindful approach is to notice, "I am experiencing anger. What is the source of this anger? Is it a valid response to the situation, or is it a residue of something else? How might this anger influence my potential actions?" This practice of observing thoughts and emotions as transient mental events, rather than immutable truths about oneself, creates psychological distance. This distance is vital for disengaging from habitual patterns of reactivity and opening up space for more considered deliberation. It allows for a clearer assessment of the problem, untainted by the immediate emotional charge.

Furthermore, mindful decision-making emphasizes the **consideration of broader implications**. In many high-stakes environments, decisions have ripple effects. A tactical choice on the battlefield might impact civilian populations or diplomatic relations. A business decision can affect employees, customers, and the wider economy. The contemplative practice of broadening one's perspective is invaluable here. It encourages the decision-maker to move beyond the immediate, tactical goals and consider the ethical dimensions, the long-term consequences, and the impact on all stakeholders. This requires cultivating a sense of responsibility that extends beyond oneself and one's immediate objectives. It's about asking not just, "What is the best way to achieve my goal?" but also, "What is the most ethical and beneficial way forward for everyone involved?"

This expanded awareness often involves **seeking diverse perspectives**. A truly wise decision rarely emerges from a single viewpoint. Mindfulness encourages openness to input from others, listening deeply and without prejudice to understand their insights. This means actively soliciting opinions from team members, mentors, or even those with dissenting views, and creating an environment where such contributions are valued. The ability to hold diverse viewpoints simultaneously, to weigh them without premature dismissal, and to integrate them into a coherent strategy is a hallmark of advanced decision-making. It is the strategist's understanding that the most effective plans are often forged through collaboration and the synthesis of multiple intelligences.

The practice also involves a conscious effort to **counteract cognitive biases**. Our minds are prone to numerous shortcuts and distortions that can lead to flawed judgments. Confirmation bias, for example, leads us to favor information that confirms our existing beliefs, while availability heuristic causes us to overestimate the importance of information that is easily recalled. Mindful awareness helps to identify these patterns as they are occurring. By noticing a tendency to selectively seek out information that supports a preferred course of action, or by recognizing that a vivid anecdote is unduly influencing a broader assessment, the decision-maker can take steps to mitigate these biases. This might involve actively seeking out contradictory evidence, conducting a devil's advocate role for one's own position, or grounding decisions in data rather than intuition alone.

Moreover, mindful decision-making fosters a greater capacity for **ethical reflection**. In complex situations, the right course of action is not always clear. Ethical dilemmas abound, and the pressure to compromise can be immense. A mind trained in contemplation can engage with these dilemmas with greater clarity and integrity. It allows for the examination of one's own values and principles, and for the consideration of how a potential decision aligns with them. This is not about rigid adherence to a dogma, but about a conscious and deliberate application of one's ethical framework to the practicalities of the situation. It requires an ability to sit with uncertainty, to acknowledge the potential negative consequences of any choice, and to make the best possible decision given the circumstances, while remaining true to one's core principles.

Consider the deployment of new technology in a security context. A rapid decision might focus solely on its operational advantages – enhanced surveillance, improved communication, or greater firepower. However, a mindful approach would also prompt questions about privacy implications, potential for misuse, the ethical responsibilities associated with its deployment, and the broader societal impact. This requires a deliberate stepping back from the immediate technical problem to consider the human and societal dimensions. It is the strategist's foresight, informed by a broadened ethical lens, that distinguishes a mere tactician from a truly wise leader.

The development of this capability is an ongoing process, mirroring the martial disciplines that require constant practice and refinement. It involves cultivating **patience** with oneself and the decision-making process. Rushing a decision out of impatience or a desire for immediate closure can be as detrimental as making it reactively. Mindfulness teaches the value of allowing ideas to gestate, of waiting for clarity to emerge, and of accepting that sometimes the best decision is to wait for more information or for the situation to become clearer.

This is not procrastination, but a strategic withholding of action, a deliberate cultivation of the optimal moment for intervention.

In practice, this might look like dedicating specific time for reflection before critical decisions, even if those moments are brief. It could involve structured journaling, where one articulates the problem, lists potential solutions, notes down internal reactions, and considers long-term consequences. It might involve practicing brief mindfulness exercises – such as focusing on the breath for a minute – before engaging in a difficult conversation or reviewing a complex proposal. These small, consistent practices build the capacity to access a state of mindful awareness when it is most needed.

The outcome of integrating mindfulness into decision-making is a shift from *reacting* to *responding*. A reactive response is automatic, often driven by immediate stimuli and past conditioning. A mindful response, conversely, is chosen. It is the result of a deliberate process of observation, reflection, and consideration. This allows the mindful warrior to navigate complex situations with greater wisdom, resilience, and ethical grounding. They are less likely to be derailed by unexpected challenges or to make decisions based on flawed assumptions or emotional turbulence. Instead, their choices are characterized by a considered clarity, a strategic foresight, and an underlying ethical coherence. This is the essence of wisdom born of awareness – the capacity to make sound judgments, not just because one has access to information, but because one possesses the inner clarity and discernment to process that information effectively and ethically. It is the strategist's ultimate tool, honed through the discipline of contemplation, enabling them to act with purpose and precision in an ever-changing world.

Chapter 7: Sustaining the Campaign: Long-Term Mastery and Continuous Growth

The journey of self-mastery, like any protracted campaign, demands an unwavering commitment to maintaining morale and preventing the insidious erosion of motivation. It is a truth etched into the very fabric of history, whether recounting the arduous campaigns of ancient armies or the relentless pursuit of excellence in personal or professional endeavors: endurance is often the most critical determinant of success. The initial fervor, the electrifying spark of a new objective, can carry an individual through the early stages. However, as the path lengthens, as obstacles multiply and the immediate rewards seem to recede, the insidious creep of fatigue and doubt can begin to undermine even the most resolute spirit. This is the inherent challenge of the "long war"—the sustained effort required for mastery and continuous growth.

To navigate this prolonged engagement, one must adopt strategies that mirror those employed by seasoned military leaders managing extended operations. Foremost among these is the discipline of **pace management**. Just as a force on a lengthy march cannot afford to expend all its energy in the initial days, an individual on the path of self-mastery must learn to regulate their efforts. This involves a conscious understanding of one's own energetic reserves, recognizing that pushing too hard, too early, can lead to exhaustion and a precipitous drop in performance, often necessitating a prolonged recovery period. Instead, a sustainable rhythm is key. This means developing an intuitive sense of when to exert maximum effort and when to conserve energy, when to push through discomfort and when to allow for rest and recuperation. It is a delicate balancing act, akin to a long-distance runner calibrating their stride to ensure they have the stamina for the entire race, not just the first few miles. This requires honest self-assessment and a willingness to adapt one's approach based on internal feedback. Ignoring the early signs of fatigue—the mental fog, the increased irritability, the waning enthusiasm—is akin to ignoring a battlefield wound; it will only worsen if left unattended.

Crucial to this sustainable pace is the practice of **energy management**. This extends beyond merely physical exertion. In the context of self-mastery, energy encompasses mental, emotional, and even spiritual reserves. Just as a soldier might guard their rations and maintain their equipment diligently, the mindful warrior must be equally attentive to the factors that replenish and deplete these vital energies. This involves identifying and minimizing sources of unnecessary drain. Are there relationships or commitments that consistently leave you feeling depleted? Are there thought patterns or internal dialogues that consume excessive mental bandwidth without yielding productive outcomes? Proactive identification and mitigation of these energy sinks are paramount. Conversely, it is equally important to cultivate and engage in activities that actively recharge these reserves. These are not mere indulgences but strategic investments in long-term capacity. This might include engaging in hobbies that foster a sense of flow, spending time in nature, nurturing supportive relationships, or dedicating time to contemplative practices that restore inner equilibrium. The goal is to create a virtuous cycle where effort is balanced by rejuvenation, ensuring that the capacity for sustained engagement is not compromised.

The psychological dimension of maintaining motivation over extended periods is equally critical. One of the most potent tools in this regard is the **celebration of milestones**. The human psyche is often driven by a sense of progress and accomplishment. In the absence of tangible markers of advancement, motivation can falter. Therefore, it is essential to intentionally break down the overarching campaign of self-mastery into smaller, achievable objectives. Upon reaching these intermediate goals, taking the time to acknowledge and celebrate them is not an act of vanity, but a strategic imperative. This acknowledgment can take many forms: a quiet moment of reflection on progress made, a shared acknowledgement with a trusted confidant or mentor, or a small, personally meaningful reward. These milestones serve as critical touchpoints, reinforcing the validity of the effort and providing tangible evidence of forward momentum. They are the rallying points that rekindle enthusiasm and provide the psychological impetus to press onward. Without them, the journey can begin to feel like an endless, unrewarded slog, a perception that can quickly extinguish the flames of dedication.

Furthermore, the practice of **reframing challenges as opportunities for growth** is indispensable. In any long-term endeavor, setbacks are inevitable. The difference between those who persevere and those who falter often lies in their perception of these adversities. Instead of viewing obstacles as insurmountable barriers or definitive failures, the mindful warrior learns to see them as valuable data points, as opportunities to refine their strategy, deepen their understanding, or strengthen their resilience. This requires a shift in mindset, moving from a fixed perspective that sees failure as a permanent state to a growth-oriented mindset that embraces challenges as integral to the learning process. When a particular approach fails to yield the desired results, it is an invitation to analyze what went wrong, to adapt the strategy, and to try again with newfound knowledge. This iterative process of trial, error, and adaptation is the very essence of mastery. It is through confronting difficulties, analyzing them objectively, and learning from them that one truly builds the robust capacity required for sustained achievement. Each challenge overcome becomes a testament to one's growing strength and adaptability, further fueling the motivation to continue.

Drawing parallels from military history, consider the logistical and psychological demands placed upon soldiers during protracted campaigns. Victories, even minor ones, were amplified and commemorated to maintain troop morale. Rations, though often meager, were meticulously managed to ensure sustenance. Downtime, though limited, was utilized for rest, repair, and mental recalibration. These were not mere incidental factors but fundamental elements of strategic planning for sustained operations. Similarly, the pursuit of self-mastery requires a disciplined approach to managing one's own resources—physical energy, mental focus, and emotional resilience—with the same level of strategic foresight.

The concept of **revisiting core motivations** also plays a pivotal role in sustaining effort over the long haul. As the demands of the campaign continue, it is natural for the initial impetus to fade or become obscured by the day-to-day grind. Therefore, periodically returning to the fundamental "why" behind the pursuit is essential. What was the initial vision that sparked this journey? What values are being honored or expressed through this commitment? What ultimate purpose does this effort serve? Engaging in practices that reconnect one with these core drivers can be incredibly powerful. This might involve journaling about one's long-term aspirations, visualizing the desired future state, or engaging in conversations with mentors or peers who can help remind you of your original intentions. When the path becomes arduous, remembering the foundational reasons for embarking on it can provide the strength to endure. It transforms the effort from a series of disconnected tasks into a meaningful, purposeful endeavor.

Moreover, the cultivation of **patience and self-compassion** is crucial. The "long war" of self-mastery is not a race against others, but a deeply personal journey of development. There will be times when progress feels frustratingly slow, when plateaus seem to stretch on indefinitely, or when old habits resurface with surprising tenacity. In these moments, self-criticism can be a significant demotivator. Instead, adopting a stance of self-compassion—understanding that imperfection and struggle are inherent parts of the human experience—is vital. This does not mean abandoning standards or lowering expectations, but rather approaching oneself with the same kindness and understanding one would offer a close friend facing similar challenges. This approach fosters a more resilient and forgiving mindset, allowing for setbacks to be processed constructively rather than allowing them to derail the entire endeavor. Patience, in this context, is the understanding that mastery is a process that unfolds over time, not an overnight transformation. It is the ability to remain committed to the journey, even when the destination is not yet clearly visible.

The application of these principles can be observed in individuals who have achieved profound mastery in various fields. Consider the dedication of a classical musician who practices scales and arpeggios for hours daily, even after decades of performing. Their motivation is not solely the pursuit of the next performance, but a deep-seated love for the craft, a commitment to continuous refinement, and an understanding that even the most accomplished artist benefits from consistent, disciplined practice. Similarly, a scientist dedicating years to research, facing numerous failed experiments, is driven by a profound curiosity and a belief in the ultimate value of their discoveries, even if those discoveries are hard-won and take years to materialize. They understand that the "long war" against the unknown requires sustained effort, punctuated by small victories and lessons learned from every setback.

Ultimately, sustaining motivation and preventing burnout in the long campaign of self-mastery hinges on a strategic, mindful, and compassionate approach. It requires recognizing that this is not a sprint but a marathon, demanding careful pacing, diligent energy management, the intentional celebration of progress, a resilient mindset that reframes challenges, a clear connection to one's core motivations, and a healthy dose of patience and self-kindness. By integrating these principles, the aspiring individual can transform the arduous journey into a sustainable and ultimately rewarding expedition, ensuring that the pursuit of growth and mastery endures.

The strategic advantage of cultivating a robust support network cannot be overstated when undertaking any long-term campaign, especially one as intricate and demanding as self-mastery. While the preceding discussions have focused on internal disciplines—pace management, energy regulation, and the psychology of sustained motivation—the external dimension of support is equally critical. A lone warrior, however skilled or determined, operates at a significant disadvantage. Conversely, a unit that trusts and relies upon its comrades possesses a force multiplier that can overcome seemingly insurmountable odds. In the context of personal growth, these comrades are our allies, forming a vital network that provides encouragement, accountability, and the invaluable benefit of diverse perspectives.

The genesis of a strong support network lies in identifying potential allies. These are individuals who, by nature or by circumstance, resonate with your aspirations and demonstrate a capacity for genuine engagement. They might be friends who cheer your successes and offer solace during your stumbles, family members who believe in your potential even when you doubt it, or colleagues who share similar professional ambitions and understand the unique pressures you face. Beyond these familiar circles, allies can also emerge from unexpected places: fellow participants in a workshop, members of a shared interest group, or even individuals encountered through online communities who exhibit a spirit of mutual upliftment. The key is to look for those who exhibit not only a willingness to listen but also the capacity to offer constructive feedback and empathetic support. These are individuals who can see your strengths even when you are bogged down by your weaknesses, and who are invested in your growth beyond mere superficial encouragement. They are the ones who will challenge your assumptions, question your limiting beliefs, and gently steer you back onto your intended course when you stray.

Cultivating these relationships requires deliberate effort and a genuine investment of time and emotional energy. It is a reciprocal endeavor; just as you seek support, you must also be prepared to offer it. This means being present for your allies, celebrating their victories with as much enthusiasm as you hope for your own, and extending a helping hand when they face their own challenges. Active listening is a cornerstone of this cultivation. When an ally shares their struggles or aspirations, offer your undivided attention. Ask clarifying questions, validate their feelings, and refrain from immediately jumping in with unsolicited advice unless it is explicitly sought. This fosters a sense of trust and mutual respect, building the foundation for deeper connection. Furthermore, transparency and vulnerability can act as powerful bonding agents. Sharing your own journey, including your doubts and setbacks, can create an environment where others feel safe to do the same, deepening the sense of shared experience and collective effort.

The strategic value of this network becomes acutely apparent when confronting the inevitable blind spots that accompany any pursuit of mastery. Our own perspectives, while often deeply held, are inherently limited. We may be so engrossed in a particular approach or so convinced of our own understanding that we fail to see alternative pathways or recognize detrimental patterns in our behavior. Allies, possessing different vantage points, can illuminate these obscured areas. A friend might observe a recurring behavioral pattern that is hindering your progress, a pattern you yourself have overlooked. A mentor might offer a strategic insight born from their own experience, an insight that could dramatically alter the trajectory of your efforts. This exchange of perspectives is not about criticism; it is about collective problem-solving and shared wisdom. When you can present a challenge or a plateau to your network, you are essentially crowdsourcing solutions, tapping into a collective intelligence that is far greater than your own isolated capacity.

Accountability is another crucial function of a robust support network. In the long campaign of self-mastery, the temptation to relax, to procrastinate, or to revert to comfortable, albeit less effective, habits can be immense. Allies can serve as the external anchors that keep you tethered to your commitments. This is not about external pressure in a negative sense, but about the shared understanding and commitment to progress. Setting clear, agreed-upon goals with trusted allies—whether it's a weekly learning objective, a fitness target, or a deadline for a creative project—creates a framework of mutual accountability. Knowing that someone else is aware of your goals and will likely inquire about your progress can be a powerful motivator. This can be structured through regular check-ins, shared progress reports, or simply a commitment to be honest with each other about adherence to plans. The psychological impact of this shared commitment is significant; it transforms a personal endeavor into a shared mission, where your progress reflects not only on yourself but also on the trust placed in you by your allies.

Moreover, a diverse support network offers a rich tapestry of experiences and viewpoints that can significantly enhance the learning process. If your network consists solely of individuals who think and act precisely like you, you will likely receive affirmation but little genuine challenge or novel perspective. A truly effective network is comprised of individuals with varied backgrounds, skill sets, and life experiences. This diversity ensures that you are exposed to a wider range of ideas, potential solutions, and critical analyses. For instance, an engineer might approach a problem with a systematic, analytical mindset, while an artist might bring a more intuitive, creative perspective. A seasoned entrepreneur might offer insights into risk management that a novice might not consider. By actively seeking out and engaging with individuals who represent different facets of human experience and expertise, you broaden your own understanding and capacity for innovation. This is akin to a military commander seeking counsel from specialists in logistics, intelligence, and communications; each brings a unique and vital contribution to the overall strategic picture.

The act of nurturing these relationships also fosters a sense of shared purpose, which can be incredibly fortifying during difficult times. When you are part of a community of individuals striving for growth and betterment, there is a collective energy that can propel you forward. This shared purpose can manifest in various ways: collaborative learning projects, mutual encouragement during challenging phases, or even simply the shared understanding that each of you is engaged in a meaningful pursuit. This sense of belonging and shared endeavor combats the isolation that can often accompany the solitary pursuit of mastery. It reinforces the idea that you are not alone in your struggles or your aspirations, and that your efforts contribute to a larger, positive movement. This communal aspect can re-energize flagging spirits and provide the resilience needed to overcome setbacks. It is the shared camaraderie of soldiers on a long campaign, knowing they are fighting for a common cause and supporting each other through the trials.

When identifying potential allies, it is important to assess not just their positive attributes but also their capacity for constructive feedback. Not everyone who offers support does so effectively. Some may be overly effusive, providing encouragement without critical insight, while others may be overly critical, offering negativity without balanced support. The ideal allies are those who can offer both encouragement and astute observation, who can celebrate your successes while also gently pointing out areas for improvement. This requires discerning individuals who are emotionally intelligent and possess the ability to communicate feedback with tact and respect. Learning to receive such feedback gracefully is equally important. Resist the urge to become defensive. Instead, view constructive criticism as a gift—an opportunity to refine your approach and accelerate your growth. Ask clarifying questions, consider the feedback objectively, and thank the individual for their insight, even if it is initially difficult to hear.

The process of building and maintaining this network is an ongoing one, requiring continuous effort and attention. It is not a static structure but a dynamic ecosystem that thrives on consistent engagement. Regularly scheduled touchpoints, whether they are informal coffee meetings, structured accountability check-ins, or simply periodic calls, are essential for keeping the lines of communication open and the relationships strong. It also involves being attuned to the needs of your network. Sometimes, an ally might be going through a particularly challenging period and will require more support. Being there for them, offering practical assistance or simply a listening ear, strengthens the bonds of reciprocity. This commitment to mutual support ensures that the network remains a vibrant and reliable resource for everyone involved.

Furthermore, leveraging your network effectively involves understanding its collective strengths and weaknesses. If you identify a gap in your own knowledge or skills, consider which ally might be best positioned to offer guidance or collaboration in that specific area. Similarly, when an ally faces a challenge that aligns with your own expertise, proactively offer your assistance. This strategic utilization of the network maximizes its benefits for all members. It's about recognizing that each person in your network brings unique value, and the art of effective support lies in knowing how and when to tap into that value, and when to offer your own.

In essence, building a support network is not merely a helpful adjunct to the journey of self-mastery; it is a fundamental strategic imperative. It transforms the often solitary and arduous path into a collaborative expedition, where shared encouragement, mutual accountability, and diverse perspectives serve as powerful engines for progress. By consciously identifying, cultivating, and leveraging these alliances, individuals can not only enhance their resilience and accelerate their growth but also discover the profound satisfaction that comes from pursuing mastery in the company of trusted comrades. This network becomes a vital resource, a source of strength, and a testament to the power of human connection in the pursuit of personal excellence.

The pursuit of mastery is not a destination to be reached, but rather an ever-evolving landscape, a continuous expedition into the uncharted territories of knowledge and skill. To assume that one has arrived, that the learning has ceased, is to invite stagnation and obsolescence. In the grand campaign of self-development, the most significant strategic advantage lies in embracing the unwavering commitment to continuous learning. This is the unending frontier, a realm where intellectual curiosity serves as our primary reconnaissance tool, constantly seeking new information, refining existing understanding, and adapting to the inevitable shifts in the operational environment. It is the recognition that mastery is not a static achievement, but a dynamic process, a perpetual state of becoming.

This mindset of perpetual learning is rooted in a deep understanding of the nature of knowledge itself. Knowledge is not a finite resource that can be fully acquired and then set aside. Instead, it is a vast, interconnected web, constantly expanding and reconfiguring itself. Fields of study evolve, new technologies emerge, and societal understanding shifts. To remain relevant, to continue to grow, we must actively engage with this dynamism. This requires more than passive consumption of information; it demands an active, intentional process of acquisition, synthesis, and application. It means cultivating an insatiable appetite for understanding, a drive to explore beyond the superficial, and a willingness to challenge our own preconceived notions. This intellectual hunger is the fuel that propels the lifelong learner forward, ensuring that the campaign for mastery never truly ends.

Effective learning strategies are the tactical tools that facilitate this ongoing acquisition of knowledge. While innate intelligence plays a role, it is the deliberate cultivation of effective learning methodologies that truly unlocks potential. One fundamental strategy is the principle of spaced repetition, a technique that leverages the natural forgetting curve of the human brain. By revisiting information at increasing intervals, we strengthen the neural pathways associated with that knowledge, moving it from short-term recall to long-term retention. This is particularly potent for factual knowledge, definitions, and foundational concepts. Imagine preparing for a complex certification exam or attempting to master a new language; consistent, spaced review of vocabulary, grammar rules, and core principles will yield far more robust and enduring results than cramming. This method transforms passive memorization into an active engagement with the material, building a solid bedrock of understanding.

Beyond rote memorization, active recall is another cornerstone of effective learning. Instead of passively rereading notes or textbooks, learners are encouraged to actively retrieve information from memory. This can be achieved through self-quizzing, flashcards, or even simply trying to explain a concept to oneself without referring to external aids. The effort involved in retrieving information strengthens its encoding in the brain, making it more accessible later. For instance, after reading a chapter on strategic planning, an individual might close the book and attempt to outline the key phases, identify the essential components of each phase, and recall the primary challenges associated with its implementation. This active retrieval process reveals knowledge gaps far more effectively than simply assuming comprehension after a single reading. It forces engagement at a deeper cognitive level, solidifying understanding and identifying areas requiring further attention.

Furthermore, the power of teaching and explaining concepts to others cannot be overstated as a learning accelerator. When we are tasked with articulating a complex idea to someone else, we are compelled to organize our thoughts, simplify intricate details, and identify the most critical elements. This process, often referred to as the protégé effect, forces us to confront any fuzziness in our own understanding. If you're learning a new software application, attempting to guide a colleague through its features, you'll quickly discover which steps you haven't fully internalized or which nuances you've overlooked. This act of explanation serves as a powerful form of self-assessment and reinforces learning through the act of communication. It transforms the learner from a passive recipient into an active disseminator, solidifying their own grasp of the subject matter.

The importance of staying updated in one's field or area of interest is paramount in maintaining relevance and fostering growth. The pace of change in most professional domains and areas of intellectual pursuit is relentless. Technologies evolve, best practices are refined, and new research constantly emerges. To remain a practitioner or an informed individual in any given area requires a conscious effort to remain current. This might involve subscribing to industry journals, following thought leaders on professional platforms, attending webinars, or participating in relevant conferences. For example, a software developer must keep abreast of new programming languages, frameworks, and security protocols. A financial analyst needs to monitor economic indicators, regulatory changes, and emerging investment strategies. Failing to do so is akin to a military unit relying on outdated maps and obsolete equipment; it leads to strategic disadvantages and potential operational failure.

Integrating new information into existing frameworks is the crucial next step after acquiring knowledge. Information rarely exists in isolation. Our minds are sophisticated networks of interconnected concepts and experiences. The true power of learning lies in our ability to connect new insights with what we already know, creating a richer, more nuanced understanding. This process of synthesis involves identifying how new data aligns with, contradicts, or expands upon existing mental models. It's about building bridges between disparate pieces of information, forming a cohesive and comprehensive picture. For instance, if one has a foundational understanding of project management principles, learning about agile methodologies involves not just memorizing new terms like sprints and backlogs, but understanding how these concepts adapt or offer alternatives to traditional waterfall approaches. This integration allows for more sophisticated problem-solving and strategic decision-making.

This integration is often facilitated through critical thinking. Critical thinking involves analyzing information objectively, evaluating its credibility, identifying biases, and understanding its implications. It's the intellectual rigor that allows us to discern valuable insights from noise. When presented with new research, a critical thinker will question the methodology, consider the sample size, and evaluate the conclusions in the context of existing knowledge. They will not accept information at face value but will engage with it, dissecting it to understand its underlying assumptions and potential impact. This disciplined approach ensures that the knowledge we acquire is robust, reliable, and genuinely useful. It prevents the haphazard accumulation of facts without a coherent structure, ensuring that our learning contributes to true mastery.

Adaptability is a direct outcome of a well-honed continuous learning mindset. In a world characterized by flux, the ability to adapt is not merely advantageous; it is essential for survival and success. When individuals and organizations commit to learning, they are, by definition, preparing themselves for change. They are building the mental agility to respond to new challenges, embrace new opportunities, and pivot when necessary. Consider the rapid advancements in artificial intelligence. Those who actively learn about its capabilities, ethical implications, and potential applications are far better equipped to navigate its integration into their work and lives than those who ignore it. This proactive engagement with emerging trends, driven by a learning imperative, fosters resilience and ensures that individuals remain not just relevant, but also at the forefront of their respective fields.

To foster this spirit of continuous learning, it is beneficial to actively seek out diverse learning environments and approaches. While formal education provides a structured foundation, informal learning opportunities are equally, if not more, important for ongoing growth. This can include reading widely across different disciplines, engaging in mentorship relationships, participating in online courses, listening to podcasts, or even learning a new practical skill like gardening or woodworking. Each of these experiences offers unique perspectives and develops different cognitive abilities. For example, learning a musical instrument not only enhances auditory processing and fine motor skills but also instills discipline and patience – traits invaluable in any long-term pursuit. Similarly, engaging with literature from different cultures can broaden one's understanding of human experience and offer novel insights into social dynamics.

The integration of new information into existing frameworks can also be viewed through a strategic lens, akin to intelligence gathering and analysis in a military campaign. New intelligence (information) must be processed, cross-referenced with existing intelligence (prior knowledge), and then analyzed to inform strategic decisions (actions and future learning). This requires a structured approach. One effective technique is concept mapping, where key ideas are visually represented and connected, illustrating relationships and hierarchies. This helps in understanding the architecture of a subject and how new elements fit into the overall structure. Another method is the use of analogies and metaphors, which can bridge the gap between unfamiliar concepts and existing understanding, making complex ideas more accessible and memorable.

Furthermore, cultivating intellectual humility is intrinsically linked to the commitment to continuous learning. Intellectual humility is the recognition that one's knowledge is limited and that there is always more to learn. It is the antidote to intellectual arrogance, which can blind individuals to new information and opportunities for growth. A truly humble learner approaches new information with an open mind, willing to be corrected or to revise their understanding. They are less likely to dismiss opposing viewpoints and more inclined to engage in respectful dialogue. This open-mindedness is a fertile ground for learning, allowing new seeds of knowledge to take root and flourish. Without it, even the most diligent learner can find their progress stalled by the walls of their own ego.

The practical application of learned knowledge is the ultimate test of its efficacy and a vital part of the learning cycle. Knowledge that remains theoretical and is never put into practice risks becoming inert. Applying new skills and insights in real-world scenarios allows for testing, refinement, and deeper understanding. If one has learned about effective communication techniques, the true learning occurs when those techniques are employed in a difficult conversation, a team meeting, or a client presentation. The feedback received from these practical applications – the observed reactions, the outcomes achieved – provides invaluable data for further learning and adjustment. This iterative process of learning, applying, and reflecting is the engine of true mastery. It ensures that knowledge is not just acquired but internalized and made actionable.

Moreover, to truly embrace continuous learning, one must cultivate a habit of reflection. Regularly setting aside time to think about what has been learned, how it has been applied, and what insights have been gained is crucial. This reflection can take many forms: journaling, meditation, or simply quiet contemplation. It's in these moments of introspection that connections are made, patterns are identified, and deeper understanding emerges. For instance, after a challenging project, reflecting on what went well, what could have been done differently, and what new skills were acquired provides a roadmap for future improvement. This meta-cognitive practice – thinking about one's own thinking and learning – is a powerful tool for optimizing the entire process.

The landscape of knowledge is not static; it is a dynamic battlefield where new information constantly skirmishes with outdated paradigms. To remain a master strategist in this environment, one must adopt the posture of a perpetual student, an explorer of the intellectual frontier. This involves actively seeking out new information through diverse channels, diligently applying effective learning strategies to absorb and retain that information, and critically integrating it into one's existing understanding. The ultimate goal is not just to acquire knowledge, but to cultivate the mental agility, adaptability, and intellectual humility that characterize a truly masterful mind. This commitment to continuous learning is not merely a component of the campaign for self-mastery; it is its very essence, the unending process that ensures growth, relevance, and enduring excellence. It is the perpetual reconnaissance and engagement on the frontier of knowledge, ensuring that our strategic advantage is never compromised by the passage of time or the evolution of the world around us.

The pursuit of mastery, often perceived as a solitary quest for individual excellence, transcends the boundaries of personal achievement to become a powerful catalyst for broader impact and a lasting legacy. As we navigate the intricate pathways of self-development, a crucial inflection point arrives when our honed skills and expanded understanding can be leveraged for purposes far exceeding our immediate needs. This is the moment we transition from mastering for ourselves to mastering for a greater purpose, transforming our personal campaigns into endeavors that resonate beyond our own lives and contribute meaningfully to the collective. It's a strategic shift in perspective, recognizing that the discipline, resilience, and insight cultivated through mastery are potent tools for positive change in the world around us.

At its core, this elevated stage of mastery is driven by a profound connection to one's values. What truly matters? What principles guide our decisions and shape our aspirations? Understanding these fundamental values is the bedrock upon which a meaningful legacy is built. When our pursuit of mastery is aligned with deeply held beliefs – be it integrity, compassion, innovation, or service – our efforts gain an intrinsic motivation that fuels sustained engagement. This alignment ensures that the energy and focus we direct towards skill development are not merely for the sake of proficiency, but for the sake of advancing something we believe in. For instance, an individual mastering the intricacies of sustainable agriculture might be driven by a core value of environmental stewardship. Their mastery, therefore, is not just about growing healthier crops, but about contributing to a more sustainable planet for future generations. This conscious linking of skill acquisition with core values transforms the practice of mastery into a purposeful act of contribution.

The impact of mastery naturally extends to our immediate circles – our families, friends, and colleagues. When we embody the principles of continuous learning, discipline, and strategic thinking in our personal lives, we become living examples of what is possible. This influence can be subtle yet profound, inspiring those around us to pursue their own growth and to consider the broader implications of their actions. A parent who consistently demonstrates a commitment to learning and self-improvement, for example, can instill a similar value in their children, shaping their approach to education and personal challenges. Similarly, a leader in a professional setting who champions a culture of learning and empowers their team to develop new skills fosters an environment where collective growth and innovation can flourish. This ripple effect, initiated by personal mastery, is the initial outward projection of our influence.

Beyond these immediate spheres, the aspiration to contribute to a larger purpose beckons. This might manifest in various forms, from community involvement and social entrepreneurship to advancing knowledge in a particular field or advocating for important causes.

The skills and insights gained through mastery provide the necessary foundation to engage effectively in these endeavors. A skilled communicator, for instance, can amplify the message of a non-profit organization, raising awareness and mobilizing support. An individual who has mastered data analysis can apply their expertise to understand and address complex societal issues, such as public health or economic inequality. The key here is to identify how our unique capabilities can best serve the needs of a community or a cause larger than ourselves. It involves looking outward and discerning where our honed abilities can make the most significant difference.

Consider the strategic deployment of expertise. Just as a military commander deploys forces to achieve specific objectives, an individual committed to a greater purpose strategically deploys their mastered skills. This requires identifying the most pressing needs and challenges within a chosen area of impact and then devising plans to address them. For example, a master carpenter might volunteer their skills to rebuild homes in a disaster-stricken area, or a seasoned educator might mentor aspiring teachers in underserved communities. These actions are not mere acts of charity; they are strategic applications of expertise, leveraging honed abilities for maximum positive effect. The planning and execution involved in such endeavors mirror the strategic thinking required in any complex campaign, emphasizing the need for foresight, resourcefulness, and adaptability.

The concept of legacy is intrinsically linked to enduring impact. A legacy is not solely about what we accumulate during our lifetime, but about what we leave behind – the positive changes we facilitate, the knowledge we impart, and the inspiration we provide. When our mastery is directed towards a greater purpose, we are actively shaping the future, leaving an indelible mark on the world. This could involve contributing to scientific discovery, advancing artistic expression, fostering social justice, or nurturing the growth of future generations. Each of these contributions, born from a commitment to mastery aligned with purpose, creates a lasting testament to a life well-lived and a campaign well-fought. The impact may not always be grand or widely recognized, but its value lies in its authenticity and its contribution to a more positive trajectory.

Living a life of meaningful contribution also involves a continuous process of recalibration and refinement. As we engage with the world and apply our mastered skills, we gain new insights and encounter new challenges. This feedback loop is essential for ensuring that our efforts remain relevant and effective. It requires a willingness to learn from our experiences, to adapt our strategies, and to remain open to new perspectives. For example, an entrepreneur who has mastered the art of business development might find that their initial business model needs to evolve to meet changing market demands or societal expectations. This adaptability, fueled by a commitment to their larger purpose, allows their impact to endure and adapt over time, ensuring that their contribution remains significant.

The inner drive for mastery, when connected to a greater purpose, becomes a potent force for good. It transforms the pursuit of personal excellence into an outward-reaching mission. The discipline cultivated through rigorous practice becomes the discipline required to persevere through complex social challenges. The strategic thinking honed in skill development becomes the strategic thinking needed to navigate intricate systems for positive change. The resilience built through overcoming personal learning plateaus becomes the resilience required to face systemic obstacles. This is the essence of mastering for a greater purpose: utilizing the full spectrum of our developed capabilities not just for our own advancement, but for the betterment of the world around us.

Furthermore, the act of sharing our mastery amplifies its reach and impact. When we are willing to teach, mentor, and guide others, we empower them to achieve their own potential and contribute to their own chosen purposes. This can take the form of formal instruction, informal mentorship, or simply leading by example. The knowledge and skills that might have remained concentrated within an individual are disseminated, creating a multiplier effect that extends our influence far beyond our direct involvement. Imagine a master craftsman who takes on apprentices, not only teaching them their trade but also imparting the values of dedication and craftsmanship. This act of knowledge transfer ensures that the skills and ethos of mastery are perpetuated, benefiting future generations and the craft itself.

The process of identifying this greater purpose is as much a journey of self-discovery as it is an outward-looking assessment. It requires introspection into what ignites our passion, what problems we feel compelled to solve, and what kind of world we wish to help create. This internal compass, guided by values and aspirations, points us towards opportunities for meaningful contribution. It's about recognizing that our unique talents and developed skills are gifts that can be shared to enrich the lives of others and to advance collective goals. The synergy between personal mastery and a sense of purpose creates a powerful momentum, driving individuals to greater heights of achievement and impact.

Ultimately, a life dedicated to mastering for a greater purpose is a life of profound fulfillment. It is the recognition that true excellence is not just about personal accomplishment, but about making a positive difference. The challenges encountered in pursuing such a purpose are often greater, demanding more of our resolve and ingenuity. Yet, the rewards are immeasurably richer. The satisfaction derived from seeing one's skills contribute to a meaningful outcome, from empowering others, and from leaving a positive legacy far surpasses the fulfillment of mere individual achievement. It is the realization that our campaign for mastery has become a force for good, a testament to the power of human potential when directed towards a noble cause, ensuring that our efforts echo long after we are gone. This is the ultimate strategic victory: mastery applied not just for proficiency, but for profound and lasting positive impact.

The journey toward mastery, when pursued with intention and dedication, invariably leads to a pivotal realization: the profound value inherent in imparting that cultivated wisdom to others. This is not merely an act of generosity; it is a strategic imperative for the enduring impact of any discipline, movement, or body of knowledge. It signifies the maturation of the master, transitioning from the solitary pursuit of personal excellence to becoming a conduit for the perpetuation and evolution of that excellence. The lessons learned, the obstacles overcome, and the insights gleaned through years of dedicated practice are not meant to be hoarded but shared, acting as a vital catalyst for the growth of those who will follow. This phase represents the ultimate fulfillment of the mastery campaign, where one's own development becomes the foundation for empowering the development of others, thereby extending the reach and reinforcing the legacy of the mastered craft.

At the heart of this endeavor lies the art and science of mentorship. Effective mentorship is far more than simply dispensing advice; it is a dynamic process of guiding, supporting, and challenging another individual to unlock their own potential and navigate their unique path to mastery. A mentor acts as a seasoned guide, one who has traversed the challenging terrain and can illuminate the pitfalls and shortcuts, not by dictating the route, but by helping the mentee discover their own optimal course. This requires a deep understanding of the mentee's current capabilities, their aspirations, and their learning style. It involves active listening, asking probing questions that encourage critical thinking, and providing constructive feedback that fosters growth without stifling initiative. A true mentor cultivates autonomy, equipping their mentee with the tools and confidence to eventually surpass their guide. Consider, for instance, the development of a skilled artisan. A master sculptor might not simply demonstrate the precise angle for striking a chisel, but rather explain the principles of stone grain, the physics of impact, and the artistic intention behind each cut, allowing the apprentice to internalize these concepts and apply them with their own emerging understanding. This transfer of knowledge is nuanced, focusing on the 'why' behind the 'how,' fostering a deeper, more intuitive grasp of the craft.

The principles of effective mentorship are deeply rooted in empathy and a genuine belief in the mentee's capacity for growth. A mentor must be willing to invest their time and energy, recognizing that the development of another is a worthy investment that yields returns far beyond their immediate personal gain. This often involves sharing personal experiences, including failures and setbacks, which can be invaluable learning opportunities for the mentee. Vulnerability and authenticity build trust, creating a safe space for the mentee to experiment, take risks, and learn from inevitable mistakes. This relational aspect of mentorship is as crucial as the technical or strategic knowledge being transferred. It is about building a partnership, fostering a collaborative environment where both mentor and mentee learn and grow. Think of the military strategist who trains junior officers. While the technical aspects of battlefield command are paramount, the mentor also imparts the values of leadership, the ethical considerations of decision-making under pressure, and the importance of caring for one's troops. These intangible elements are often learned through observation, dialogue, and the mentor's own lived example.

Teaching, in its most impactful form, is an extension of mentorship, focusing on the systematic transmission of knowledge and skills. It requires a mastery of not only the subject matter but also of pedagogical principles. An effective teacher understands that learning is not a passive reception of information but an active process of construction. This means designing learning experiences that are engaging, relevant, and challenging, catering to different learning styles and paces. It involves breaking down complex concepts into digestible components, providing opportunities for practice and application, and creating mechanisms for assessing understanding and providing feedback. The teacher, much like the mentor, must be adept at diagnosing learning needs and tailoring their approach accordingly. The digital age has further democratized the forms of teaching, with online courses, webinars, and digital tutorials becoming powerful tools for disseminating expertise globally. However, the core principles remain: clarity, engagement, practice, and feedback. A seasoned programmer, for example, might not only teach the syntax of a new language but also explain the underlying architectural principles, the common design patterns, and the best practices for writing efficient and maintainable code, thereby equipping their students with a holistic understanding.

Furthermore, the process of teaching itself can serve as a powerful reinforcement of the teacher's own mastery. The act of articulating complex ideas, anticipating student questions, and explaining concepts from multiple perspectives forces a deeper engagement with the material. It compels the teacher to refine their understanding, identify gaps in their own knowledge, and develop new ways of conceptualizing the subject. This symbiotic relationship between teaching and learning is a hallmark of continuous growth. The master who teaches often finds their own mastery deepening, their insights sharpened by the questions and challenges posed by their students. This iterative process of instruction and learning creates a virtuous cycle, elevating both the teacher and the learner.

Beyond formal teaching and mentorship, there is the broader concept of inspiring through example. Often, the most profound lessons are learned not through direct instruction but through observation and emulation. Masters who embody the principles they espouse – integrity, dedication, resilience, and a passion for learning – serve as powerful role models. Their commitment to their craft, their consistent pursuit of excellence, and their ethical conduct create an inspiring narrative that can motivate others to strive for similar standards. This is particularly potent in leadership roles, where the leader's behavior sets the tone for an entire organization or community. A leader who demonstrates unwavering commitment to a vision, even in the face of adversity, can inspire loyalty, dedication, and a collective drive towards achieving shared goals. This inspirational influence is often subtle, woven into the fabric of daily interactions, yet its impact can be immense.

The fulfillment derived from contributing to the growth and mastery of others is a unique and deeply rewarding aspect of the mastery journey. It is a transcendence of ego, a recognition that one's own success is amplified when it contributes to the success of others. This fulfillment stems from witnessing the spark of understanding ignite in a mentee's eyes, seeing a student overcome a difficult challenge, or observing a protégé apply lessons learned to achieve their own significant goals. It is the realization that one's efforts have a ripple effect, extending influence and impact far beyond what would be possible in isolation. This sense of contributing to something larger than oneself, of perpetuating a tradition of excellence, and of nurturing future generations of practitioners is a profound source of satisfaction. It is the ultimate validation of one's own mastery – the ability to effectively transfer that mastery, ensuring its continuity and evolution.

This contribution to the growth of others also necessitates a commitment to nurturing environments conducive to learning and development. This might involve creating formal training programs, establishing communities of practice, or simply fostering a culture of continuous learning within one's sphere of influence. It requires recognizing that different individuals learn and grow at different rates and in different ways, and therefore, a flexible and adaptable approach is essential. Providing access to resources, opportunities for experimentation, and constructive feedback are all crucial elements in cultivating a fertile ground for mastery to flourish in others.

The legacy of a master is not solely defined by their individual achievements but by the enduring impact they have on the collective body of knowledge and practice they inhabit. By effectively sharing their wisdom, mentoring aspiring practitioners, and inspiring new generations, they ensure that their contribution transcends their own lifetime. This act of passing on wisdom is a strategic imperative for the long-term health and evolution of any field. It is the continuation of the campaign, not through direct personal engagement, but through the empowerment of others to carry the banner forward. The master, having completed their individual campaign, becomes the architect of future campaigns, laying the groundwork and providing the essential guidance for those who will build upon their foundation. This final phase of mastery is, therefore, the most impactful, as it ensures that the pursuit of excellence continues, adapted and enhanced by each successive generation, a testament to the enduring power of shared knowledge and inspired growth.

Chapter 8: The Integrated Self: Living a Life of Purpose and Mastery

The pursuit of mastery, as we have explored, is a multifaceted journey. It encompasses not only the disciplined refinement of skills and the strategic application of knowledge but also a profound inner cultivation. It is here, at the nexus of inner awareness and outer action, that the seemingly disparate disciplines of strategic thinking, honed through centuries of military doctrine, and mindfulness, rooted in contemplative traditions, reveal their profound synergy. Far from being opposing forces, these two domains act as complementary pillars, supporting a robust and integrated approach to navigating life's complexities and achieving a state of balanced mastery.

Military strategy, at its core, is about anticipating challenges, assessing capabilities, and formulating plans to achieve objectives. It demands foresight, meticulous preparation, and the ability to adapt to dynamic environments. This requires a clear understanding of one's own strengths and weaknesses, as well as those of adversaries or competing forces. It involves scenario planning, risk assessment, and the development of contingencies – all exercises in projecting oneself into future possibilities and making informed decisions in the present. Think of the meticulous planning that precedes a complex military operation. Every variable is considered: terrain, weather, enemy disposition, logistical support, and the potential for unforeseen events. This structured approach to problem-solving cultivates a mental discipline that prioritizes clarity, logic, and a comprehensive understanding of the operational landscape. It instills a habit of thinking ahead, of analyzing cause and effect, and of developing a coherent, actionable plan. This strategic mindset is invaluable in any domain, equipping individuals with the mental architecture to break down large goals into manageable steps, identify potential obstacles, and chart a course towards desired outcomes.

However, the most brilliant strategy is rendered ineffective if it cannot be executed with precision and adaptability in the face of real-world friction. This is where mindfulness enters as a critical enabler. Mindfulness, the practice of paying attention to the present moment non-judgmentally, cultivates a heightened awareness of one's internal and external environment. It allows for a deeper understanding of one's own thought processes, emotional states, and physical sensations. In a strategic context, this translates to an enhanced ability to remain calm and focused under pressure, to observe unfolding situations with clarity, and to respond effectively rather than react impulsively. Consider the battlefield commander whose meticulous plan encounters an unexpected enemy maneuver. A strategically minded individual might have anticipated such a possibility, but it is the mindful practitioner who can remain centered amidst the chaos, accurately assess the new reality, and adjust their plan without succumbing to panic or rigid adherence to the original course. This present-moment awareness allows for a more nuanced interpretation of events, enabling the strategic mind to pivot and adapt with agility.

The integration of these two disciplines creates a powerful feedback loop. Strategic planning provides the framework and direction, ensuring that efforts are purposeful and aligned with overarching goals. Mindfulness, in turn, provides the clarity and presence of mind necessary to navigate the complexities of execution. A strategic plan can outline the ideal path, but mindfulness allows one to recognize when the path deviates and to make the necessary course corrections. This interplay is not merely about efficiency; it is about resilience. When faced with setbacks, a strategist might analyze what went wrong and revise the plan. A mindful individual, however, can also observe their own emotional response to the setback, preventing it from derailing their overall progress. They can acknowledge frustration or disappointment without being consumed by it, thereby maintaining the mental equitability required for sustained effort.

This synergy extends to decision-making. Strategic thinking encourages a rational, analytical approach, weighing pros and cons, and considering long-term consequences. Mindfulness complements this by fostering an awareness of intuitive insights and gut feelings, which can often arise from subconscious processing of vast amounts of information. By cultivating both analytical rigor and intuitive awareness, individuals can make more holistic and effective decisions. A military strategist might use data and historical precedent to evaluate a course of action, but a mindful approach might also highlight an subtle unease or a strong sense of alignment with a particular option, even if it's not immediately quantifiable. This integration allows for decisions that are not only logically sound but also resonant with a deeper understanding of the situation and one's own capabilities. It's about marrying the head with the heart, the rational with the intuitive, to arrive at the most robust conclusion.

The disciplined preparation inherent in strategic thinking also finds its counterpart in the mindful cultivation of mental and emotional resilience. Just as a military unit trains rigorously to prepare for the rigors of combat, individuals who integrate mindfulness into their lives build an inner capacity to withstand stress, manage adversity, and maintain equanimity in challenging circumstances. This inner preparedness is a form of strategic advantage, allowing one to perform at a higher level, regardless of external pressures. The ability to consciously regulate one's internal state, to remain present and focused when faced with distractions or difficulties, is a direct outcome of mindful practice. This translates into sustained performance, improved concentration, and a greater capacity for problem-solving, all of which are essential components of mastery.

Furthermore, the principles of adaptability, so central to effective military strategy, are deeply enhanced by mindfulness. Strategy often involves planning for contingencies, recognizing that even the most well-laid plans can be disrupted by unforeseen events. Mindfulness cultivates the mental flexibility to adjust to these disruptions without losing sight of the ultimate objective. It allows one to remain open to new information and to shift perspective when necessary, recognizing that rigidity in the face of change is a recipe for failure. This is akin to the concept of "wu wei" in Taoism, which emphasizes effortless action in alignment with the natural flow of events. Mindfulness provides the awareness to perceive this flow, while strategic thinking provides the ability to navigate it purposefully.

Consider the process of leadership. A strong leader requires both a clear vision and the ability to inspire and guide others through complex processes. Strategic planning provides the vision – the clear articulation of goals and the roadmap to achieve them. Mindfulness, however, allows the leader to connect with their team on a deeper level, to understand their needs and concerns, and to communicate with authenticity and empathy. A leader who is strategically brilliant but lacks mindful awareness may struggle to build trust or foster collaboration. Conversely, a leader who is mindful but lacks strategic direction may be well-intentioned but ultimately ineffective. The integration of both allows for leadership that is both visionary and grounded, inspiring and effective. This is about leading not just with intellect, but with presence and genuine connection.

The practice of self-reflection, a cornerstone of both strategic analysis and mindful awareness, further solidifies this integration. Regularly reviewing past decisions and actions, identifying what worked and what didn't, is a crucial strategic exercise. Mindfulness deepens this by encouraging an honest and compassionate examination of one's own motivations, biases, and patterns of behavior. This introspective process allows for continuous learning and improvement, ensuring that strategies are not only effective in the moment but also contribute to long-term personal growth and mastery. It's about understanding not just the external landscape, but the internal landscape that shapes our responses to it.

The overarching goal of this integration is to cultivate a state of "aware mastery" – a capacity to engage with the world with both purpose and presence. It is about being able to plan for the future while fully inhabiting the present, to act decisively while remaining open to adjustment, and to achieve objectives without sacrificing inner peace or ethical integrity. This holistic approach recognizes that true mastery is not solely about external achievement, but about the integrated development of one's capabilities and one's inner life. It is the realization that the most effective strategies are born from a clear mind, a focused intention, and a deep connection to the present moment. By weaving together the structured discipline of strategy with the liberating awareness of mindfulness, we create a potent framework for navigating life's inherent challenges, embracing its opportunities, and ultimately, living a life of purpose and profound mastery. This fusion allows us to move beyond mere tactical execution to a more comprehensive and resilient approach to all endeavors, transforming how we plan, how we act, and how we ultimately, lead our lives.

The culmination of our exploration into the integrated self, as informed by the rigorous discipline of strategic thinking and the profound presence of mindfulness, ultimately points towards a singular, compelling destination: a life imbued with genuine purpose and profound meaning. While mastery of skills and strategic acumen are undeniably valuable, they remain incomplete if not anchored to a guiding star – an unwavering alignment with what we hold most dear, our core values. To live a life of purpose is to ensure that every action, every decision, and every strategic endeavor serves a higher, personally resonant objective. It is to move beyond the reactive management of circumstances and toward the proactive creation of a life that reflects our deepest principles and aspirations. This is the ultimate aim of self-mastery: to forge an existence that is not only effective and resilient, but also deeply authentic and intrinsically fulfilling.

The journey to this purposeful existence begins with a deliberate and often challenging process of self-discovery. It requires us to peel back the layers of societal conditioning, external expectations, and ingrained habits to unearth the fundamental beliefs and principles that truly define us. Identifying these core values is not a passive act; it demands introspection, honesty, and a willingness to confront uncomfortable truths about ourselves and our motivations. What truly matters to you? What principles guide your decisions when no one is watching? What causes stir your passion and evoke a sense of righteous indignation or profound joy? These are not abstract philosophical questions, but practical inquiries that form the bedrock of a life lived with intention.

Consider the act of defining one's core values as akin to establishing the foundational principles of a strategic campaign. Just as a military operation requires a clear objective and a set of guiding operational parameters, a purposeful life needs clearly articulated values that dictate the direction and nature of our endeavors. These values act as an internal compass, providing unwavering direction even amidst the fog of uncertainty and the pressures of external demands. They are the non-negotiables, the ethical anchors that ensure our actions remain consistent with our innermost sense of what is right and important. For some, values like integrity, honesty, and fairness might be paramount, forming the unyielding basis of all their interactions and decisions. For others, compassion, service, and contributing to the well-being of others might be the guiding lights. Still others may prioritize creativity, innovation, personal growth, or courage. The specific constellation of values is unique to each individual, and its power lies in its authenticity and its deep resonance with one's inner self.

The process of identifying these values can be approached through various contemplative and strategic methods. One effective approach is to reflect on moments of peak fulfillment and profound dissatisfaction in your life. When have you felt most alive, most engaged, and most truly yourself? What were the underlying principles or beliefs that were being honored in those moments? Conversely, when have you felt most drained, most conflicted, or most inauthentic? What values were being violated or ignored? By dissecting these pivotal experiences, you can begin to identify the core tenets that either nourish or deplete your spirit. Another method involves envisioning your ideal future self and the legacy you wish to leave behind. What qualities would that future self embody? What impact would you have made on the world? The answers to these questions often point directly to your most deeply held values.

Furthermore, a strategic review of your commitments and how you currently spend your time can reveal significant insights into your actual, rather than aspirational, values. Do your daily actions and the allocation of your resources (time, energy, attention) genuinely reflect the principles you believe are most important? Often, there is a significant gap between the values we profess and the way we live. This discrepancy is not a cause for self-recrimination, but rather a powerful signal that a recalibration is needed. A mindful examination of your schedule, your interactions, and your priorities can highlight areas where you are living in accordance with your values and areas where you may be compromising them, perhaps out of habit, fear, or a lack of clarity.

Once identified, the critical step is to actively and consciously align your actions with these core values. This is where the disciplined practice of integrating strategy and mindfulness becomes paramount. Your personal strategy is not merely about achieving external goals; it is about designing a life that is a coherent expression of your deepest principles. This means making deliberate choices in every area of your life – your career, your relationships, your personal development, and your engagement with the wider world – that honor and uphold your values.

Consider how this alignment manifests in professional life. If you value integrity, then decisions regarding business practices, client interactions, and personal conduct must always prioritize honesty and ethical behavior, even when faced with opportunities for short-term gain that might compromise these principles. If you value innovation, then your work life should actively seek out opportunities to learn, experiment, and contribute new ideas, rather than settling into a comfortable but stagnant routine. If you value service, then your professional path should ideally lead you to roles where you can contribute to the well-being of others or to a cause larger than yourself. This alignment transforms a career from a mere means of earning a living into a powerful vehicle for expressing your purpose.

In personal relationships, aligning actions with core values means ensuring that your interactions with loved ones are characterized by the principles you hold dear. If you value open communication and honesty, then you commit to speaking truthfully and listening attentively, even when it's difficult. If you value compassion and empathy, then you strive to understand and support your loved ones, offering kindness and support in their times of need. If you value personal growth and mutual support, then you actively encourage and celebrate the development of those close to you, fostering an environment where each person can flourish.

The mindful component is crucial in ensuring that this alignment is not a rigid, forced adherence, but a fluid and conscious expression of your authentic self. Mindfulness allows you to remain aware of your values in the moment of decision and action. It provides the clarity to recognize when an opportunity or a situation is in conflict with your principles, and the inner strength to make a choice that honors your values. For example, if you value authenticity, mindfulness can help you recognize when you are tempted to say or do something that feels inauthentic or performative, giving you the space to choose a more genuine response.

This process of alignment is not a one-time event, but an ongoing, dynamic practice. Life is constantly presenting us with new challenges, opportunities, and evolving circumstances. Our values, while fundamental, may also deepen and refine over time as we gain new experiences and insights. Therefore, regular introspection and strategic review are essential to ensure that our actions remain in sync with our current understanding of ourselves and our most important principles. This might involve periodic retreats for deeper reflection, journaling practices to track alignment, or even conversations with trusted mentors or friends who can offer perspective.

The power of living a purpose-driven life, where actions are aligned with core values, extends far beyond mere personal fulfillment. It cultivates a profound sense of internal coherence and resilience. When your outward actions are a true reflection of your inner principles, you experience a deep sense of integrity that is inherently grounding. This inner coherence acts as a buffer against the inevitable stresses and uncertainties of life. You become less susceptible to external validation or criticism, as your sense of worth is derived from living in accordance with your own deeply held beliefs, rather than from the opinions of others.

Moreover, this alignment fosters a powerful sense of agency and control over your life. Instead of feeling like a passive participant being swept along by the currents of circumstance, you become the active architect of your own experience. You understand that while you may not always control the external events that occur, you always have the power to choose how you respond to them, and crucially, to ensure that your responses are guided by your core values. This empowers you to navigate challenges with a steady hand, to make difficult decisions with conviction, and to pursue your goals with unwavering determination, knowing that your efforts are contributing to a meaningful whole.

The strategic dimension of this purposeful living involves not only the identification of values but also the conscious design of systems, habits, and long-term plans that actively support their expression. This might involve structuring your daily routine to incorporate activities that nourish your values, such as dedicating time for creative pursuits if you value creativity, or engaging in acts of service if you value compassion. It could also involve making strategic career choices, choosing relationships that are supportive of your values, or even deciding where to live based on the alignment between your principles and the community.

Mindfulness plays a vital role in ensuring that these strategic choices are made with clarity and presence. It allows you to observe the subtle signals of your inner wisdom, to discern between fleeting desires and enduring values, and to make choices that are not driven by impulse or external pressure, but by a deep, considered understanding of what truly matters. When faced with a decision that may pull you away from your values, mindfulness provides the mental space to pause, to connect with your inner compass, and to choose the path that honors your authentic self.

Ultimately, a life lived with purpose, where actions are seamlessly aligned with core values, is a life of mastery in its most profound sense. It is the mastery of self, the ability to direct one's own life with intention and integrity. It is the mastery of circumstance, the capacity to navigate the complexities of the world with wisdom and resilience. And it is the mastery of meaning, the creation of an existence that is not only successful by external metrics but is also deeply rich, fulfilling, and authentically yours. This integration of purpose, values, strategic action, and mindful awareness forms the essence of the integrated self, leading to a life of enduring significance and profound personal fulfillment. It is the ultimate expression of living intentionally, ensuring that each day is a step closer to the person you aspire to be and the life you truly wish to lead. This is not merely about achieving goals; it is about becoming the person who is capable of living a life that truly matters.

Navigating the inevitable currents of complexity and uncertainty that define modern existence requires a cultivated inner landscape. It's not about eliminating challenges, for they are intrinsic to the human experience, but about developing the capacity to move through them with a steady hand and an unyielding spirit. This is where the synthesized wisdom of strategic foresight and mindful presence truly shines, offering not just survival, but a flourishing existence even in the face of adversity. The agility we've discussed, the capacity to pivot and adapt, is not merely a tactical advantage; it is the cornerstone of personal resilience. It is the understanding that rigidity in the face of change is a prelude to fragility. Think of it like a seasoned sailor navigating a storm. They don't fight the waves head-on with brute force; rather, they understand the nature of the wind and water, adjusting their sails, trimming their course, and anticipating the shifts. Similarly, our internal strategic compass, informed by our core values, allows us to make necessary adjustments without losing sight of our fundamental direction.

Maintaining composure amidst chaos is not an innate trait for most; it is a cultivated skill. When faced with unexpected setbacks, the primal instincts can trigger a cascade of fear, anxiety, and a desire to retreat. This is where the mindful pause becomes indispensable. Before reacting, taking a deep, conscious breath can interrupt the automatic stress response. This brief interlude allows the prefrontal cortex, the seat of our rational thought and decision-making, to re-engage. It's in this space that we can shift from a purely reactive state to a more considered, strategic one. Consider a critical business negotiation that takes a sudden, unfavorable turn. The immediate urge might be to lash out or concede defeat. However, by employing a mindful pause, one can acknowledge the surge of emotion without being dictated by it, assess the new landscape, and then formulate a measured, strategic response that still aligns with long-term objectives. This isn't about suppressing emotion, but about understanding its role and ensuring it serves, rather than sabotages, our goals.

The ability to make sound decisions under pressure is a hallmark of integrated self-mastery. Often, under duress, our cognitive bandwidth shrinks, and we tend to rely on heuristics and shortcuts that may not always serve us best. Mindfulness training expands this capacity by enhancing focus and clarity, even when external stimuli are overwhelming. It cultivates an awareness of our own mental states, allowing us to recognize when we are becoming clouded by stress or emotion and to consciously bring ourselves back to a state of clear observation. Strategically, this means developing a framework for decision-making that can be applied even when the stakes are high. This might involve creating pre-defined criteria for evaluating options, identifying potential risks and mitigation strategies in advance, or having a trusted advisor to consult during critical junctures. For instance, in a medical emergency, a seasoned doctor, despite the high-pressure environment, relies on their extensive training and established protocols to make life-saving decisions. This framework, built upon years of learning and practice, allows for effective action even when faced with immense stress.

Bouncing back from adversity, or resilience, is more than just enduring hardship; it's about learning, adapting, and emerging stronger. This is where the concept of "post-traumatic growth" finds its practical application. Adversity often shakes the foundations of our assumptions and beliefs. While this can be destabilizing, it also presents an opportunity for profound re-evaluation and growth. The strategic mind looks for lessons in every setback, analyzing what went wrong, what could have been done differently, and how to apply these insights to future challenges. Mindfulness, in this context, helps us to process the emotional impact of setbacks without getting stuck in rumination or despair. It allows us to acknowledge the pain or disappointment, but then to gently redirect our attention towards solutions and future possibilities.

Consider a project that fails to meet its objectives. A reactive response might involve blaming external factors or individuals. A strategic, resilient response involves a thorough post-mortem analysis. What were the critical decision points? Where did the execution falter? What unforeseen variables were at play? By dissecting the failure objectively, one gains valuable intelligence for future endeavors. Simultaneously, practicing self-compassion through mindfulness allows for the processing of any personal feelings of inadequacy or frustration associated with the failure, fostering the emotional fortitude to move forward with renewed determination. This doesn't mean ignoring mistakes, but rather reframing them as learning opportunities rather than insurmountable obstacles.

The principle of antifragility, introduced by Nassim Nicholas Taleb, is particularly relevant here. Antifragile systems are those that actually benefit from shocks, volatility, and stressors. While we may not always achieve true antifragility in every aspect of our lives, we can certainly cultivate a disposition towards it. This involves actively seeking out challenges that stretch our capabilities, rather than shying away from them. It means embracing a growth mindset, where difficulties are seen as opportunities to strengthen our skills and expand our capacity. Strategically, this could involve taking on a project that is slightly beyond our current comfort zone, or deliberately exposing ourselves to new environments and perspectives. Mindfully, it involves cultivating an inner calm that allows us to engage with these challenges without being overwhelmed.

The concept of grace in navigating complexity speaks to an ease and elegance in the face of difficulty. It's not about appearing effortless, but about possessing an inner poise that allows for effective action without undue internal struggle. This grace is born from a deep well of self-awareness, a clear understanding of one's values and capabilities, and the practice of mindful presence. When we are deeply connected to our purpose, the inevitable obstacles become less about personal affronts and more about challenges to be overcome in service of that purpose. This reframing diminishes the emotional charge associated with difficulties, allowing for a more objective and efficient response.

Imagine a leader facing a significant organizational crisis. Instead of succumbing to panic or defensiveness, a graceful response involves clear communication, decisive action, and a steady reassurance of the team. This outward composure is a direct reflection of their inner state, cultivated through consistent practice of mindfulness and strategic foresight. They understand the steps required to address the crisis, they can anticipate potential ripple effects, and they can manage their own emotional responses to inspire confidence in others. This isn't about suppressing fear, but about acknowledging it and choosing to act in alignment with their role and responsibilities.

Furthermore, the integration of strategy and mindfulness equips us to not only withstand the pressures of complexity but to actually leverage them for growth. The dynamic tension inherent in challenging situations can be a powerful catalyst for innovation and deeper understanding. By approaching complexity with curiosity rather than apprehension, and by maintaining a focus on our core objectives while remaining flexible in our methods, we can transform potentially debilitating situations into springboards for progress. This requires a conscious shift in perspective – viewing chaos not as an enemy, but as an inherent characteristic of a living, evolving system, and recognizing our capacity to find order and purpose within it. The integrated self, therefore, is not one that avoids difficulty, but one that is adept at dancing with it, transforming it, and ultimately, thriving because of it. This dance requires preparation, practice, and an unwavering commitment to inner alignment, enabling us to move through life's intricate patterns with both strength and serenity.

The essence of navigating complexity with grace and resilience lies in the cultivation of an unshakeable inner equilibrium, a state that allows for clear perception and effective action even when the external environment is turbulent. This equilibrium is not a static achievement but a dynamic process, continuously honed through the synergistic application of strategic thinking and mindful awareness. It is about developing the mental agility to adapt to unforeseen circumstances without compromising core principles, and the emotional fortitude to remain centered amidst external pressures. When faced with chaos, the tendency can be to react impulsively, driven by fear or a sense of overwhelm. However, the integrated self understands the power of the pause. This brief, deliberate moment of stillness, facilitated by mindfulness, provides the crucial cognitive space to move from a reactive state to a proactive one. It is in this pause that we can access our strategic frameworks, allowing us to analyze the situation objectively, identify our objectives, and chart a course of action that aligns with our values.

Consider a scenario where a critical project deadline is suddenly moved up, presenting a seemingly insurmountable challenge. The initial reaction might be panic, leading to rushed, error-prone work and increased stress. However, by consciously employing the mindful pause, one can acknowledge the surge of adrenaline and anxiety, take a calming breath, and then engage the strategic mind. This might involve re-evaluating existing resources, identifying potential bottlenecks, prioritizing essential tasks, and communicating proactively with stakeholders about revised timelines and expectations. This approach transforms a potentially disastrous situation into a manageable challenge, demonstrating grace under pressure and resilience in the face of unexpected demands. The strategist doesn't shy away from difficulty; they leverage it as an opportunity to refine their plans and demonstrate their capabilities.

Emotional fortitude, a key component of resilience, is directly nurtured by the mindful practice of observing and understanding one's emotional landscape without being controlled by it. This means recognizing feelings of frustration, disappointment, or fear as transient states, rather than defining truths. By acknowledging these emotions with non-judgmental awareness, we create a buffer between the stimulus and our response. This allows us to engage with challenges from a place of grounded strength rather than reactive vulnerability. Strategically, this emotional resilience is crucial for maintaining long-term commitment to goals, even when faced with setbacks. It prevents discouragement from derailing progress and enables a consistent, focused approach towards desired outcomes.

Think of an athlete preparing for a major competition. They undergo rigorous physical training, but equally important is their mental preparation. Mindfulness practices help them manage performance anxiety, stay focused during crucial moments, and bounce back from errors during the competition. The strategic element comes into play in their game plan, their understanding of their opponents, and their ability to adapt their tactics on the fly. If they make a mistake, their mental training allows them to quickly let go of the frustration and refocus on the next play, demonstrating both emotional resilience and strategic adaptability. This ability to rebound is not about pretending the setback didn't happen, but about processing it effectively and channeling that energy into constructive action.

Bouncing back from adversity, or resilience, is not simply about returning to a previous state; it's about transforming through the experience. Each challenge, when approached with a strategic mindset and mindful awareness, becomes an opportunity for learning and growth. This involves a commitment to post-event analysis, not for the purpose of assigning blame, but for extracting valuable insights. What lessons were learned? How can these lessons be integrated to improve future performance and decision-making? This continuous improvement loop is fundamental to building robust resilience. The strategic mind actively seeks these lessons, while the mindful awareness ensures that the emotional residue of the adversity does not impede the learning process.

For example, a startup facing a significant funding shortfall must not only strategize on how to secure new investment but also analyze the reasons for the initial setback. Was the business model flawed? Was the pitch inadequate? Was the market timing off? A mindful approach to this analysis allows the founders to engage with these difficult questions without succumbing to self-recrimination. They can objectively assess the situation, identify actionable steps for improvement, and communicate their revised strategy with renewed confidence. This process of reflection and adaptation is what builds true resilience, enabling the venture to navigate future financial storms with greater preparedness and wisdom.

Furthermore, the integration of these two powerful disciplines allows for a profound sense of agency, even in the most unpredictable circumstances. While we cannot always control the external events that befall us, we retain the ultimate power to choose our response. This choice, when guided by a clear understanding of our values and a strategic perspective, becomes the bedrock of our resilience. It is the recognition that even in the face of overwhelming odds, we possess the inner resources to navigate with intention and to emerge from challenging experiences with greater strength and insight. This proactive engagement with life's complexities, rather than passive endurance, is the essence of living with both grace and resilience. It transforms the inevitable friction of existence into a catalyst for personal evolution, allowing us to not only withstand the storms but to learn to dance in the rain. The ability to maintain this inner equilibrium, this unwavering composure, is a testament to the power of a truly integrated self. It is the capacity to be fully present in the moment, to assess the situation with clarity, and to act with purpose, thereby transforming the often-turbulent waters of life into a course that leads towards greater self-mastery and fulfillment. This ongoing practice of mindful strategy allows us to face uncertainty not with trepidation, but with a quiet confidence, knowing that we possess the inner tools to navigate whatever lies ahead.

The journey toward an integrated self is not a destination to be reached, but a continuous unfolding, a vibrant engagement with the tapestry of existence. At its core lies the profound practice of presence, the art of being fully alive in each unfolding moment. This is not a passive state, but an active, conscious choice to immerse ourselves in the richness of our experiences, no matter how mundane they may seem. It is the antithesis of living on autopilot, of letting days blend into a monotonous blur, only to find ourselves wondering where the time has gone. True mastery, in this sense, is synonymous with experiencing life fully, savoring the sweetness of joy, acknowledging the sting of sorrow, and finding meaning in the quiet hum of the ordinary.

This practice begins with a conscious intention to shift our awareness from the relentless march of the future or the lingering echoes of the past, to the vibrant reality of the present. It is about cultivating a deep, appreciative curiosity for what is happening right now. Consider the simple act of drinking a cup of tea. In our hurried lives, this often becomes a perfunctory act, a means to an end. But by bringing our full attention to it, we can transform it into a rich sensory experience. Notice the warmth of the mug in your hands, the subtle aroma that rises with the steam, the complex layers of flavor that unfold on your tongue, the way the liquid warms you from the inside out. Each sip becomes an opportunity for mindful engagement, a small anchor in the present moment. This isn't about forcing ourselves to feel something profound; it's about simply noticing what is already there, unadorned and authentic.

The cultivation of presence extends beyond sensory experiences to our interactions with others. How often do we find ourselves half-listening to a loved one, our minds already rehearsing our response or drifting to a pending task? True connection, the kind that nourishes the soul and strengthens relationships, requires our undivided attention. When we are fully present with another person, we offer them the gift of our complete awareness. We listen not just to their words, but to the nuances of their tone, the unspoken emotions conveyed through their body language, the deeper currents of their meaning. This deep listening fosters understanding, empathy, and a sense of genuine connection. It allows us to move beyond superficial exchanges to a place of authentic communion, where both parties feel seen, heard, and valued. Imagine a conversation with a friend who is sharing a personal struggle. If your mind is elsewhere, grappling with your own anxieties or planning your next move, you miss the subtle cues of their distress, the silent pleas for comfort and support. But if you can set aside your internal chatter and offer them your full presence, you create a space of safety and trust, enabling them to feel truly understood and less alone. This is the power of being present in our relationships, transforming routine interactions into opportunities for deep human connection.

This ongoing practice also involves a deliberate engagement with our physical sensations. Our bodies are constant conduits of information, offering us a rich, nuanced feedback loop about our internal and external world. Yet, we often move through our days disconnected from this vital source of wisdom. We might feel a twinge of discomfort, a growing tension in our shoulders, or a subtle ache, but we push through, ignoring these signals until they become more insistent. By intentionally tuning into our physical selves, we can develop a more intimate relationship with our bodies, learning to interpret their messages and respond to their needs with greater wisdom. This might involve simple practices like paying attention to the rhythm of our breath, noticing the subtle shifts in our posture, or becoming aware of the physical sensations associated with different emotions. For instance, recognizing that anxiety often manifests as a tightness in the chest or a churning in the stomach can be the first step in learning to manage these feelings more effectively. By acknowledging these physical cues without judgment, we can begin to understand their origins and develop strategies to alleviate them, rather than suppressing them.

Furthermore, the practice of presence teaches us to appreciate the inherent beauty and wonder that exists in the seemingly ordinary aspects of life. So much of our dissatisfaction stems from a constant seeking of the extraordinary, a belief that true happiness lies just beyond our current reach. We chase grand experiences, overlooking the quiet miracles that surround us every day. The intricate pattern of veins on a leaf, the fleeting dance of sunlight on a wall, the sound of rain pattering against the windowpane – these are moments of quiet magic that we often miss when our attention is elsewhere. By consciously bringing our awareness to these subtle details, we begin to reframe our perception of reality. We discover that life's richness is not solely confined to peak experiences, but is woven into the very fabric of our everyday existence. This shift in perspective fosters a profound sense of gratitude and contentment, as we learn to find joy not in the accumulation of external achievements, but in the simple act of fully inhabiting our lives.

This practice of presence is not a static achievement; it is a dynamic, evolving skill that requires consistent cultivation. It's akin to tending a garden; without regular care, the weeds of distraction and rumination will inevitably take root. Therefore, establishing daily rituals that support this practice is essential. These might include brief periods of meditation, mindful walking, or simply dedicating a few minutes each day to sit in quiet observation, without any agenda or expectation. The key is regularity and a commitment to gently redirecting our attention whenever it wanders. Even when our minds are overwhelmed by thoughts or worries, the act of noticing this distraction and then consciously returning our focus to the present moment is, in itself, a powerful exercise in presence. Each time we do this, we strengthen our capacity for mindful awareness, building an inner resilience that allows us to remain anchored even amidst the storms of life.

The integration of this mindful presence into every facet of our lives transforms the very nature of mastery. It moves from a performance-based achievement to a state of being. It means that the pursuit of goals is not a race against time, but a deeply engaged process. Whether we are learning a new skill, navigating a complex project, or simply engaging in a routine task, bringing our full attention to it imbues the activity with a sense of purpose and aliveness. This is not about eliminating challenges, but about meeting them with a clear, focused, and engaged mind. The satisfaction derived from a task completed with mindful intention is far deeper and more enduring than that gained from mere completion. It is the satisfaction of having fully participated in our own lives, of having savored each step of the journey.

Consider the process of learning a new language. A purely strategic approach might focus on memorizing vocabulary and grammar rules, aiming for fluency as quickly as possible. While effective, this can often lead to a sterile, mechanical acquisition of the language. By contrast, integrating presence into this process means truly listening to native speakers, immersing oneself in the sounds and rhythms of the language, and experimenting with speaking, even if imperfectly. It involves finding joy in the nuances of pronunciation, appreciating the cultural context embedded in the words, and engaging with the language as a living, breathing entity. This approach not only accelerates learning but also fosters a deeper connection to the culture and people who speak it, transforming a task into a rich and meaningful experience.

Similarly, in the realm of professional life, the practice of presence can revolutionize our approach to work. Instead of viewing work as a series of demands to be met or a means to an end, we can approach each task with focused intention. This means being fully present during meetings, engaging actively in discussions, and contributing thoughtfully. It means dedicating our full attention to the task at hand, minimizing distractions, and striving for quality in our execution. This not only enhances productivity and effectiveness but also fosters a sense of fulfillment and purpose in our professional endeavors. When we are present in our work, we are not merely going through the motions; we are actively shaping our contributions and finding meaning in the process itself. This shift from a task-oriented to a presence-oriented approach transforms the work experience from one of obligation to one of engagement and contribution.

This continuous practice of presence also imbues our relationships with a deeper layer of authenticity. When we are fully present with our partners, children, friends, or colleagues, we create an environment of genuine connection and trust. We offer them the space to be themselves, without judgment or the pressure to perform. This allows for vulnerability and intimacy to flourish, strengthening the bonds between us. It means being truly there for someone, not just physically, but emotionally and mentally. It's about putting down the phone, making eye contact, and offering your complete attention, showing them that they are your priority in that moment. This simple, yet profound, act of presence can be the most powerful gift we give to those we care about, fostering deeper understanding and more meaningful connections.

Moreover, by anchoring ourselves in the present, we cultivate a profound sense of inner peace and equanimity. The constant striving, the anxieties about the future, and the regrets of the past often create a turbulent inner landscape. Presence acts as an antidote to this internal chaos. By consciously returning our attention to the here and now, we create a sanctuary of calm within ourselves, a space where we can observe our thoughts and emotions without being swept away by them. This is not about suppressing our feelings or pretending that difficulties don't exist, but about developing the capacity to acknowledge them with clarity and detachment. It allows us to respond to life's challenges from a place of grounded strength, rather than reactive reactivity.

Think of a sailor navigating a rough sea. While the waves may be turbulent and the wind strong, the skilled sailor remains focused on the task at hand – steering the boat, adjusting the sails, and maintaining a steady course. Their presence is not about denying the storm, but about engaging with it fully, making the necessary adjustments with calm awareness. Similarly, when we practice presence, we acknowledge the challenges and uncertainties of life, but we choose to meet them with our full attention and a steady inner compass. This allows us to move through life's complexities with a sense of grace and resilience, transforming potential sources of stress into opportunities for growth and learning.

The cumulative effect of this ongoing practice is the cultivation of a life lived with intention and depth. It is about recognizing that each moment holds the potential for richness, for learning, for connection, and for joy. By committing to being present, we are not merely completing tasks or fulfilling obligations; we are fully inhabiting our lives, savoring the journey, and discovering the profound beauty that lies within the ordinary. This dedication to presence is the hallmark of a truly integrated self, one that is not just striving for mastery, but is living it, moment by conscious moment. It is the continuous unfolding of our potential, expressed not in grand gestures, but in the quiet, consistent commitment to experiencing life fully, as it unfolds. This practice ensures that self-mastery is not a distant summit to be conquered, but an ongoing, vibrant way of being.

The journey toward a truly integrated self, as we have explored, is not a static achievement, a pinnacle scaled and then admired from afar. Instead, it is a dynamic, ever-evolving campaign – an ongoing mission that demands our sustained commitment, our strategic foresight, and our unwavering dedication. This is the essence of lifelong growth, the relentless pursuit of becoming more, of refining our capabilities, and of deepening our understanding of ourselves and the world around us. It is the understanding that mastery is not a singular victory, but a continuous state of engaged learning and mindful application.

To embrace this ongoing mission is to view personal development not as a series of discrete achievements, but as a perpetual process of strategic engagement. Just as a seasoned military commander constantly analyzes the evolving battlefield, adapting tactics and refining strategies, so too must we approach our personal growth. This requires a proactive stance, an internalizing of the principle that stagnation is the enemy of progress. We must cultivate a mindset where every experience, every challenge, and every interaction serves as an opportunity for learning and refinement. This isn't about dwelling on perceived shortcomings, but about identifying areas for enhancement with the clarity of a seasoned strategist, and then meticulously planning and executing the steps required for improvement. It's about recognizing that the skills and insights that served us yesterday may need to be augmented or entirely reinvented to meet the demands of tomorrow.

This commitment to lifelong growth is fundamentally about embracing a spirit of continuous learning. It means actively seeking out new knowledge, even in areas that lie outside our immediate comfort zones or current expertise. Think of it as expanding your operational theater. The more diverse your understanding, the more adaptable and resilient you become. This could manifest in various forms: delving into subjects that pique your curiosity through books and research, engaging in courses or workshops to acquire new skills, or seeking out mentors who possess wisdom and experience in areas you wish to develop.

The key is to remain perpetually curious, to ask "why?" and "how?" with an insatiable hunger for deeper comprehension. This intellectual curiosity fuels the engine of personal evolution, ensuring that our understanding of the world and our place within it remains vibrant and relevant.

Moreover, this ongoing mission necessitates the diligent application of mindful awareness to every facet of our lives. We have discussed the power of presence, but its true efficacy lies in its consistent, deliberate application. It is the disciplined practice of bringing our full attention to whatever we are doing, whether it's a complex strategic decision or a simple everyday task. This means not only being present *during* learning, but also being present in the *execution* of what we have learned. It's the difference between knowing a tactical maneuver and flawlessly executing it under pressure. This requires constant vigilance against the insidious creep of distraction and the comforting allure of autopilot. We must actively cultivate the habit of checking in with ourselves, of ensuring that our attention is anchored in the present moment, allowing us to engage with tasks fully and effectively. This consistent application transforms knowledge into wisdom, and potential into actualized capability.

Consider the analogy of a high-performance athlete. Their journey is not defined by winning a single championship, but by the relentless pursuit of incremental improvements. They engage in rigorous training, analyze their performance data, seek feedback from coaches, and constantly refine their techniques. They understand that even at the peak of their performance, there are always avenues for further development. This same dedication must be applied to our personal and professional lives. We must regularly assess our progress, identify areas where we can optimize our approach, and be willing to adapt our strategies as circumstances change. This might involve setting aside dedicated time for self-reflection, perhaps weekly or monthly, to review our goals, evaluate our efforts, and recalibrate our focus. This disciplined self-assessment is crucial for ensuring that our "campaign" remains on track and that we are making consistent, meaningful progress.

The essence of this ongoing mission also lies in embracing challenges as opportunities, rather than obstacles. Every setback, every unexpected difficulty, is a potential training ground for enhancing our resilience and strategic thinking. Instead of viewing failure as a terminal event, we must learn to analyze it objectively, to extract the lessons it offers, and to integrate that knowledge into our future actions. This is the hallmark of a seasoned strategist – the ability to learn from every engagement, to adapt to unforeseen circumstances, and to emerge from adversity stronger and more capable. This requires a certain psychological fortitude, a willingness to confront discomfort and to persist even when faced with significant resistance. It's about understanding that the most profound growth often occurs when we are pushed beyond our perceived limits.

Furthermore, this commitment to lifelong growth requires us to actively seek out constructive feedback and to receive it with an open mind. Often, our own blind spots prevent us from seeing areas where we can improve. Input from trusted colleagues, mentors, friends, or even objective data can provide invaluable insights. The ability to listen without defensiveness, to consider the feedback thoughtfully, and to act upon it where appropriate is a critical component of continuous development. This is not about accepting every piece of advice uncritically, but about developing a discerning ear and a willingness to integrate valuable perspectives into our own strategic planning. It's about understanding that our personal "intelligence gathering" is enhanced by the perspectives of others.

This concept of an "ongoing mission" also speaks to the iterative nature of personal development. It's rarely a linear progression. There will be periods of rapid advancement, followed by plateaus or even perceived regressions. The key is to maintain momentum and to not be discouraged by these fluctuations. Each phase offers its own unique learning opportunities. A plateau might be an indication that a new approach is needed, a recalibration of strategy. A perceived regression might simply be a necessary period of consolidation, where the lessons learned are being integrated at a deeper level. By maintaining a long-term perspective and a commitment to the overall mission, we can navigate these natural cycles of growth with greater equanimity and resilience.

The strategic element of this lifelong journey is crucial. It involves not just reacting to circumstances, but proactively shaping our development. This means setting clear, ambitious goals, breaking them down into manageable steps, and developing well-defined action plans. It's about foresight – anticipating future needs and proactively acquiring the skills and knowledge to meet them. For example, if you recognize that a particular industry is evolving rapidly, a strategic approach would involve identifying the emerging skills and knowledge that will be in demand and beginning to cultivate them well in advance. This proactive preparation ensures that we are not caught off guard by change, but are instead positioned to capitalize on new opportunities.

This ongoing commitment also involves cultivating a deep sense of self-awareness. Understanding our strengths, our weaknesses, our values, and our motivations is fundamental to charting a meaningful course of personal growth. It allows us to align our development efforts with what is truly important to us, ensuring that our "campaign" is not just about improvement, but about growth in directions that are both personally fulfilling and strategically sound. This self-awareness is not a one-time discovery, but a continuous process of introspection and observation. It's about regularly checking in with our internal compass to ensure we are still moving towards our desired north star.

Furthermore, the integration of mindful awareness into this ongoing mission transforms how we experience our efforts. It imbues even the most routine tasks with a sense of purpose and engagement. When we are present in our work, our learning, and our relationships, we are not just performing actions; we are actively participating in the unfolding of our lives. This presence allows us to savor the process of growth, to find satisfaction in the effort itself, and to appreciate the incremental progress we make along the way. It shifts the focus from a future outcome to the richness of the present moment, making the journey itself a source of fulfillment.

This perspective frames our personal development as a strategic campaign, a dedicated effort to realize our full potential. It is a commitment to continuously honing our skills, expanding our knowledge, and deepening our self-understanding. By embracing this mindset, we are not simply striving for mastery; we are actively living it, moment by conscious moment. This enduring commitment ensures that our lives are characterized by purpose, effectiveness, and a profound sense of inner peace, as we navigate the ever-changing landscape of existence with strategic clarity and mindful intention. It is a lifelong endeavor, a testament to the human capacity for growth, adaptation, and the persistent pursuit of becoming the best version of ourselves. The mission is ongoing, and the potential for realization is, in essence, limitless. We are the commanders of our own growth, the architects of our evolving selves, and the dedicated participants in the grand campaign of a life well-lived. This continuous dedication to learning and self-refinement is not merely a strategy for success; it is the very essence of a life lived with purpose and mastery. It is the ongoing commitment to showing up fully, to learning consistently, and to evolving intentionally, ensuring that the journey itself is as rich and rewarding as any destination we might aspire to reach. This is the ultimate expression of an integrated self – one that is perpetually engaged in the vital work of becoming.

References

Clausewitz, Carl von. On War.

Kabat-Zinn, Jon. Wherever You Go, There You Are: Mindfulness Meditation in Everyday Life.

Lencioni, Patrick. The Five Dysfunctions of a Team: A Leadership Fable.

Sun Tzu. The Art of War.